MW00994618

The Other Side of Hell

by
Bob Adamov

Packard Island Publishing

Other *Emerson Moore* Adventures by Bob Adamov

Rainbow's End	Released October 2002
Pierce the Veil	Released May 2004
When Rainbows Walk	Released June 2005
Promised Land	Released July 2006

Next *Emerson Moore* Adventure
Tan Lines   To be released Summer 2009

The following publication provided reference material:

The Ice of Lake Erie Around South Bass Island by Thomas Huxley Langlois and Marina Holmes Langlois, Copyright 1985 The Ohio State University

ISBN: 0-9786184-1-6
ISBN: 978-0-9786184-1-4

Library of Congress Number: 2008923186

Cover art by Red Incorporated

Cover photo by Bob Adamov

Submit all requests for reprinting to:
BookMasters, Inc.
PO Box 388
Ashland, Ohio 78735

Published in the United States by:
Packard Island Publishing, Wooster, Ohio

www.bookmasters.com
www.packardislandpublishing.com
www.BobAdamov.com

First Edition – June 2008

Printed in the United States

Acknowledgements

Internationally-acclaimed underwater videographer, Roger Roth, had sent me a video of the *Tibetts,* a Soviet missile frigate, which was sunk off of Cayman Brac by the Caymanian government. After viewing it, I called Roger and told him I had a plot and let's go to the Cayman Islands to research it, which we did in December 2005. I'd like to thank Roger for his invaluable research and coaching, especially with the dive sequences.

I also would like to express my appreciation to Put-in-Bay's legendary island singer and rogue, Mike "Mad Dog" Adams, for his coaching and "starring role" in the novel. Nancy and Jay Easterbrook, owners of DiveTech on Grand Cayman, were also key supporters of my efforts and editors of the dive sequences.

Roger, Mad Dog and Nancy were instrumental in setting up meetings for me in the Cayman Islands. Their help made it possible for me to meet and interview the following characters: treasure hunter "Mongo" Ben Marich, Arie Barendrecht at Cobalt Coast Dive Resort, Durty Reid Dennis of Durty Reid's Bar and Grill, Steve Foster of Foster Foods Fair Ltd., Mark Rice of Rice Communications, "Barefoot Man" George Nowacki, Adrien Briggs with Sunset House, Patrick Kenney with Tortuga Divers, Cathy Church of Cathy Church's Underwater Photo Centre & Gallery, Derek Haynes of the Royal Caymanian Police, Rod McDowall with Red Sail Sports, and Ted Kravakis at the Ministry of Banking and Finance.

For the ice stories on Put-in-Bay, a special thank you to Mayor Mack McCann, Jeff Koehler, DairyAir Bob Wernecke and ice fishing guide John Hageman.

I'd also like to extend my appreciation to my team of editors: Claudine Kriss, Roger Roth, Hank Inman of Goldfinch Communications, Cathy Marchese, Julie Davis, Mike "Mad Dog" Adams, Sam Adamov, and the one and only Joe Weinstein.

Dedication

This book is dedicated to my beautiful, loving and caring sweetheart, Cathy Marchese.

The Lake Erie Islands Historical Society will receive a portion of the proceeds from the sale of this book.

For more information, check these sites:
    www.Divetech.com
    www.MikeMadDogAdams.com
    www.Cobaltcoast.com
    www.Put-in-Bay.com

They that wait upon the Lord shall renew their strength; they shall mount up with wings as eagles; they shall run, and not be weary; and they shall walk, and not faint.
– Isaiah 40:31

Wonders of the Oceans

For eons, our oceans have been the most stable ecosystems on earth. Water temperatures, salinities, and amounts of sunlight have changed little through this time lending to the development and stability of the marine life we have come to love as scuba divers. But divers aren't the only ones who need to be aware of and protect this stability.

In the past few decades, numerous practices have had adverse affects on our oceans. These include, but are not limited to shark-finning, bottom-trawling, long-lining; over-fishing that does not support sustainability of many species, by-catch waste, and more. Shark finning is removing the apex predators from marine ecosystems, which will soon cause a total imbalance in the food web. Bottom trawling devastates marine habitats on the seafloor, and the tonnage of by-catch that is thrown over-board is mind-boggling.

Because of irresponsible dumping, our oceans now have eddies of garbage floating in them that stretch for hundreds of miles that most people don't even know about. An example of this is the "Eastern Garbage Patch" located 800 miles north of the Hawaiian Islands. Much of this patch is made up of non-biodegradable plastic.

Coastal development of resorts and hotels is causing silt runoffs worldwide that are smothering, choking, and ultimately killing corals and sponges. With the disappearance of these coral and sponge habitats, other marine creature populations are diminishing. Better development planning is necessary to alleviate this catastrophe from getting worse.

For our own protection, we need to preserve our ocean environments, which are instrumental in keeping carbon dioxide levels within the limits we need to live. We need to help sustain marine population levels in order to continue to have fish in our diets, keeping us healthy. We need to learn more about the oceans and fall in love with them.

Why should we learn more about the oceans and fall in love with them? Jacques Cousteau once wisely stated, "People protect what they love."

Roger Roth
Underwater Videographer
May 2008

Lake Erie Islands

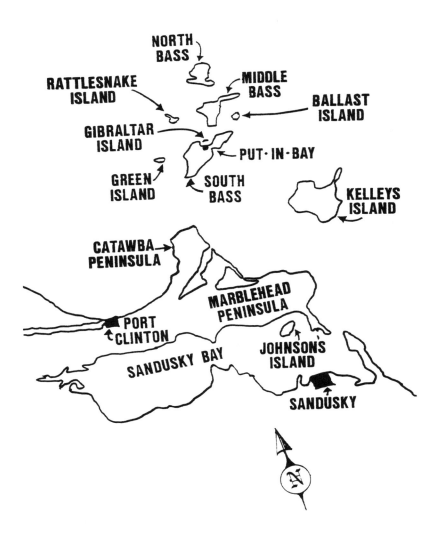

South Bass Island

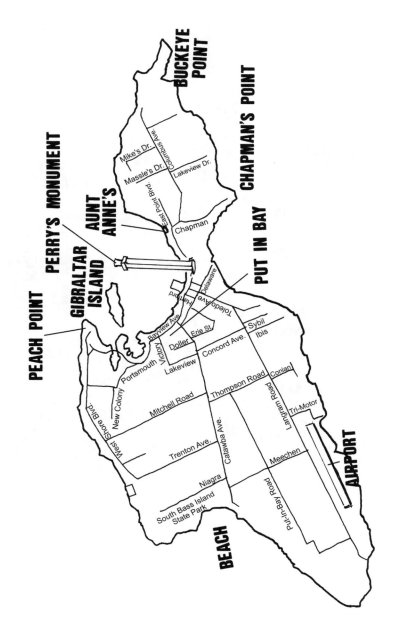

Grand Cayman Island

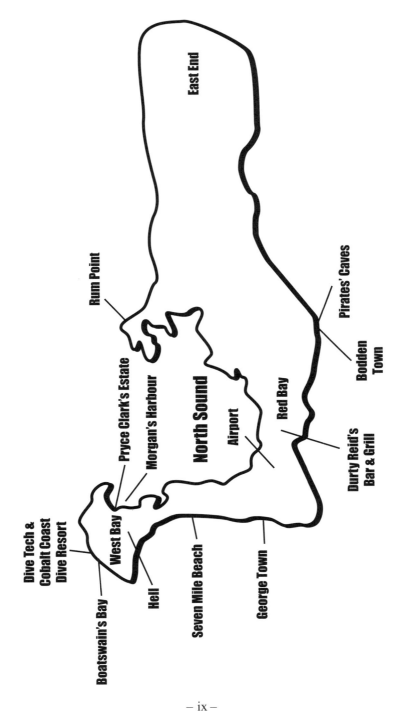

- East End
- Rum Point
- Pirates' Caves
- Bodden Town
- Pryce Clark's Estate
- Morgan's Harbour
- North Sound
- Red Bay
- Airport
- Durty Reid's Bar & Grill
- Dive Tech & Cobalt Coast Dive Resort
- West Bay
- Boatswain's Bay
- Hell
- Seven Mile Beach
- George Town

Off the Cayman Islands
Late 1944

Flashes of lightning and the ominous booms of thunder filled the dark stormy skies as the solitary Henkel seaplane struggled on its critical rescue mission through the torrential downpour. The tropical storm's winds buffeted the small plane and threatened to dismember its fragile wings from its fuselage. The plane bobbed up, down, and sideways as the rain pelted it.

"Nein!" the German pilot said grimly to himself as he struggled to control his seaplane. He had been muttering to himself for the last hour about the storm, which had moved in more quickly than he had anticipated. It had captured him and his plane in its turmoil.

The seaplane's engines sputtered as the pilot wrestled to nurse the last vestige of power from its weakening engine. As he adjusted the fuel mix, the pilot thought to himself how he had been foolhardy to insist that the captain allow him to carry out his mission. Earlier, he had convinced the captain to launch the small plane from the freighter even as the weather began to worsen and, with full knowledge, that the repair work to the seaplane's engine had not been completed.

The captain and the pilot had recognized the dire circumstances they were in from the previous night's storm. One of the ship's engines had been lost in the middle of that storm's fury, bent on sending another victim to the deep. To make matters worse, the ship had been caught by a rogue wave and its steel plates aggressively assaulted. As the ship rose on one wave and thrust sideways, her steel hull had been subjected to stress levels for which it had not been designed. Rivets had popped and several plates had twisted, allowing seawater to flow into the hull.

The crew had rushed to the forward hull in a futile attempt to stop the water's invasion of the ship. Standing next to the captain, the pilot had heard the reports. He knew the dangerous situation in which they had found themselves. With strict orders to maintain radio silence and the secrecy surrounding the ship's mission, they had no way to cry out for help to any passing vessels. The only real hope was if the seaplane could take off before the next storm broke and seek assistance from a German submarine resupply ship.

The pilot had studied the charts and resupply ship schedules. He had seen that a German submarine resupply ship was scheduled to be nearby. If he could find it before the next storm, he'd direct it to his ship for assistance.

The pilot had wiped several beads of sweat from his brow as he straightened his body from the chart table, which he had been bent over. Looking out of the chart room and through the wheelhouse, his eyes had scanned the darkening horizon. It foretold of another furious storm. The humidity was stifling as he drew a breath of the room's stale air and stepped out onto the deck.

Standing at the rail, he had contemplated the risk. He had to take it, even if it only slightly increased the odds for salvaging their ship and its precious cargo. The Fuhrer would have expected them to commit any sacrifice. He had approached the captain and explained that he needed to go for help.

The captain had shaken his head from side to side. He didn't want the young man to risk sacrificing his life, but the pilot was persistent.

The captain had looked straight into the eager eyes of the pilot just as he had looked into the eyes of many others, who had served him during the war. Most of the time, he had listened and reluctantly given them his permission. And most of time, the young men died.

The pilot had seen the captain's hesitation and appealed on behalf of his shipmates, hoping that the captain would relent on the basis of the number of lives at risk.

Reluctantly, the captain had nodded his head and given the 25-year-old pilot the order to launch the seaplane. The pilot had rushed off to his waiting plane to prepare it for a quick launch before the storm struck.

An hour and a half had passed since the plane was launched and the pilot had failed to sight the resupply ship. It then dawned on the pilot that the ship may have moved out of the area when the storm approached. The pilot cursed himself for not considering the possibility of the resupply ship taking such action. His only choice now was to point his plane toward the nearest landfall which were the Cayman Islands.

Within the next hour, the storm had blown in and the pilot's hopes had risen, but were just as quickly dashed as the engine coughed, sputtered and died twice. The pilot had been successful in restarting the engine on both occasions. He looked at the approaching landfall along the edge of the southern horizon and hoped he would be able to attain his destination. Ditching a plane in a turbulent sea during a storm was always a difficult and dangerous alternative, even if the plane was a seaplane.

The pilot thought he could see the swells breaking on the reefs, which protected the north side of Grand Cayman. It was then that the plane's engine sputtered one last time and it lost height in a downdraft. The pilot feverishly tried to restart the engine, but it would not cooperate. Setting his eyes on the beach, he fought to maintain his altitude as he tried to put the plane into a long glide. He wanted the glide to carry him to the beach, but his efforts were in vain in light of the strong headwind he encountered.

In a matter of minutes, the small seaplane crashed into the sea, short of the sandy beach. The tired pilot fought valiantly to control the landing, but the plane hit the water as a large wave caught one of the pontoons, causing the plane to flip over and slide upside down into the sea.

The pilot struggled to release the now jammed hatch as water began to fill the cockpit. His efforts were fruitless. He began to choke and gasp as liquid death poured into his solitary cell. Fighting to free himself until the very end, the pilot drowned as the plane sunk.

The seaplane, the pilot, and his ship never reached their destinations.

Two Days Earlier
Northeast of the Cayman Islands

The pride of the Kreigsmarine's pirate fleet of German surface raiders was the *Achilles*. And the reason for its success was her quiet and thoughtful captain, Karl Koehler. Koehler's reputation was known throughout the Kreigsmarine. He had the uncanny ability to effectively disguise his surface raider into a seemingly innocent freighter and take advantage of unsuspecting victims. This, in turn, resulted in multiple sinkings of Allied commercial vessels and capturing numerous prize ships.

The *Achilles* steamed the mid-Atlantic and the southern Atlantic looking for prey. When she spotted a likely target, she'd draw abreast of the unsuspecting victim. Then, her crew would raise the German naval ensign with its large ominous swastika and drop her plywood sides to reveal her bristling armament and herself as one of the premier surface raiders in Hitler's pirate fleet.

The *Achille*s was well equipped as a vessel, ready to mask her identity. She could raise or lower masts and funnels and alter her profile with dummy bows and structures. Her wardrobe included an assortment of flags from neutral countries so that she could approach her prey as a neutral vessel.

She was originally an express freighter, a 7,862-ton vessel that was 500 feet long and 60 feet wide. Her top cruising speed was 25 knots. This hunter-killer had six 5.9-inch guns, hidden on deck and ready for action. Also concealed on her decks were a 75-mm gun, two twin 37-mm guns and four 20-mm guns. Below the waterline, were four 21-inch torpedo tubes, two on each side of the ship.

Below deck and in cargo hold #2 was a Henkel He 114B seaplane. Using a crane, the crew could lift it from the hold and place it in the water. Usually the raider carried two seaplanes, but it was decided to sacrifice one for this mission in order to have more space for their valuable cargo. The seaplanes were usually used as scout craft to scour the surrounding area for potential targets and also to identify enemy warships.

On other missions, she was known to carry up to 92 mines for deposit in enemy shipping lanes. This mission was different. Rather than using her stealth to seek enemy victims, she would be using her stealth to avoid detection and safely deliver her valuable cargo.

It was due to his success and the Allied advance into Germany that Koehler and his ship had been given a secret assignment and now found themselves headed into the South Atlantic. Loaded in their cargo hold were crates containing gold, which the Nazis had stolen from countless banks throughout Europe. The gold was being transported to Argentina where the Nazis would secrete it for a new Reich.

On three occasions, ships on the horizon surprised them. Not wanting to raise any suspicions nor cause a ship to send out radio messages if the *Achilles* suddenly changed direction and steamed away, the crew had resorted to subterfuge when ships passed dangerously close to the raider.

While the majority of the crew stood at their battle stations, ready to drop camouflage and open fire, the rest of the crew created the subterfuge. They played their ruse to the end with several of the crew roving the decks in civilian disguise and waving at the passing vessels. One crewmember, reluctantly dressed as a female, pushed a baby carriage around the deck. To the passing ships, it gave the appearance of a neutral freighter making her way peacefully. And it worked.

In addition to avoiding enemy warships, the crew had to avoid contact with other German raiders. Their mission was so secret that the other raiders had not been advised and could view the *Achilles* as an interesting target. Even though Koehler could resort to using signal flags in order to avoid breaking his mandate of radio silence, he was under strict orders not to communicate with other raiders. If he did, it would only raise questions in the minds of the other raiders' captains and spread throughout the Kreigsmarine.

Koehler turned his eyes to the deck below and smiled as he saw the crew conducting their duties. Lookouts were posted. All seemed to be going well. Koehler was anxious to complete this mission. He longed for action and couldn't wait to unload his valuable cargo in Argentina and return to raiding.

His attention was distracted when he saw the dark clouds on the horizon and billowing thunderheads. It appeared that they would be heading into a serious tropical storm. Turning on his heels, he strode into the wheelhouse.

Off the Coast of Cuba
1960

The *Murask*, a Brigadier Type II Class frigate and also known as patrol vessel #380, was part of the convoy making its way to Havana. She was one of several frigates escorting the convoy of

Soviet freighters. The decks of the freighters contained several covered, long cylindrical objects. These objects were the focus of international discussion and heightened tension between the White House and the Kremlin.

The Kennedy administration was rattling their sabers and Khrushchev was standing defiant. The U-2 photos of the Soviet missile sites in Cuba and continued missile shipments were taking the world to the brink of a nuclear war.

From the bridge of the *Murask*, Captain Petr Russinoff grimly eyed the U.S. Navy destroyers, which were steaming parallel to and shadowing the convoy.

"If only the Americans knew what we had on board," Russinoff mused with a sly grin on his face.

"What is that, Captain?" his first mate asked.

"Nothing. Nothing." Changing the topic, he spoke seriously, "Maintain your course. I'm returning to my cabin, should you need me."

"Yes, sir!"

Russinoff left the bridge and walked down the companionway to his quarters. He realized that he must be careful when he mused aloud. Only he knew about that secret cargo, which had been skillfully concealed on board his ship. When the time was right, he would be ordered to use it against the Americans. He smiled as he opened his cabin door and thought about the dangerous maelstrom he'd release upon receipt of the order, an order that Khrushchev and only Khrushchev could give. It would have a devastating effect upon the population of the United States.

Havana, Cuba
1996

The late afternoon sun seemed to heat up the hot air even more as the old Cadillac pulled to the curb in front of Havana's airport. In the back seat were two Soviet Naval officers. Commander Ivan Katzukov was looking forward to the flight to Moscow and a return to his family. Since the Cuban Missile Crisis, he had been the fourth captain assigned to the *Murask*.

With dissolvement of the U.S.S.R. and the closing of the old Soviet base in Cuba, the two frigates, the *Murask* and missile frigate #356, were being decommissioned and their crews repatriated to the newly created Russian Republic. As duties were wrapped up, crew members were flown out of Cuba. After Katzukov and seven crew members departed today, only Katzukov's second in command would remain to conduct one crucial task before flying out the next day.

Grasping his brief case, Katzukov stepped out of the car. His second-in-command, Vasiliy Zarubkin, followed him closely. Zarubkin had joined his ship two years earlier and had served him well.

"Good day for a flight," Zarubkin said as he joined his captain on the curb.

"Yes, it is." Katzukov glanced skyward at the brilliant blue Cuban sky. He was going to miss this assignment in the Caribbean.

The driver pulled two large suitcases from the car's trunk and deposited them on the curb next to Katzukov. He then returned to the car to wait for Zarubkin to reenter.

"Captain, you said you had one last assignment for me?"

The captain looked directly into Zarubkin's eyes for a moment, then lowering his voice, replied, "Yes, my dear Vasiliy." The captain motioned Zarubkin to move closer to him. "I am going to entrust you with a state secret. You cannot share this with anyone, but I need you to act upon this tomorrow. Only you and no one else should be around the ship when you do this." He leaned forward and whispered his instructions to his comrade.

Zarubkin's eyes widened as he heard the instructions. "How long have you known that this was on board?" Zarubkin asked fretfully.

"Since I took command. You must understand that I was sworn to secrecy."

"I do," Zarubkin fidgeted. He thought about the deadly consequences to the crew and himself should an accident have happened and the evil whirlwind had been unleashed. A cold chill ran up his spine as he thought about his task.

"Do you have any questions as to how you are to handle this?" Katzukov looked seriously at his friend.

"No, sir. I will be very careful in disposing of it."

"Bury it deep in the jungle. There will be little danger then of someone finding it and using it."

"I'll follow your orders." Zarubkin tried to conceal his nervousness, but Katzukov still sensed it.

"Good, then I will wish you well. I am sure our paths will cross again, but who knows with the turmoil in the homeland today."

They were returning to their respective provinces and did not know when they would see each other again.

"I will do my duty."

Yes, you will, Katzukov thought as they shook hands. Katzukov picked up his suitcases and walked into the terminal. It was better that this task be assigned to Zarubkin. After all, he was not married and did not have children. Katzukov didn't disclose to Zarubkin that his original orders were for him to handle the disposal himself. But he didn't want to place himself in danger. It was the first time that Katzukov had disobeyed an order.

Shaken, Zarubkin entered the car and settled into the back seat.

"Where to?" the driver asked.

Zarubkin gave the driver directions to a seedy bar that he had frequented from time to time. He decided to have one last drunk in the event that something went amiss the next day. Zarubkin didn't know it at the time, but he was about to enter dangerous waters.

After leaving the airport and entering the city, the taxi careened down several narrow streets and pulled to an abrupt stop in front of the bar. Zarubkin paid the driver and dismissed him.

Zarubkin's insides were in turmoil as he entered the worn building and took a wobbly seat at the bar. He threw a wad of cash on the bar and ordered his first drink. For the next hour, the 47-year-old Zarubkin downed a variety of drinks, from Russian vodka to island rum. His vision began to cloud, as did his judgment.

He tossed more crumpled cash on the bar as he downed another shot of vodka and wiggled his head from side to side in an effort to shake the fuzziness from his vision. The slender built Russian was enjoying his buzz.

"Hello, señor," a voice whispered sensually in his ear.

Zarubkin turned slowly to his right to find the source of the voice. With distorted vision, he saw a slightly overweight Cuban woman with long dark hair and brown eyes. Her lips were painted in high gloss red. She was wearing a faded blue blouse, held together by one button, which strained to contain her ample bosom. Below the blouse, she wore a colorfully patterned skirt and red heels.

"May I join you?" she cooed. She had been watching the Russian Naval officer since he entered the building. She had also seen the wads of cash that he had been throwing on the bar as well as the heavy drinking. She bided her time as she watched him drink and planned on when she would approach him. She knew how to stalk her prey. That's how she made her living.

The bartender winked slyly at her as he refilled the shot glass. "Señor, this one is on the house," he said. In the past, he had seen Maria Alvarez draw unsuspecting drinkers into her web like a black widow spider. As long as he didn't interrupt her plans and looked the other way, he usually ended up with a large tip from her. The tip would be delivered to him the next day after she had "collected" her fees.

In his dazed state, Zarubkin allowed his reddened eyes to freely look the woman up and down. Not bad, he thought to himself. Of course, in his state, any woman would look appealing. "Sit right here," he answered as he patted the bar stool next to him.

Alvarez surprised Zarubkin by scooting the bar stool a little closer to him before plopping her ample bottom on it. She crossed her leg, allowing her fleshy thigh to come into view. She leaned in to Zarubkin as she slipped one chubby arm around his shoulder and began to stroke the back of his neck.

Her sensuous strokes on his neck sent warm feelings down his spine. He smiled as he asked, "Drink?"

"That would be nice!"

Turning to call the bartender, Zarubkin was surprised to find him standing in front of him. "Give the lady whatever she wants."

"Señorita?" The bartender already knew what she would ask for, but had to play his part in this charade.

"Tequila."

The bartender turned and reached for her special bottle on the top shelf.

"And what is this pretty lady's name?" Zarubkin slurred his words.

"Maria." She didn't have to force the return smile. She knew that she had selected the right prey.

" I'm Vasiliy."

"You're Russian?" she asked although the uniform already revealed his nationality to her.

"Yes," he responded as the bartender returned with her drink and placed it in front of her.

Alvarez picked up the shot glass and threw her drink down. Then she returned the empty glass to the bar, smacking her lips as she did. "May I have another?" she asked as she leaned further into Zarubkin and began to slowly rub her left breast on his right arm.

Zarubkin grinned as his dulled mind shifted to think about the evening's possibilities. He liked what she was doing with her breast. "Yes," he said as he threw his vodka down his throat. "And bring me another, too," he ordered the bartender.

A new sensation now distracted Zarubkin. Alavrez's right hand had begun to rub the top of his right thigh. He beamed as he placed his hand on her thigh and returned the sensation. She, in turn, allowed her hand to drift on to his inner thigh and languidly stroked it, sending electrifying shivers sensuously up his body. Uncontrollably, he emitted a low moan.

"You like that?" she asked, already knowing the answer.

He couldn't talk. Slowly, Zarubkin nodded his head. His eyes were closed and heavy with desire. He was on his way to la-la land.

The bartender returned with the refills and quietly set them in front of them. He didn't want to interrupt her evil maneuvers.

Alvarez removed her hand from his thigh and picked up his shot glass. "Here, let me do this for you," she said as she picked up his drink and lifted it to his lips. "Drink it down."

As Zarubkin opened his mouth and swallowed, Alvarez bent close to his right ear. She purred, "There are other things that you could let me do to you, too. I'm sure that you would enjoy them."

Before Zarubkin could respond, Alvarez's pink tongue darted out. It found its target. It penetrated his ear, sending more electrifying feelings through his body. He moaned in response.

"I have a room we could go to if you'd like," she offered as she allowed her puffy lips to sexily slide across his right cheek. Zarubkin turned suddenly and tried to kiss her lips, but she quickly pulled back.

"Uh, uh," she said with a demure look, enticing Zarubkin. "Only if we go to my room." She abruptly withdrew all physical contact with him and threw down her shot.

Zarubkin didn't like the interruption to the sensations flooding his body. He reached out to draw her back to him.

Pushing his hands away, she said, "No, no. Only if we go to my room." She looked at him and waited to see if he would take the bait.

She didn't have to wait long. He devoured the bait and threw more cash on the bar. "That should take care of the bill," he said as the bartender magically appeared and scooped up the cash.

"Let's go visit that room," Zarubkin said with a drunken grin.

Alvarez was proud of herself. Her approach worked every time for her. She slid off the bar stool, allowing more thigh to show as she teased her unsuspecting prey. "Here, let me help you," she said as the drunken Zarubkin tried to stand. He wobbled and almost fell, but Alvarez steadied him as she placed one arm around his waist.

"There we go. Don't want you to fall and hurt yourself. We've got plans for tonight, don't we, Basil?" she cooed.

"Vasiliy," he corrected her as he felt her left breast swell against his arm again.

"Vasiliy," she said, but to herself she thought, who in the hell cares.

Zarubkin was so drunk and enraptured by her attention that he failed to notice that she was walking him toward the rear door of the bar. He also didn't notice that she threw a wink over her shoulder to the bartender, who was already picking up her special tequila bottle. He carried it to the sink and refilled it with water. Then, he replaced it on the shelf so that it would be ready for her next victim. He did this for several of his lady "clients," knowing that he would be tipped for his help.

As Zarubkin and Alvarez stumbled out of the rear door, a figure arose from a small table in a shadowy corner of the bar. He had been watching Zarubkin and had seen Alvarez approach him to practice her trade. He had settled back in his chair and nursed his drink. He would wait until the right moment presented itself. He was a very patient man.

He finished his drink and walked to the door. Stepping through it, he saw the couple walking unsteadily around the corner. He quickly stalked after them. It wouldn't take him long to catch up to them.

The next morning, a warm drizzle did little to provide relief to the high humidity of the previous day. The rain-washed away some of the dust and litter in the streets and back alleys. In one alley, it did little to wash away the blood caked on the face of a man whose eyes stared lifelessly into the rain.

The blood originated from a deep wound at the top of his head and covered the scratch mark trails left on both cheeks by a pair of long fingernails. Alvarez had been interrupted in her robbery attempt when Zarubkin screamed out and the pipe connected with his head, causing the bloody wound. Zarubkin had crumpled in a heap on to the dusty alley where he died.

Alvarez had turned to look at the figure, who had followed them and was now holding the pipe in his hand. "You didn't have to do that!" she said.

Two steely eyes glared at her in response.

"Who are you?" she asked as the two eyes narrowed and she saw the figure in front of her begin to lift the pipe over his head. "I'll share what I've taken from him." There was no change in the figure's demeanor. She pushed the cash toward him. "No, you take it all," she cried out as the pipe swung down abruptly and connected with her temple. Her lifeless body dropped next to Zarubkin's.

The figure reached down and pried the wad of cash from her clenched hand. Casually, he tossed the pipe into the alley and walked away, counting his evening's take.

When the bartender read about the murders in the newspaper, he shrugged his shoulders as he realized his big tip wouldn't be forthcoming. He reached for her bottle on the top shelf. Taking the cap off, he emptied the water into the sink and tossed the empty bottle in the trash. Glancing at the empty space on the top shelf, he wondered how long it would be before another Alvarez walked in and made a similar arrangement with him. Probably not long, he thought to himself.

He was going to miss Alvarez. She had been very generous with her tips, more so than the other ladies. This was the first time that Alvarez hadn't completed her part of their arrangement. He didn't know that this was also the first time that Zarubkin failed to complete a mission. Zarubkin's failure would have dire circumstances in the future.

Several Years Later
The Round House
Put-in-Bay, South Bass Island

Between Cleveland and Toledo and off the Catawba Peninsula, which juts into Lake Erie like a long finger pointing the way to paradise, is a group of alluring islands. Like magnets for fun seekers, they attract people from throughout the Midwest. Pre-eminent among these emerald-like islands is South Bass Island and its crown jewel, the quaint resort town of Put-in-Bay. It is located on the north side of the island and is widely known as the "Key West of the Midwest."

Using the Jet Express from the mainland, visitors enter Put-in-Bay's sheltered harbor with Gibraltar Island on the starboard side and East Point on the port side. They are welcomed by a large array of watercraft at anchor or at the docks. As visitors disembark from the Jet Express, they observe the partying on the boats at the nearby docks and hear the air filled with shouts as scantily clad male and female bodies sensually gyrate to the loud music coming from the expensive boats' equally expensive sound systems. It's another Put-in-Bay weekend of escape from the reality of life.

Visitors cross busy Bay View Avenue and walk through the shaded DeRivera Park, which is bounded on three sides by a mixture of bars, restaurants and gift shops. On the far side of the park and running parallel to Bay View is the village's main street, Delaware.

The centerpiece of Delaware is the architecturally unique Round House Bar. It's a bright red, wooden, circular building with a silver domed roof. A large white-railed porch, adorned with stars and stripes banners, offers a respite from the heat. At the ends of the porch are mounted two flags, one is the United States flag; the other is the Canadian flag.

From the ceiling of the Round House hangs a red, white and blue striped canopy, which is held in place by a wooden bicycle wheel with lights. The circular interior walls are constructed of plaster and are adorned with murals painted by the late Canoe Bob. They contain familiar scenes of the islands like the Ford Trimotor plane, the Battle of Lake Erie, sailboats, and steamers in the harbor.

The popular resort bar's afternoon crowd broke into applause when legendary island entertainer, Mike "Mad Dog" Adams, entered the room from a doorway to the right of the semi-circular bar. Carrying his guitar, the tall, powerfully built and rugged Mad Dog made his way past the female bartenders and climbed the stairs to the large stage perched above the top shelf liquor. As he climbed the stairs, his female admirers screamed at the top of their lungs and waved copies of the Men of Put-in-Bay calendar, which they wanted him to autograph. He was Mr. July and his bare barrel chest dominated the page.

Today, this bearded pirate was attired in a stars and stripes dew rag and a gold earring dangled from his left ear lobe. His billowy linen shirt was unbuttoned halfway down his muscular chest, revealing a gold coin hanging from a gold chain. He had discovered the coin while diving off the Cayman Islands a few years earlier.

This entertainment machine had opened nationally for major musical acts such as Johnny Cash, Loretta Lynn, Jerry Lee Lewis and the Oak Ridge Boys. He had been named as top entertainer in Ohio by one of the major Cleveland radio stations. He was also known throughout the Caribbean for his acts in the winter months, a musical Caribbean cruise he sponsored each February out of Miami and his antics during Put-in-Bay Days in Key West. In the Cayman Islands, Mad Dog had been lauded as the Pirate Comedy King during Mardi Gras festivities and had participated in Pirates' Week events.

Every afternoon from May through September, Mad Dog entertained his Round House audience with a mixture of comedy and songs. His repertoire included songs he had written as well as rock & roll, country and island type songs like those of Jimmy Buffet.

Approaching the stage microphone, Mad Dog adjusted his guitar and surveyed his afternoon audience. A smile crossed his face as he saw many of the 300 patrons, who packed the bar and dressed in pirate attire for the weekend. He threw an ornery wink at one sexily attired wench and, with a twinkle in his eye, opened his afternoon show.

"By a show of hands, how many of you have never been here before?" he asked.

About a third of the room raised their hands while the others shouted, "Yeah!"

"How many of you have been here before?"

"Yeah!" boisterously shouted the return visitors as they raised their hands.

"How many of you don't know where you are or how you got here?" Mad Dog yelled as his face broke into a confidant smile.

The crowd responded with another "Yeah!"

"And how many of you just don't give a damn?"

Again the crowd yelled back to the singer.

"You guys want to have a good time?"

"Yeah!"

"Then, let's get the hell out of here!" Mad Dog teased. "Don't forget that every day above ground is a good day. So, let's have a little fun! You ready?"

"Yeah," the crowd roared.

"Put-in-Bay is the only place where the taxi drivers' motto is 'We drink and drive so you don't have to!'" The crowd chuckled as Mad Dog continued, "I was riding my bike around the island today and got pulled over by a Put-in-Bay policeman for crashing a stop sign. When he recognized me, the officer asked me to say something funny. I said, 'You're good looking!'"

The crowd roared.

"Put-in-Bay is the only place where the hotel delivers a bottle of wine to my room by throwing it through the window!"

Laughter filled the room as Mad Dog's eyes settled on one young patron who had extremely spiked hair. "What the hell happened to your hair?"

The patron smiled weakly.

"That will teach you to never call the guy who cuts your hair a fag."

The crowd tittered.

Looking at a guy wearing a loud shirt, Mad Dog yelled, "Nice shirt! Is it made from the Norwegian flag?"

Amidst the laughter, Mad Dog zeroed in on another patron in a loud shirt. "You know, my grandmother had a couch made out of the same material!"

Surveying his audience again, he cooed as he looked at the wenches, "Don't we have some pretty wenches here today? What do you say me buckos?"

The men responded wildly.

Arching his right eyebrow, Mad Dog snarled, "Arrrrrrrgh, I think me be inviting some of them to walk me plank!"

The crowd roared as two wenches in front of the stage briefly bared their chests to the entertainer. Mad Dog smiled and looked over the audience. "What can I say guys, they do this to me all the time. But I never get tired of it!" He let a large smile cross his face as he looked at one of the wenches. "I wish you were the pony in front of Wal-Mart, then I could ride you all afternoon for a quarter," he grinned with a salacious look as the packed bar filled with more laughter.

He reached over to a nearby table and picked up a waiting shot glass. It was filled to the brim. He turned back to the audience as he began to raise the glass to his lips. Before downing his shot, he shouted his legendary, German drinking chant as the audience joined in.

"Ziggy, Zaggy, Ziggy, Zaggy, Hoy, Hoy, Hoy!
  Ziggy, Zaggy, Ziggy, Zaggy, Hoy, Hoy, Hoy!
 Ein, Zwei, Drei!"

He and the audience downed their drinks as the bartenders scurried to refill them. Mad Dog threw his shot glass to the floor behind him. By the end of the afternoon, there would be a dozen shot glasses littering the floor. Mad Dog began to strum his guitar as he broke into one of his popular island songs.

A figure standing near the front door turned and exited the Round House. He had been walking by and stopped in for a moment to enjoy the opening of Mad Dog's show. He was smiling as he walked east along Delaware Avenue as he thought about his friend, Mad Dog. Little did Mad Dog's audience realize that Mad Dog had been an ex-Navy SEAL early in his career. He had been in and out of some sticky situations in that role.

The tanned, 6-foot-2 figure with glossy black hair and dark brown eyes smiled as he walked past the island's Village Bakery and Sandwich Shoppe, home of the best pies on the island. He waved at its high-energy owner, Pauline, who was conversing with Maggie and Linda from the Chamber of Commerce office next door.

Pauline returned the wave as Maggie, who could never let an opportunity to jab Emerson Moore pass by, yelled out, "Hey Emerson! Got any beads?"

Her ornery sister, Linda, added, "Want to earn some beads?"

Emerson Moore responded "Any time with you, Linda." Smiling, *The Washington Post* investigative reporter crossed the street and climbed into his aunt's golf cart. He had become fond of his three lady friends and enjoyed their good-natured teasing.

As he started the golf cart and pulled into the street to head to Aunt Anne's house on East Point, he thought back again to Mad Dog and his undercover work. Mad Dog had often told Emerson that he did his best Put-in-Bay work under covers.

February
Put-in-Bay

Since Lake Erie is the shallowest of the Great Lakes, it gets the most extensive ice-cover of any of the Great Lakes. The Lake is fed from the Detroit River on the western end as well as numerous streams and rivers. This stream of water passes eastward and under the ice to its outlet on the Niagara River through Niagara Falls.

South Bass Island, located in the middle of western Lake Erie, has many coves in which sheet ice may grow. It also has shorelines with projecting points, which stop and amass wind-driven ice floes. Major currents move eastward and westward by the islands and through the South Passage between the south side of the island and the mainland as well as the North Passage between the island's north side and Middle Bass Island.

Ice most often forms in late December or January with the formation of splash-ice on the cliffs and the beaches. Chilling of the lake's surface water is expedited by snowfall and cold nights, causing a thin cover of sheet ice to form on the lake. This sheet ice is further augmented by expanding ice crystals below the ice sheet as well as freezing rain, snow and frost on the ice's surface.

While new ice is being added onto the bottom of the sheet ice, the top surface suffers losses to its integrity through melting and vaporization. Sheet ice can be broken up by storms during the winter season. The resulting ice floes may shift and freeze together to form new ice covers.

Winter snowfall in the group of islands clustered in the western basin of Lake Erie can be relatively mild compared to the lake effect snow dumping on Cleveland and even more so on Buffalo. The wintry storms typically move eastward and pick up moisture as they cross Lake Erie, then bury the snow belt, which runs from Cleveland through Erie to Buffalo.

The converse can be true if the wind blows in from the east. Then, Put-in-Bay and Toledo get hammered like Buffalo. Snow on Put-in-Bay's main tourist strip on Delaware Avenue can be as high as three feet.

The biggest threat to the 400 hardy islanders, who live on South Bass Island year round, is the strong wind. It can send temperatures plunging. The second biggest threat is the ice. What may have been safe ice one day may have become unsafe the next day as a result of changing weather conditions.

New and clear ice is typically strong ice whereas cloudy ice signals air and weak ice. Ice formed from muddy water and after a strong blow attracts the sun's warmth and will weaken and melt faster than other types of ice. As the ice cracks, fissures occur and typically run parallel to the shoreline. This is a result of changing water levels and the ice's thermal expansion and contraction. Some fissures appear annually in the same places due to regular movement of the water currents.

Inexperienced ice travelers are unaware of the dangerous currents in the channels and over reefs. These currents flow under the ice and erode the ice from underneath. In some places the ice may be six inches thick. But in others, the current can erode the ice, making it dangerously thin. Thin ice can be like a death trap, waiting for its next victim to plunge through.

East winds will cause the lake's water level to fluctuate and water will seep through cracks in the ice and lay on top of the ice, causing it to sag from the weight. A layer of drifting snow can then cover the area and freeze, but an unsuspecting person driving through this type of ice will break through to the lake bottom.

One might perceive that the easiest route over the ice to Put-in-Bay from the mainland is from the Miller Ferry terminal on the

Catawba Peninsula's north side to Lime Kiln Dock on the southeast side of South Bass Island. That's where perceptions can get people in trouble. There's a strong current between those two points, the South Passage, which can undermine the rigidity of the ice.

Each year, experienced islanders test the ice and mark safe routes between the two points, often using recycled Christmas trees. At certain times of the year and after a good freeze, it's not unusual to see islanders drive their vehicles across the ice as they pick up supplies. Some of the more adventuresome islanders drive out on the ice in vehicles with the doors removed so they can exit quickly if their vehicles break through the ice. It's not unusual to see four-wheeler ATV's with 20 gallon plastic drums attached to the front and rear so that they'll float in the event they crash through the ice.

When it warms in late winter, ice molecules go through a change. The change diminishes their strength and moves them from a horizontal orientation, which supports weight to vertical strength, which does not. The warming air can also change solid ice to a slush pack, like walking through a melting snow cone. As ice cracks and separates, strong blowing winds can create ice shoves as tall as the gazebo in DeRivera Park.

Another danger occurs when ice breaks apart and ice fisherman with their shanties and vehicles are cast adrift in the lake. Many times, the stranded fisherman are on their cell phones giving rescuers directions by using their handheld GPS units. Sometimes, islanders will use their hovercraft to rescue stranded fisherman and then return to the floating ice floe and take ownership of the abandoned vehicles and shanties.

From the air, Coast Guard helicopters can spot the cracks in the ice and, using their speakers, warn fisherman below. They usually close off with, "We can pick you up now or your body later." That message seems to drive home the seriousness of the situation.

Heavy east winds will allow ice to break free and push it westward and away from the islands. Once, 40 ice shanties drifted west off of Rattlesnake Island to West Sister Island and then a few days later eastward to Green Island. During the voyage, some of the shanties sunk, some were crushed and a few remained intact for salvagers to recover.

A fun event for islanders as the ice breaks apart in Put-in-Bay's harbor is ice cake jumping. Islanders of all ages carefully jump from one ice cake to another as a crowd gathers to watch. It teaches respect for the ice and is relatively safe in the shallower harbor area although missing an ice cake dumps the jumper into frigid water. If the wind is blowing strong, it isn't unusual to see some islanders doff their coats and hold them aloft like sails. Once the wind filled their handheld coats, their makeshift sailing vessels take them across the harbor.

On this cold February day, islanders watched as one of the planes from Dairy Air's fleet, the island's only island-based airline service, circled over several of the ice shanties as it returned from a flight to the mainland for supplies and passengers. The rambunctious airline owner, Denny Watson, was on a mission and looking for one particular customer.

Emerging from one of the ice fishing shanties in an area known as Chryslerville, was island ice fishing guide, Pat Chrysler. Chrysler had heard the plane's engines as it circled and stepped out to wave at his old friend. He also knew what his friend was bringing him. He looked skyward as Watson opened the pilot's side window, allowing cold air to rush into the cabin, much to the dismay of one of his passengers.

"Oh," she started, "it's too cold."

"Patience, my dear. Patience," the pilot replied as he grabbed the five white McDonald's bags containing Egg McMuffins. Extracting two Egg McMuffins, he casually tossed them out the open window. "Got to check the windage," he explained to his chilled passenger. He watched as they dropped and splattered on the ice. He knew that the first two were always sacrificed to Chrysler's two Yellow Labs.

He then twisted the top of each bag shut so that the excess bagginess created enough aerodynamic drag to slow the McMuffins descent for a soft landing on the ice. To keep the bags closed, he tied plastic yellow caution tape to them. The yellow tape would act as a streamer when the bag was dropped and assist Chrysler in locating his breakfast. He lined up the plane for a run and tossed the five bags, one at a time, out the window. The bags gracefully floated to the waiting and very hungry ice fishermen.

Chrysler waved a thank you to Watson who responded by dipping his wings and closing the window, much to the relief of his passenger, as he headed to the Put-in-Bay airport.

"In the summer, I'll tie a few ice cream bars inside of a white kitchen trash bag and drop it across the bow of his fishing boat," Watson told his passenger, who was still trying to recover from the blast of cold air.

The previous day, a visiting fisherman and his two dogs strolled away from their ice shanty and its relatively safe ice. Unknowingly, they ventured onto thin ice. The ice beneath them gave way like a trap door, plunging the three of them into the freezing water. They began splashing and thrashing about as the shock of the fall took the fisherman's breath away.

The fisherman worked hard to push his dogs out of the water and onto the ice, but as he worked, hypothermia began to set in. It was always a race against time when you fell through.

Too late, the fisherman remembered that he had an emergency whistle hanging around his neck. He reached for it and began to feebly blow for help. He had exerted so much energy in pushing his dogs onto the ice that he was in a much weakened state. The advancing hypothermia didn't help matters either.

No one heard the low blasts from his whistle as the man sank into unconsciousness and began to sink from the weight of his waterlogged clothing. The two dogs seeing their master in distress, jumped back into the frigid lake water in an attempt to rescue him.

Three hours later, several ice fishermen found him and his two dogs. It was too late. The fisherman was pronounced dead at the scene. So were the dogs.

A week earlier, an experienced ice resident, after several hours of drinking at one of Put-in-Bay's bars, started a late night trek from Put-in-Bay to Middle Bass Island. Despite invitations to spend the night from several of the Put-in-Bay residents, he decided to brave the frigid west wind, which was blowing snow almost horizontally, and walk home. It was a walk that he had made without incident for years. However, this night was going to be an exception.

Because of the blowing snow, he missed the Christmas tree-marked path and walked out onto thin ice over the current. He plunged through the ice and into the cold water. He was fortunate that the current did not sweep him away from the hole and he was able to quickly resurface due to the flotation device he was wearing.

Reaching for his ice picks, which hung from a piece of twine around his neck, he struggled to plant them on the surface of the ice. As he did, he kicked his legs to bring his body horizontal to the ice and was able to slowly pull himself out of the water and onto his belly as he made forward progress with the ice picks. Once he was on ice, which would support him, he rolled over and away from the thin ice.

Cautiously, he moved away from the hole and stood. He gathered his thoughts while he determined his exact location with the handheld GPS he had retrieved from his pocket. Now sober as a result of his near encounter with death, he realized how far off the path he had wandered. Using his GPS, he slowly made his way through the blinding snowstorm to the path and continued his journey home to Middle Bass Island and a warm fireplace.

This night, a snowmobile, pulling a small skid, was speeding across the lake. There was a nor'easter blowing snow horizontally. The three occupants, two on the snowmobile and one on the skid, were returning from doing repair work for Cary and Ralph Butler on the Catawba Peninsula.

Ralph had retired from the Miller Ferry, which served as the shortest route to South Bass Island. The Butlers were known for their hospitality, but especially for making a fine Catawba wine. In appreciation for the repair work, they graciously offered wine and hot-out-of-the-oven bread to their friends. Time and weather had been forgotten as the three drank a little too much of the couple's Catawba grape wine and consumed portions of the hot bread, saturated in melting butter.

Islander Buzz Barton was driving the snowmobile. Wine was his weakness and he had imbibed more than the others. Seated behind him was Emerson Moore, who had also volunteered to help on the home repair project.

In the skid, being pulled by the snowmobile, was part-time island dock worker and full-time bartender, Carl Deitz, who had elected to winter at Put-in-Bay this year and skip his annual bar tendering gig in Key West. Deitz also had too much wine that evening.

They were a little more than a half-mile northwest of Catawba Peninsula when Barton abruptly brought the snowmobile to a halt. With the engine idling, he stood up, wobbling as he did.

"What's wrong?" Emerson queried.

"Drank too much. Got to take a piss," Barton replied as he stepped off and walked a few paces away.

"Make sure you aim downwind," Deitz chortled from the skid as the frigid wind blew in from the east.

"I'll be doing well to unbutton and unzip all this gear before I wet myself," Barton retorted as he struggled to unzip his snowmobile suit. "Thought I could make it home, but nature calls, boys."

Emerson heard Deitz getting up from the skid and was surprised when he walked by and settled into the seat, that Barton had vacated.

"What are you doing?" Emerson asked as the heavyset Deitz plumped his large frame in front of him. Emerson had to scoot back a few inches to give Deitz extra room.

"I've always wanted to drive one of these at night across the ice. It'd be better if I drove the rest of the way home. He's had too much to drink."

Squinting through the furious snowstorm, Emerson cautiously replied, "This is not good weather to experience your first night drive."

Deitz kept his sullen thoughts to himself although he was on the verge of unleashing a series of expletives at Emerson. When he drank, he had a tendency to become mean and want to do things his way. His mind was made up, he was going to drive and no one would budge him from his seat at the controls.

Both of their heads turned to look at Barton, who continued to wobble as a yellow stream of urine hit the ice. "I'm writing my name in the ice," Barton tittered. It was a guy thing.

When he finished urinating, he turned and saw Deitz at the controls. "And what in the hell do you think you're doing there?"

"My turn," Deitz grinned. "You've had too much wine and I've waited on you enough over the years to know when I need to drive you home. Tonight's one of them nights."

"Nah, too dangerous. You don't know the way. And you can't see the way. Ice is too dangerous. You can drive another night," Barton cautioned.

"Emerson, you've been on the trail before. You know the route, right?" Deitz turned halfway around to look at Emerson.

"I've been on it several times. As long as I can see the markers, we'd be all right. But in this driving snow, no one is going to see the markers. Let Buzz drive," he replied. Inner alarm bells were going off in Emerson's brain. There was no way that any-one in his right mind would let Deitz pilot the snowmobile. His experience with ice didn't come close to matching Barton's.

There had been an early thaw in the last week and patches of open water. A new cold front had moved in that morning, caus-ing a layer of thin ice to form over the open water.

"Like I said, too dangerous," Barton said as he returned to the side of the snowmobile and began to dislodge Deitz from his seat. Deitz gave a good-natured shove back at Barton. Suddenly, Barton's feet slipped out from under him and he crashed onto the ice. His head hit the ice with a large thud, knocking him unconscious. At the same time, his head landed in the area where he had just urinated, erasing his name, which he had so artfully written.

"Not a good move, Deitz," Emerson said as he leapt from the snowmobile and knelt by Barton's side. "Buzz, you okay? Can you hear me?" he asked as he moved Barton's body away from the yellowed ice.

Barton's only response was a moan.

Emerson glared at Deitz. "Don't just sit there! Help me move him to the skid."

Deitz stood and walked over to Barton. "Looks like Buzz has a buzz on." He snorted out loud.

Emerson glared at Deitz as he motioned him to help. The two men laid Barton on the skid and tried to make him as comfortable as possible.

"Better tie him on," Deitz said. "Don't want him falling off while we're flying across the ice."

"I don't know about that," Emerson said. Emerson knew the danger of going through the ice. A person needed to be able to extricate himself quickly if he went through the ice.

Deitz ignored him and picked up several pieces of twine from the skid. He began to secure Barton. "We'll just use a few pieces." Deitz began to secure Barton. "Got a knife? I need this cut."

Emerson produced a knife from his pocket and cut the twine. Twice more, he cut the twine as Deitz worked feverishly in the growing wind. Emerson returned the knife to his pocket as Deitz spoke, "We better get going."

"Go slow. We don't want to stray outside of the trail markers," Emerson cautioned as he took his seat behind Deitz.

Grinning as he adjusted his goggles, Deitz raced the engine a couple of times and then eased the snowmobile forward. After glancing back at Barton, Deitz picked up speed.

"Slow down," Emerson shouted in Deitz's ear.

Deitz ignored him and they raced through the growing snowstorm toward South Bass Island. Due to their consumption of wine and the reduced visibility in the snowstorm, neither Deitz nor Emerson realized that they were veering off the trail. As they raced along the trail, they both mistook a shadow as one of the Christmas trees marking it. This mistake took them from the safety of the trail toward unsafe ice.

As they flew across the ice, Emerson realized that he hadn't seen another Christmas tree in a while. He was just about to comment to Deitz when the snowmobile crossed freshly frozen thin ice. The ice gave way, plunging the snowmobile and the attached skid into the frigid water.

As they sunk, Emerson pushed away from Deitz, who was struggling to free himself. With his heart jump-started by falling through the ice, Emerson produced his knife from his pocket and felt his way back to the attached skid as they sank. He quickly sliced the three strands of twine securing Barton. With the growing weight of his wet snowmobile suit, Emerson grasped one of Barton's arms and began to swim upwards.

He was thankful for his scuba training in that he felt that he was better able to handle a dangerous situation like this. But he also realized that getting to the surface quickly was not his only concern. He had to find the opening that they had crashed through.

As he swam upward through the black water, he glanced downward, trying to spot Deitz. He couldn't see him through the darkness. All of a sudden his hand struck the ice overhead. He leveled off and began to search for the opening, but time and air were running out. He pulled Barton up and grasped his legs around him. Then with as much strength as he could muster, he propelled both of his arms through the thin covering of ice above him. Fortunately, he broke through.

Gasping for breath, Emerson reached for Barton and relieved his weakening legs. He brought Barton's head above water. He tried to shove Barton out of the water onto the ice, but the ice broke. Desperately, with hypothermia setting in, he kept pushing Barton onto the ice. The ice continued to break under his weight.

Finally the ice held a portion of Barton's body. Emerson carefully pushed the rest of Barton's body onto the thicker ice. Fatigued, Emerson looked around the open water and tried to spot Deitz. He didn't see him. He considered trying to dive underwater and to locate him, but cast aside that thought as foolhardy. There would be little chance that he could locate Deitz in the dark water.

A cough caused Emerson to turn his head toward Barton. Barton coughed again and his body moved. Emerson resolved to pull himself out of the water. With his left hand, he grabbed one of the spikes from the rope hanging from his neck. He planted it into the ice. It held. He then swung his body parallel to the ice and tried to roll out of the water as he drove the other spike into the ice with his right hand. He couldn't quite make it and slipped back into the water.

Emerson repeated the procedure and this time it was successful. As he rolled onto the ice, he continued his momentum and rolled further away from the open water. Stopping, he reached for one of Barton's legs and pulled Barton farther onto the safer ice.

Barton began coughing up more water and moaned feebly.

"Hang in there, Buzz. You'll be okay," Emerson encouraged him through chattering teeth.

With his strength completely drained, Emerson didn't think twice about trying to stand and go for help. Instead, he wrapped his arms around Barton and tried to do his best to keep him warm. They would spend the night on the ice with hopes of a rescue when the sun broke.

"We'll make it, Buzz." Emerson murmured.

Barton and his wife had befriended Emerson when he had moved to the islands. They had spent time fishing, boating, water skiing and ice fishing together. On one of their evening ice fishing trips, Emerson had commented about living on the island during the winter. He had told Barton, "It's so quiet after the lake freezes that you can hear the snowflakes falling in the woods when you walk."

Barton's four children had grown close to Emerson. The youngest child, Cortnee, had been especially fond of Emerson. He had taken time with her when he visited to join her for her imaginary tea parties.

Emerson tried to sleep but the cold penetrated him like a sharp knife. As the night passed, Emerson went in and out of consciousness. At times, he was tormented by nightmares of his 16-year-old cousin's death in one of the island's caves and how helpless he had felt when he stayed with his cousin as he died. Those haunting dreams flooded his mind. Finally, he fell into unconsciousness.

The storm ended, leaving an eerie stillness over the lake's ice.

Seven hours later, the quiet of an early morning's bright blue sky was disturbed by the noise of two U.S. Coast Guard rescue helicopters. They were searching the ice for the missing men or for evidence showing snowmobile tracks disappearing into open water. They had been alerted to commence a search when the missing men's friends and families reported them unaccounted for. The worst was feared.

One of the copters slowed and began to descend. It had spotted two bodies huddled together a mile off the marked trail. As the helicopter landed to recover the bodies, it radioed its location, so that the rest of the rescuers could narrow their search for the third person.

Two Weeks Later
Early Morning
Key West, Florida

Carefully, the intruder jimmied the door lock and forced open the door of the trailer in the United Street trailer complex. It made a small noise as he pushed it open.

"Careful, mon," his accomplice cautioned in his heavily accented Jamaican voice.

"Shhhh!" the first man said quietly as he carefully peered into the trailer. The water in the shower was still running and an evil smile crossed his face. Their patience had paid off. They had been crouched next to the trailer for the last two hours and hoping its occupant, their target, would arise and shower.

With his handgun sweeping the room, the first assassin stepped slowly into the trailer's main living area. Walking carefully through the cluttered kitchen, he paused to listen to the shower. He moved into the narrow hallway. At the end, he noticed that the door to the master bedroom was slightly ajar.

Pausing outside the bathroom door, his hand reached for the doorknob. Gripping it and, at the same time, aiming the gun at chest level, he easily turned the knob. Hot steam from the shower waffled through the air as he smiled and pulled the trigger three times. The silenced weapon coughed quietly as its bullets were discharged and penetrated the shower curtain with deadly force.

As he leaned into the bathroom to pull back the shower curtain and finish his victim, he heard a voice.

"Looking for me?"

The gunman whirled to face the now open bedroom door. Framed in the doorway was a powerfully built, blonde-haired, 39-year-old man. The confident grin on his face went well with his cocky attitude. In his hand, he was holding a .45 and it was pointed at the gunman. Panicking, the gunman abruptly raised his gun and fired quickly, missing his target's head by inches. At the same time, the intended victim fired. The narrow hallway was filled with the noise from the explosive fire of the .45.

The gunman's head rocked backwards from the force of the .45's bullet hitting his forehead and he dropped his gun. He staggered backward several steps. In a moment, his body joined his gun on the floor.

"You should have knocked," the ex-Navy SEAL smiled. Noticing a movement, he leapt over the fallen gunman, and quickly moved toward the kitchen. Seeing the second assassin swing his gun to bear on him, he dropped as a gunshot flew overhead. Rolling across the floor and around the kitchen counter, he surprised the gunman.

"Missed me," he grinned nonchalantly as he unleashed a shot from his prone position. The bullet spun the gunman backwards and out the trailer door. Standing, he walked to the doorway and scanned the area outside of his trailer. Seeing no threats to his safety, Sam Duncan walked down the steps and bent over to examine the second gunman. His shot had found its mark. The second gunman was also dead. "Sometimes you wish you weren't so deadly accurate," he mused aloud to himself as he wished that he had been able to take one alive for questioning.

Taking another look around to make sure that no one else was there, he began going through the dead gunman's pockets. He found rental car keys, an airline ticket and a piece of paper with an old photo of Duncan and Duncan's Key West address. "That photo doesn't do me justice. I'm much better looking than that," he muttered as a smile crossed his face and he stood.

Reentering the trailer, he paused a moment to reset the alarm in his trailer door and, then walked into the hallway where he went through the pockets of the other assailant. Duncan then returned to his kitchen area where he picked up the phone and called the Key West Police.

As the dispatcher answered, Duncan could hear the sirens from police cars, which had probably been dispatched to investigate the source of the gunfire in the trailer park. Duncan asked for Harley Rupert, who had an office there.

Rupert was a DEA agent who had worked with Duncan on a number of drug busts and had been involved with Duncan and Emerson Moore a while back on the heist of Mel Fisher's treasure during the middle of Hurricane Charley.

"Harley Rupert here," the deep voice answered. The bearded man with long, black curly hair eased his 300-pound body back into his chair.

"Harley, it's Sam."

"Morning, Sam. What's going down?" his voiced boomed.

"Key West's best are on their way to my place. You can hear the sirens coming."

Rupert's voice became serious. "What have you done now?" he demanded.

"I had two hired gunslingers after me this morning."

Rupert sat upright in his chair. "You okay?"

"Not a scratch."

"Doesn't surprise me. And how are your two visitors?"

"They didn't make it."

Rupert paused. "That doesn't surprise me either. It would have been nice to question them."

"Yeah, it would have."

"Know them?"

"No." Duncan paused, then continued. "They're Jamaican."

"Locals?"

"Nope. Found rental car keys in the one's pocket. He had an airline ticket stub in his other pocket."

"Kingston, then?"

"One did."

"What about the other?"

"Funny thing. He had a ticket from Grand Cayman."

"Grand Cayman?"

"Yeah. The two are fairly close together. Jamaica is east of the Cayman Islands," Duncan reminded Rupert. "They run drugs to the East End of the Caymans."

"Tell me something I don't know," Rupert fidgeted. Duncan knew that Rupert had a strong knowledge of the Caribbean islands because of his involvement with drug interdiction.

"You think this is connected to that big deal we busted?" Rupert wondered aloud to Duncan.

"Could be. It cost them a bundle."

"What do you need me to do?"

"Let the chief know so that the boys go easy on me." Duncan was referring to Key West Chief of Police, Luis Sorrento.

"Sure, I can do that," Rupert responded.

Two police cars were pulling into the lane, which led to Duncan's trailer.

"Thanks." Duncan paused for a moment. "Harley, there's one thing I almost forgot to mention."

"Yeah. What would that be?"

"One of the gunmen had another photo in his pocket."

"Who was it?"

"You. Talk to you later." Duncan hung up.

Stunned, Rupert stood from his chair. A number of scenarios ran through his mind as he hurried his bulky frame to Sorrento's office.

Before stepping outside, Duncan playfully picked up a teddy bear from his kitchen counter. "You certainly earn your keep," he said as he examined the wireless miniature surveillance camera set in the bear's right eye. The monitor was set in Duncan's bedroom from where he could quickly identify anyone walking into his trailer unannounced as friend or foe. He set the bear on the counter, facing the doorway, and winced when he saw that one of his Bose speakers had a bullet hole. Shaking his head, he walked out to greet the arriving police officers.

Sloppy Joe's Bar
Later That Day

Sloppy Joe's Bar at the corner of Duval Street and Greene Street was already crowded as locals and island visitors converged to celebrate the start of three days of festivities for Put-in-Bay Days. Lake Erie's Put-in-Bay had a long-standing reputation as the Key West of the Midwest and each summer reciprocated with Key West Week.

The bar's owner, Joe Russell, had been a close friend of Ernest Hemingway when the author lived in Key West. Besides being a bar owner, a charter boat captain, and rumrunner, Russell had also been the author's boat pilot and fishing companion.

Sloppy Joe's was Hemingway's local hangout and was also one of the key locations for the weeklong Ernest Hemingway Days activities each July. The event, directed by Key Wester Carol Shaughnessy and Lorian Hemingway, Hemingway's grand-daughter, included an Ernest Hemingway look-a-like contest, the running of the bulls, a fishing tournament, author presentations, a Hemingway play by Canadian actor and playwright Brian Gordon Sinclair, and a short story competition.

The open doors and windows allowed the cool ocean breeze to penetrate the darkened bar, with its high ceilings and walls adorned with pictures of Hemingway. Emerson Moore was seated at the bar where he had a good view of the raised stage in the rear of the bar. He had flown to Miami from Cleveland with Mad Dog and the two had rented a Jeep Wrangler for the scenic, four-hour drive through the Keys to Key West. Emerson was nursing a Seven and Seven as Mad Dog talked backstage with several other visiting Put-in-Bay performers - Pat Dailey, Bob Gatewood, Ray Fogg, and Pete & Wayne.

Earlier in the day, Emerson had visited with Kim Fisher at the Mel Fisher Treasure Sales where they recounted the heist of the treasure during Hurricane Charley two years earlier. Emerson had a deep admiration for the Fisher family and their unswerving perseverance to locate the wreck of the *Atocha* and discover its treasure. During their discussion, Kim had invited Emerson to visit the *Atocha* site and dive for treasure since it was still a working treasure recovery site. Emerson had readily accepted the invitation and was going to dive the site the next day.

Feeling someone nudge his arm, Emerson turned and saw a somewhat reserved Sam Duncan. This was totally out of character for his usually vivacious friend.

"Sam the man has arrived! Now the party can start!" Emerson said as he tried to liven up his somber friend. It had no effect.

After Duncan sat on the adjoining bar stool and placed his drink order, Emerson asked, "What's wrong? I've never seen you like this."

"Had an interesting visitor this morning."

"Oh?"

"Let me correct that. I had two interesting visitors."

"Female?" Emerson teased his skirt-chasing friend.

The question brought a small grin to Duncan's face. "Not this time, E."

The barmaid returned with his drink and bent over to serve it to Duncan. Duncan's eyes quickly took in her ample cleavage before she straightened. "I had a visit from two Jamaican hit men."

Emerson's eyes widened. "And you were the target?"

"Yeah, but I turned it on them. The prey became the hunter," he grinned as he recalled how he had handled the situation. "I blew it. They're both dead, but I suspect I know who sent them."

"Some woman's husband?" Emerson asked teasingly.

"I wish."

For a brief moment, Emerson saw the old gleam return to Duncan's eyes.

"I've been involved in a case off and on. Drug interdiction stuff." He tipped his glass back and took a large swallow before continuing. "I caused a lot of heat on this guy's sources in Jamaica." He emptied his glass. "He doesn't like my interference. It cost him millions."

"I'd guess not." Emerson thought a moment before speaking. "You okay?"

"Yeah. I wanted to take the guys alive, but I didn't think. I just reacted." Duncan then recounted the morning's events to Emerson.

"You were lucky," Emerson observed when Duncan completed his tale.

"No, just prepared," Duncan responded firmly. "Today's technology can make a difference in living or dying. But first, you've got to use the stuff." Eyeing a tall blonde female as she walked by, Duncan asked, "Enough talk about me. How are you doing since your ice adventure?"

Emerson didn't say anything as a cold shudder ran through his spine despite the warm Florida air.

"You okay, E?" Duncan asked.

"Yeah. It's tough. It hasn't been that long ago."

"Don't want to talk about it?"

"Probably should." Emerson caught Duncan up on the events of that tragic night when the three men broke through the ice.

"How long were you in the hospital?"

"Too long. I hate those places. Not that they don't do a good job, I just don't like being there."

"Yeah, other than going to a hospital to have a baby, it's not typically a good reason that you have to go. "

"And look who's talking about babies!" Emerson gave Duncan a playful shove.

"So both guys died, then?"

"Yes. My friend Barton didn't make it. I barely made it from what they told me. I guess Barton came to and crawled on top of me to help my body retain heat. That's how they found us. He was laying on top of me."

"Sacrificed himself for his friend," Duncan mused.

"Yes. 'Greater love hath no one than this, that one lay down his life for his friends. - John 15:13.'"

Duncan's eyes widened at hearing Emerson quote from the Bible. "Where did that come from, Bible boy?"

"I'll tell you about it some time." Emerson grew quiet and clammed up. This was out of character for him.

"It's about your parents, right?" Duncan probed.

Emerson didn't respond as additional memories brought dark, ominous clouds to his mind.

"Okay, I get the picture. You don't want to talk about it."

"Sam, that's a story for another day," Emerson said through clenched teeth.

Duncan backed off and returned to the ice disaster. "That Barton sounded like a good man."

"A very good man. His family and I were very close. It's hard facing them. You think about what you could have done different. You wonder why it was him and not you who died. My mind was all messed up. It was difficult seeing his family and the other islanders. I had to get away and clear my mind."

"Good thing that your buddy Mad Dog had invited you on this trip," Duncan observed.

"I'll say. Do you know what Barton did for the community?"

"What?"

"In his will, Barton had set aside some funds for the mayor."

"The mayor?" Duncan sat straight up in his seat. "Were they related?"

"Wait a second. Let me finish. No, they weren't related. It seems that the two of them had a pact. Whichever was the first to die, the other would oversee a wake for him. The funds were to pay for the wake. And what a wake it was! It was an open bar at the Beer Barrel and almost every islander attended. They had an open mic and anyone could step up to tell stories about Barton. What a way to go out!"

"That is remarkable that the two of them would plan something like that."

"He was a good man. I still can't believe it happened." An uncontrollable shudder ran through Emerson's body as he again recalled the horrifying events of that night.

"Did they find the third guy?"

"Yeah. They figured out where we broke through the ice and brought in a rescue team. You remember Scuba Kat?" Emerson smiled as he asked.

Duncan smiled too. He clearly remembered the very married and beautiful scuba diver from the New Wave Dive Shop on the mainland in nearby Port Clinton. They had dived together to retrieve the two duffel bags filled with drugs a year and a half ago. All three of them had narrowly missed being killed by the two Mafiosos who had hired them. "Oh yeah, how could I forget that beauty?"

Emerson was still grinning as he recalled his friend's unsuccessful attempts when he hit on her.

"Did she dive for the body?"

"No, her husband, Rob, did."

Duncan grimaced. "She should have dumped him and run off with me!"

Emerson shook his head. "That would never happen. He's a great guy."

"And what am I, chopped liver?"

Emerson ignored the question and continued his story. "Rob teaches ice rescue and is one of the top guys in western Lake Erie. It was pretty dangerous as is any recovery under ice, but he found him. Deitz's snowmobile suit had become snagged on the snowmobile and he couldn't free himself. Rob found him in 30 feet of water."

"Tough break."

"The whole thing was a nightmare! I've been having trouble sleeping since I was released from the hospital." Emerson raised his glass and took a long swallow.

"Hitting the alcohol again?" Duncan was concerned as he recalled Emerson's drunken binges after losing his wife and son in an automobile accident.

Emerson peered over the glass's rim at Duncan. "In one word, no. It's under control. I can't let that happen like it did in the past. It's just the nightmare stuff. I guess I really needed this trip away from Put-in-Bay. It's hard not to dwell on the events of that evening when you're right there. This respite to Key West and the Cayman Islands will do me good. I needed a change of scenery."

"Got to admit that the scenery here is great," Duncan commented as he eyed two scantily attired tourists, walking into the bar.

Emerson shook his head at his woman-crazy buddy. "Hey, what happened to you and that woman with the two kids? When I was here last time, it looked like the two of you were starting to hit it off. And that one kid seemed to really take to you."

"Didn't work out. She moved back to West Virginia to be with family."

"It looked like you two were getting cozy," Emerson teased, remembering their joint deep sea fishing trip on the *Fish Check* from Garrison Bight.

"Well, we did get cozy," Duncan grinned. "It just didn't work out. In my business, I can't afford to be tied down."

"I bet."

Duncan sipped his drink. "You checked in?"

"Yeah. At the La Concha." Emerson was referring to the Crowne Plaza on Duval, Key West's tallest building. It was one of Emerson's favorite places to hang out and watch the sunsets from its rooftop patio, which provided unrestricted scenic views of Key West.

"What are your plans?" Duncan asked as he set the drink on the bar.

"I'm diving on the *Atocha* tomorrow. Kim Fisher invited me to join him."

"Sounds like fun."

"Then, I'm planning on enjoying the Put-in-Bay Days festivities. I saw a few of the other islanders are here and escaping Lake Erie's blustery winter. After that, I'm going to the Cayman Islands with Mad Dog and doing some diving there."

Duncan's head gave an involuntary twitch.

Emerson paused. "Is something wrong?"

Duncan thought a moment and decided against telling Emerson that the guy behind the assassins resided in Grand Cayman. "No, I just thought how much I enjoy the Cayman Islands."

"Why don't you join us, then? Mad Dog won't mind. You both are party animals and it'll get you away from this morning's incident."

Duncan couldn't hide the thought that flashed through his mind. "Sounds good. I can do some technical dives there."

"Let's plan on it."

The crowd started to clap as Put-in-Bay broadcast mogul, Nick James, and his attractive wife, Lyn, approached the microphone at the front of the stage to open the three-day event.

Emerson nudged Duncan. "Did you see the white PIB-TV van parked outside?"

"Yeah,"

"Nick and his wife drove it down here and are going to broadcast the event live to northeast Ohio."

"Cool!"

"Greetings from the Key West of the Midwest, Put-in-Bay. And welcome to Put-in-Bay Days here in sunny Key West!" James announced as he opened the festivities. "Okay, I see a lot of familiar faces from Put-in-Bay in the audience. If you're from Put-in-Bay or a Put-in-Bay visitor, could you stand?"

About a third of the crowded bar stood, some had to be helped to their feet due to an afternoon of drinking.

"Let's give them a round of applause for making the trek down here."

The crowded bar was filled with applause and cheers.

"Now, let's not waste any more time. To kick off Put-in-Bay Days, here's island legend and all-around-good guy, Mad Dog Adams!"

James and his wife left the stage as the brawny entertainer stepped to the mic and surveyed the audience. Spotting Emerson at the bar, he nodded his head and turned to the crowd, "How many of you know where you are right now?"

The crowd roared.

"And how many of you just don't give a damn and want to have a good time?"

The crowd shouted in response.

"That's what I thought." Mad Dog grinned as he began to play his guitar. He stopped suddenly as he spotted an attractive tourist seated near the front of the stage. "Honey," he began, "have you ever seen my show before?"

She shook her head from side to side.

"Good. Because a little later, I'm going to have you come up here and I'll let you show everybody how to blow my conch." He stooped and picked up a large conch shell, which he had set on the stage. Holding the conch shell high over his head for the audience to see, Mad Dog asked, "Isn't this conch the biggest you have ever seen?"

The audience roared their affirmation as Mad Dog brought the conch to his lips and blew a long note from it. The crowd tittered as Mad Dog leaned toward the young female and teased, "Get your lips ready." With a mischievous smile, Mad Dog broke into song.

Emerson and Duncan grinned at each other for a moment before focusing their attention on the stage. They were going to enjoy the evening's entertainment.

Grand Cayman
Caribbean

Directly 150 miles south of Cuba and 180 miles northwest of Jamaica lay the lush green Cayman Islands – Grand Cayman, Cayman Brac and Little Cayman. The three islands are perched on the top of the Cayman Ridge, a submarine mountain that runs from Cuba to Belize. The Cayman Trench, which is over four miles deep, surrounds the Cayman Islands.

Grand Cayman is approximately 22 miles long and 8 miles across at its widest point. The highest elevation is about 60 feet above sea level and the most striking topographical feature is the North Sound, a shallow reef-protected lagoon with an area of about 35 square miles.

Cayman Brac lies about 90 miles east northeast of Grand Cayman. It is about 12 miles long and a little over a mile wide. The Bluff is the Brac's most outstanding feature, rising along the length of the island and reaching a height of 140 feet at the eastern end then falling in a shear cliff to the sea.

Little Cayman is 5 miles west of Cayman Brac and is 10 miles long and 2 miles wide. It is the flattest of the three islands with its highest elevation being 40 feet. Little Cayman is separated from Cayman Brac on the east by a 7-mile wide channel.

None of islands has rivers or streams because of the porous nature of their rock base and the absence of hills or valleys. The lack of water and sediment runoff into the sea causes the water surrounding the islands to have an amazing clarity.

Discovered by Christopher Columbus in 1503, the islands were originally named Las Tortugas due to the massive turtle population. When Sir Francis Drake visited the islands in 1586, he renamed them the Cayman Islands after a native term for crocodile.

The East End of Grand Cayman marked the Northwest Passage to Cuba for treasure-laden Spanish ships from Portobello, Panama and Vera Cruz, Mexico. Low-lying Grand Cayman was the last land mass ships would sight on their way to Cuba and the entrance to the Gulf Stream for a faster voyage past the coast of Florida and into the Atlantic. When the ships sighted Bermuda, they'd turn to starboard and sail toward the Azores and then on to Spain.

The numerous reefs around the Cayman Islands, especially at the East End, have been the major factors for more than 300 shipwrecks littering its sea floor, which, in turn, caused the Cayman Islands to be known as the "Wreck Capital of the Central Caribbean."

Hitting a reef under full sail resulted in the entire hull, below the waterline, being sheered off. The remaining upper portion of the ship, now lightened by the loss of the lower hull, would continue flying over the reefs and scatter in pieces over hundreds of yards from the initial impact site. Some of the remnants would end up on the shore.

With the late afternoon sun glaring over the yardarm and blinding a ship's crew, unsuspecting ships would sail dangerously close to the reefs and find themselves impaled on the jagged Elkhorn coral. The lower decks would flood and the ship would settle on the coral. At times, ships' crews worked quickly to lighten the load by tossing cannons and heavy cargo overboard in an attempt to free the ship. Sometimes, it worked and they would sail away to a nearby bay for repairs. Other times it didn't work and the ship would be abandoned to the next storm, which would pummel it on the reef and scattered its remaining wreckage. Pieces washed ashore would be used by the Caymanians to construct homes.

One of the most notorious wrecks was "The Wreck of the Ten Sails". One night in November 1788, the *Cordelia*, the lead ship of a convoy of merchant ships bound from Jamaica to Britain, ran aground on the reef at East End. A signal was given to warn off the other ships, but was misunderstood as a call to follow closer and nine more ships sailed onto the reef. The people of East End are reported to have shown great heroism in ensuring that no lives were lost.

Some ships were deliberately run aground for insurance purposes, or enticed to their demise on the reefs by island wreckers who placed false navigation lights on shore and awaited opportunities to salvage expensive cargo.

During World War II, the desperate need for scrap metal to build ships created a business opportunity for a number of Caymanians. They'd raise old cannon, anchors and chain from shipwreck sites on the East End of Grand Cayman and from Little Cayman. Once the holds of their schooners were full, they'd sail to Florida or Alabama to collect a lucrative payment for the scrap metal.

Long known for their mastering of the seas as fishermen and turtlers, in the early 1900s many Caymanian men took to the seas as sailors aboard merchant ships, which sailed throughout the world's seas.

Over the years, the Caymans attracted a wide variety of visitors, including ships putting in to harvest the bountiful supply of turtles and fish as well as replenishing their fresh water supply. Pirates stopped to repair their ships and bury treasure.

Evidence of the pirate visits has been discovered over the years. It varied from silver coins washed up on the beaches to pirate graves, which contained armed skeletons, to caches of cutlasses and muskets. In one of the caves near Pedro's Castle on Grand Cayman, a chest containing a flintlock pistol, an old cutlass, and copper and silver coins was found.

Stories about discovering hidden treasure abound in the Caymans. One story focused on a pirate ship, which allegedly robbed a bank in Cartagena, Colombia of $3 million and then crashed on a southern Little Cayman reef. More importantly are the whispered stories of Caymanians who have discovered treasure and quietly sold it abroad to avoid paying taxes.

After particularly violent hurricanes or winter storms, wreckages are constantly buried and unburied. They can be scattered or moved hundreds of yards; sometimes they can be moved to the edge of the Trench where they plummet four plus miles below.

The rigging on the two pirate ships creaked as the vessels slowly made their way into George Town's harbor. As the wind freshened, the ships' sails snapped. The frigates had three fully rigged masts and a raised quarterdeck and forecastle. The lead ship was heavily armed with 38 cannon while the second ship carried 30 cannon. The gun crews on the forecastle of each ship prepared their cannons for firing the opening salvos.

Screaming with a bloodlust from the main deck of both ships and from the rigging was the motley dressed crew. Their stamina and bravery had been fortified by swilling rum over the last hour. They were waving their muskets and cutlasses in eager anticipation for their early afternoon raid on George Town to pillage and plunder the bay front town and kidnap the island's governor general.

High above the main deck, each ship's Jolly Roger signaled to George Town's citizens that danger was near. Below the Jolly Roger flew another flag, one that conveyed an even more menacing message. It was a red flag, signifying that no quarter would be given.

From the lead vessel's quarterdeck, bearded Captain Black Jack stood, dressed in a white linen shirt and a black waistcoat. His attire was completed by well-worn black leather boots and striped red and black trousers. From his waist hung his large sword and two pistols dangled from a rope, which hung from his massive neck. "Be ye ready?" he shouted to the main deck as he surveyed his rowdy crew.

"Arrrrrrrrgh," the crew yelled back boldly.

"We be not taking prisoners, so make sure ye kill them swiftly," he ordered.

"Arrrrrrrrgh," they responded and turned to face the approaching landfall.

As they brazenly sailed into the harbor, they came within range of Fort George, located on the waterfront. The fort's cannons opened fire on the first ship. The cannon balls whistled through the air, missing their mark and sending plumes of water high in the air around the ship. With the freshening wind, the lead ship flew quickly by the fort and neared the dock.

The second ship was also greeted by a salvo from the fort's cannon, which missed the ship and dropped harmlessly into the bay.

Captain Black Jack adroitly adjusted the wheel to position the ship for a landing at the dock, yelling to his gun crew to commence firing. The ship shuddered briefly as the two cannons fired at the town. Their shots fell short and into the water near the small beach while sending towers of spray onto the townspeople, gathered at the waterfront.

Expertly spinning the wheel while keeping an eye to his sails, Black Jack maneuvered the craft next to the dock where a squad of British Redcoats, led by the island's governor general, began to open fire. As the ship nudged against the dock and several of the crew tended to the sails, the other crew members returned fire and leaped from the ship as the second ship pulled into the dock and began unloading its bloodthirsty crew.

With cutlasses raised and muskets firing, the crews from both ships charged into the Redcoats, quickly subduing them and capturing the governor.

The watching townspeople broke into applause and cheers as the captured governor and Redcoats were marched through the crowd by the muscular pirates and buxom wenches, several of whom were scantily attired in miniskirts and black leather boots.

"How about a date?" one of the tourists yelled to one nearby wench who paraded by.

"Only in your dreams!" the longhaired blonde yelled as she dialed a number on her cell phone.

"That's the way to handle him!" encouraged a dark-complected pirate wearing a black hat and white linen shirt with brown leather breeches and black boots. He was holding a cutlass at his side.

"Thanks, Emerson."

Emerson smiled from beneath the black hat.

"Oh, thanks, Emerson," mocked a powerfully built, bearded pirate wearing a bandanna. He then turned to the nearby tourist and thrust his sword at him. "I'll make gallows meat out of ye before I'd let you date me wench."

Withdrawing into the crowd, the tourist whimpered, "Sorry, I didn't know she was with you." Seeing the steely-eyed stare from the pirate, he turned and disappeared into the crowd.

Emerson grinned, "Rescuing fair maidens, as usual?"

"It's just me nature," Mad Dog Adams said with a hearty laugh.

Emerson smiled at his rascally friend.

Through his wealth of friends, Mad Dog had been able to secure passage for Emerson and himself on board one of the pirate ships for the mock landing. The landing signaled the official start of the annual Pirates' Week in the Cayman Islands.

Each winter for the past 30 years, a brief time warp captured the Cayman Islands as costumed pirates of all ages converge for this 11-day festival filled with parades, street dances, music, food, fireworks, and heritage events throughout the districts. Visitors and locals dined on such traditional Caymanian dishes as turtle stew, crab, conch stew, fried fish, rice and beans, breadfruit and heavy cake.

"Let's see if we can get a seat at JJ Breezes." Mad Dog was pointing to a gaily-decorated three-story building with a restaurant and bar perched on the second and third stories. Its balconies were crowded with partyers.

"Looks crowded."

"Yeah, but I'll push a couple of drunks aside so we can belly up to the bar," Mad Dog teased as he turned to make his way through the crowded street as the parade started. "And if that doesn't work, I'll pull out me trusty sword and cut a swath through them!"

They quickly made their way to the second floor, ordered drinks and squeezed into a corner of the balcony overlooking the parade route.

Gaily decorated trucks pulled equally decorated trailers, which contained a variety of island life displays, music makers and a couple of beauty queens. Costumed stilt walkers mingled with children of all ages, who were marching along the waterfront road.

It couldn't have been more than 10 minutes into the parade when the incident occurred.

"My purse!" a female parade watcher screamed from the street level, near but below the balcony from where Emerson and Mad Dog were watching the parade.

A teenager had grabbed the woman's purse, which had been dangling loosely from her shoulder. Emerson had been looking in that direction and observed the theft. He saw the young man running toward JJ Breezes where he would make a right turn down a side street and disappear into the safety offered by the city.

As he raced toward the corner under JJ Breeze's balcony, Emerson catapulted himself over the rail and dropped onto the fleeing youth. The force of Emerson's fall dropped the youth to the ground, but didn't prevent him from struggling to free himself from Emerson.

A voice boomed over Emerson's head and spoke to the would-be purse-snatcher, "Easy does it son." Two sets of hands gripped the youth as the two uniformed Cayman Island police officers restrained him. Emerson stood to his feet and held the stolen purse in one hand.

"My purse. Thank you," the sweet feminine voice cooed.

Emerson turned and stared at the source of the voice. He found himself staring into two deep brown eyes. They reminded him of a doe's eyes, wide and soft. Her light chocolate skin, full lips and short black hair immediately attracted Emerson's attention as well as the attention of several nearby male onlookers. She was wearing a bright red tee shirt which hugged her ample bosom and tight jeans that looked as if they had been painted on – as was common with many of the Cayman Island women.

"Miss Denise, are you okay?" one of the police officers asked.

Denise Roberts smiled as she looked at the officer and then at the captured culprit, "I'm in a lot better shape than that boy."

I'll say, Emerson thought to himself as he looked at the beautiful woman, then at the boy in the firm grasp of the police officers.

"We'll take him in and write it up. You coming along?" one of the officers asked.

"It's supposed to be my day off," she winced in mock desperation. "Let me thank my rescuer and I'll be along shortly."

The police officers nodded and disappeared with their prisoner down the adjacent street.

"Thank you for rescuing my purse," Denise said to Emerson who had bent over to pick up his black pirate's hat. It had been knocked off his head during the scuffle.

"It was nothing," Emerson grinned. "Just thought I'd drop in," he teased.

"Are you going to stay down there all day or coming back up here?" Mad Dog's voice bellowed from the balcony above.

"I'll be right up," Emerson replied.

"And bring the babe!" Mad Dog yelled as he tipped his head back and downed another beer.

"The babe?" Denise smiled at the compliment.

"You'll have to excuse my friend. He can be a bit boisterous," Emerson said.

"I'd be happy to join you and buy you a drink. It's the least I can do to repay you." Sticking her hand out, she announced, "I'm Denise Roberts."

Swooping off his hat and bowing at the waist in one motion, Emerson replied, "I'm Emerson Moore, my lady."

"Aren't we the polite pirate?"

Emerson grinned as he straightened and placed his hand in the small of her back to guide her toward JJ Breezes. They continued to talk as they made their way through the crowded sidewalk and climbed to the second story.

"I take it that you're visiting," Denise asked as they entered the restaurant.

"Yes," he replied. "This is my first trip. My buddy, Mad Dog, is a singer and invited me to join him here."

"Is that Mad Dog Adams?"

"Yes, you know him?"

"I saw him perform at Durty Reid's last year. He's a riot!"

"That's an understatement! He can really get a crowd going," Emerson responded as he thought about his rowdy friend.

Looking at his pirate attire, she asked, "And you're here for Pirate's Week, too?"

"Yeah. We lucked out. Mad Dog was able to get us on board one of the pirate ships for the mock landing."

"You enjoy it?"

"It was way too cool. Mingling with the other pirates on board and swapping stories. And Mad Dog was the best story swapper on board our vessel."

"I bet," she responded as they reached the top of the stairs and began to walk through the crowded dining area.

"He and I are going scuba diving while we're here."

She looked around at him. "Off the wall?"

"Probably," he responded to her question about diving off the Trench's wall.

"Be careful about your depth if you're going off the wall."

"Yeah, I know. I've been told to watch it by some of the pros."

"Well, well. Look what we have here. A beautiful wench," Mad Dog started as the two approached him. "Women have a strange effect on my buddy, Emerson. When he sees one, he just jumps off of second story balconies to impress them."

"That's me, for sure," Emerson responded.

Denise smiled. "How about that drink?"

"I already have one." Emerson went to pick up his glass when he saw that it was empty. He spun his head around and looked at Mad Dog. "Any idea what happened to my drink?"

"Yeah. A midget pirate drank it."

"Right. And where is he now?"

"I told him to go smoke some ganja and he'd feel high!" Mad Dog grinned.

"Miss, can I get you anything?" the waiter interrupted their exchange.

"Sure, I'll take a Singapore Sling. Emerson?"

"Seven and Seven."

"That's a 14!" Mad Dog quipped.

Ignoring Mad Dog's comment, Emerson turned to Denise. "So you reside here?"

"Yes. I've been here for a number of years."

"Where are you from?"

She hesitated and dodged answering the questions directly. "I've lived all around the Caribbean," she answered evasively.

Emerson picked up on it right away, but allowed it to go for now. "So where do you work?"

"I'm a secretary here in George Town."

Emerson nodded his head.

"I've been there for a while and I enjoy the work. I have a great boss!"

"That's always a good thing," Emerson grinned. He was enjoying her accent and the almost musical way in which she conversed.

The waiter appeared with their beverages and set them on their table. They picked up their drinks and sipped them as they looked at the passing parade.

"And what about you, Emerson? What do you do and where are you from?"

"I'm an investigative reporter for *The Washington Post*."

Her eyes narrowed when she heard his response. "A reporter?"

Emerson nodded.

"Are you here on a story?"

"No, just escaping the harsh winter on Lake Erie." Emerson didn't feel like disclosing that he really needed to escape from the nightmares that were haunting him virtually every night.

He wondered how long until the tormenting memories from the ice tragedy would interrupt his sleep.

"Lake Erie?"

"Yes. It's one of the Great Lakes along the north coast of the United States. Right across from Canada."

"Sounds cold."

"It can be. I actually live on one of the islands in the lake's western basin."

"You're an islander, too!" she exclaimed.

"In a matter of speaking. But at this time of the year, I'd rather be an islander here where it's nice and warm," he smiled.

"Well, I should be going. I need to go to the police station. I'm sure they will have me complete some report." She rummaged through her purse and left payment for the drinks on the table as they stood.

"Thank you for the drink," Emerson said appreciatively.

"No, it is I who should be thanking you for dropping into my life today!" she quipped.

Emerson smiled.

Noticing for the first time that Mad Dog was no longer with them, she asked, "Where is that friend of yours? I'd like to say good-bye."

Quickly scanning the room, Emerson spotted Mad Dog. He was now standing by the bar. He had his arms around two women and was carrying on an animated conversation with them.

Emerson pointed. "Looks like he's busy, but we can interrupt him."

Flashing a smile at Emerson, Denise responded, "No, he looks like he's having fun."

Emerson interrupted her before she could continue. "Mad Dog has fun wherever he goes."

"I can tell," she agreed. "Thank you again." She started to walk away when she stopped suddenly. "Perhaps I will see you again. Maybe at Durty Reid's when Mad Dog sings there."

"That would be nice," Emerson said as she turned and walked through the crowd.

Morgan's Harbour
Western Grand Cayman

The two-story contemporary plantation manor house had uninterrupted views of Morgan's Harbour and the North Sound. A high white stone fence offered privacy to the luscious landscaped grounds with their meandering pathways. The grounds were covered with a velvet green lawn and flowering plants including orchids and roses. Towering palm trees, mixed with mango and banana trees, provided sanctuary for the Cayman Islands' wild parrots.

Fresh sea breezes moved through the balconies at the front and rear of the massive, 8,000-square-foot home. Next to the house was a three-car detached garage with additional living quarters overhead.

At the rear of the house, the two large French doors opened and a figure, carrying a glass of Tortuga rum, slowly walked into the covered and screened verandah. He looked down on the boats nestled at his dock and then opened the screen door. Stepping down from the verandah, he walked across the patio to a bait well, built into the patio's floor.

Crouching, he opened the bait well and extracted a bucket containing several pieces of fresh fish. He turned to face the large saltwater aquarium, which had been built into the patio and just a few feet from the inground swimming pool.

"How are my pets today?" he asked, knowing that he wouldn't get a response. Peering into the clear water, he saw a number of fish swimming around the reef, which had been carefully constructed inside the aquarium. One of the yellow snappers swam too close to the rocky reef and disappeared into the jaws of one of the three moray eels, which inhabited the reef.

The figure laughed wickedly as the eel retracted into the reef with its tasty meal. "You move just like me, my pet. Quickly and deadly," he smiled sinisterly. "Now, where are your brothers?"

He affixed a portion of fish to the end of a pole and stuck the pole into the water, close to several small underwater tunnel-like openings in the reef. It didn't take long for one of the eels to appear and snatch the free meal. He placed another piece of fish on the pole and stuck it into the water near another opening. Soon the third eel struck the offered fish and retreated.

He repeated the process four more times, then returned the bucket of fish to the bait well. The sound of approaching footsteps caused him to turn as a voice called, "Mr. Clarke."

"Yes?" Pryce Clarke answered. Clarke's dark ebony skin glistened in the late morning sunlight. He was 6 feet 3 inches tall with a lean and muscular physique. His dark eyes peered from his closely shaven head as he adjusted his lavender colored gauze shirt. His slacks were a white linen and he wore brown sandals on his feet.

Slade was Clarke's right hand man. He was as ebony skinned as Clarke, but much shorter and stouter, carrying 250 pounds on his broad frame. Attired in a well-worn and stained white tee shirt and dark blue shorts, Slade responded, "We found Arturo. He's around front in the car."

"Good." Clarke gazed across the harbor as he thought. "Have him brought here."

Slade nodded his head and disappeared around the corner of the house. In a few moments he returned, leading two of his men who were tightly gripping the arms of a struggling Arturo. They forcibly marched him around to the patio and stopped in front of Clarke for the confrontation.

"Slade, show Arturo what you showed me this morning," Clarke instructed.

Slade reached into his pocket and produced three gold coins. He held them in his outstretched hand in front of Arturo.

At the sight of the coins, Arturo's eyes widened. "I can explain."

"Not yet. You will have your chance. Where did you find these, Slade?"

"In Arturo's weight belt."

"And Slade, what made you look into his weight belt?"

"When we were working last night, I thought I saw him stuff something in the belt, so I decided to check after he dropped his weight belt and gear on board and went below. That's when I found these coins."

Clarke's eyes focused on Arturo. "Now it's your turn to talk. Why were these coins in your weight belt?"

"I was bringing them on board to turn them in and I just for-got." His eyes were wild with fear as he responded.

"Why didn't you just throw them in the bag with the rest of the coins?" Clarke asked. His voice was hard and cold.

Shaking, Arturo searched for an answer.

"I asked you why didn't you throw them in the bag?" Clarke asked again. His menacing eyes seem to penetrate Arturo's soul.

Nervously and with a quivering voice, Arturo answered, "I thought they looked special and I didn't want to mix them in with the others."

"Liar!" Clarke's comment flew through the air like a dart at Arturo. "You were going to steal them from me and you weren't smart enough to not get caught!"

Arturo hung his head, eyes downcast. His body continued to shake.

"You didn't think anyone would notice, did you?"

Arturo didn't reply. He knew that whatever he said would not be accepted. He silently awaited his fate.

"Bring him over here by the aquarium," Clarke ordered as he grabbed the fish bait from the bait well. "I think I have to show you how I deal with people, who try to steal from me." Clarke picked up a piece of the dead fish.

"Bring him closer and hold him tight."

Even though they were restraining him, Arturo struggled to free himself. As Clarke began to rub the fish over Arturo's face, Arturo twisted, trying to break loose as he realized the fate, which he was facing. When he began to scream, Slade slapped a piece of duct tape across his mouth. He had anticipated what his boss would do and had a roll with him. It wasn't the first time that he had seen this type of execution.

"Slade, secure his arms and his feet to the pole."

Working quickly, Slade followed his boss's instructions and bound the twisting Arturo, who had been forced to lie on his stomach on the patio. The three henchmen then pushed Arturo to the edge of the aquarium.

"Help me lower him into the aquarium," Clarke directed ominously.

With a desperation surge of adrenaline, Arturo surprised them by rolling away from the aquarium's edge. A quick kick to his head from Slade halted Arturo's' attempt to avert his punishment.

"Take a deep breath," Slade grinned maliciously as he commented. With that they rolled him over the edge and into the water with a splash, sending nearby fish scurrying to the corners of the aquarium.

Arturo took a large breath as he hit the water and he felt the pole push and guide him close to the rocky reef. Because of his years diving, he had trained himself to hold his breath for long periods of time. He wasn't sure how long they would keep him under before bringing him up.

His face was pushed against the sharp coral of the reef and he jerked it to the side as blood emerged from a cut on his cheek. A movement out of the corner of his eye caught his attention. At about the same time, he felt a surge of pain fill the side of his face where his cheek had once been.

A movement from the right side focused his attention and terror filled his mind as the second eel struck at his fish-swabbed face. Forgetting to hold his breath, Arturo screamed silently and bucked against the pole, which now held him and made him easy prey for the eels. The eels struck repeatedly at the drowning man.

A few minutes later, Arturo's body ceased its thrashing at the end of the pole. With the macabre punishment fatally complete, Clarke directed his henchmen, "He's dead. Take him out and to the Trench."

The three henchmen began to pull the body from the water as Clarke continued.

"Cut him three ways: long, deep and continuous. Then weight him down and toss him overboard. It'll be snack time for all the sea critters as he drops into the Trench." Clarke grinned malevolently as his men pulled Arturo's body from the aquarium and carried it away.

Another of his men appeared from the corner of the house. He was pushing a cart with six squawking chickens and approaching a fenced area 30 feet from the patio's edge.

Seeing him, Clarke spoke. "Give one to me. I'll feed him today." His morning's bloodlust was unsatisfied.

The man reached into the cage and extracted one chicken. He turned and handed it to Clarke. Grasping the bird in one hand, Clarke reached for its neck and abruptly twisted it, breaking its neck and killing it.

"So easy to kill," he muttered to himself. "Just like anyone who dares to challenge me."

He walked 10 steps and threw the dead chicken into the area surrounded by a 4-foot high, sturdy fence. "Lunchtime," he called as he watched his other pet quickly devour its meal with its sharp teeth. "You devour your food like I devour people," he said with a cocky attitude. He motioned to the man to continue his feeding and returned to the cool, air-conditioned house.

Pryce Clarke was Jamaican born and, at an early age, had become involved in petty burglaries. He soon graduated to more violent crimes and drug running. Feeling the heat from the Jamaica government, he moved to the Cayman Islands. There, he managed his Jamaican drug running from a distance and expanded his market into the Cayman Islands. Using the low profile, high powered, go fast boats known as Jamaican canoes, he ran drugs from Jamaica to waiting Cayman fishing boats off of East End. With no U.S. Coast Guard and DEA interdiction or helicopter surveillance, it was relatively easy to transport the drugs to seemingly innocent fishing vessels and run them into the East End for distribution.

After Hurricane Ivan devastated the Cayman Islands, Clarke saw an additional opportunity to increase his illegal income. With the pressing need to rebuild the Cayman Islands' damaged structures, he founded a construction company. He staffed his company with a large number of Jamaicans. In addition to making a hefty profit from his company, he also profited from each Jamaican worker. Each one, whom he brought into the Cayman Islands, provided him with a portion of their paychecks as a fee for him finding them good jobs. They also purchased their drugs from him. Clarke was benefiting handsomely on all sides. Life was getting better for Clarke.

Life got even better for Clarke when he accidentally made his big discovery.

Cobalt Coast Dive Resort/DiveTech
West Bay

Earlier in the day and before his pirate ship ride, Emerson had landed at the Grand Cayman airport and picked up his Avis rental car. Driving British style on the left side of the road, Emerson had driven west through the Seven Mile Beach area to

West Bay, past the small village named Hell and to the Cobalt Coast Dive Resort. The resort fronted Boatswain's Bay on the northwestern side of Grand Cayman Island and its North Wall, one side of the 4-mile deep Trench.

Mad Dog had suggested the mid-sized dive resort to Emerson since Mad Dog was staying with his old friend, Reid Dennis, the owner of Durty Reid's Bar and Grill. Emerson was pleased by his hotel selection, as DiveTech was located on the property. He'd planned on finishing his technical dive training through them while he was on the island.

Emerson drove the small rental car into the parking lot and parked in front of the three-story resort, painted tan and trimmed in white and aqua blue. He walked up to the inviting open-air entranceway and lobby of the building, built in the style of a Caribbean Great House. To his right, he could see Duppies' Restaurant & Bar and to the left he spotted the resort's office.

Ahead of him, he saw a number of tables and chairs, partially shaded by an overhead trellis and fronting a large swimming pool. Beyond the pool was a beach comprised of sand and rock as well as a dock leading 1,300 feet into the ocean. From the end of the dock flew a diver's flag. A ladder led into the clear, crystal blue water.

"You are here," a friendly voice with a slight Dutch accent greeted Emerson from behind.

Turning, Emerson saw the tall, gray-haired Arie Barendrecht, the congenial owner of Cobalt Coast Dive Resort.

"You must be Emerson, yah?"

Emerson smiled. Arie was as affable as Mad Dog had indicated. "Yes."

"And your drive here was with no problems?"

"No problems at all," Emerson grinned.

"Good. Let's get you settled in your room. It's upstairs."

They started up the stairs to the second floor when Emerson stopped at the landing. He was staring out at the beach. "What are those guys doing?" Emerson asked as he saw three men using flour sifters and sifting through the sand in front of the resort.

"They are looking for diamonds," Arie grinned with an air of mystery.

"Looking for diamonds?"

"Yah. There was a wedding there on the beach last night. When it came time for the groom to place the ring on the bride's finger, he dropped it in the sand. They couldn't find it last night."

"That must have ruined the wedding."

"Not really. It added to the drama in a special way."

"How's that?"

"The groom's mother used to stay here for many years until she died 10 years ago. Her son wanted to be married on the 10th anniversary of her death. He wanted the wedding to take place here since it was one of her favorite places to stay. When they lost the wedding ring, they spotted his stepfather and he was wearing the mother's wedding ring on a cord around his neck. So the stepfather took the ring off the cord, and they used the ring for the service."

"That worked out well."

"But there's more to the story."

"How's that?"

"The stepfather rarely wore the ring around his neck. When he left to go to the wedding, he walked back into his room and placed it around his neck. Otherwise, the kids wouldn't have had a ring for the wedding."

"That's spooky," Emerson commented.

"The kids said that his mother wanted to participate in the wedding and that's why this happened the way it did."

A shout came from the beach and one of the men held an object high in the air, signifying a triumphant victory. It was the ring.

Arie turned back to Emerson. "And now we have a satisfactory ending to this love story." Arie was grinning as the men raced from the beach to the waiting newlywed, who was seated next to the patio.

They arrived at Emerson's second story suite, which overlooked the ocean. Arie opened the door to the suite, revealing an island themed room filled with colorful cushions on rattan furniture and island décor. A small kitchen was in the rear of the front room.

"The bedroom is back here," Arie said as he walked down the hallway and past the bathroom.

Emerson set his laptop on the kitchen table and followed Arie into the rear bedroom, which housed two double beds.

Setting Emerson's suitcase down, Arie turned to Emerson, "I almost forgot. There's a man seated by the pool. He was asking questions about you when he arrived. I think he's dangerous," Arie said cautiously.

Arie had Emerson's full attention. "Let's go out front and you can point him out." His mind was racing. It was too soon for him to make enemies in the Cayman Islands. He had just arrived.

The two walked through the suite and out the doorway to the white railing.

"That's him there," Arie pointed to a man whose back was toward them. The man was wearing a black ball cap. "Being in this business for as many years as I have, I know people. That one, he is dangerous."

"I'll check him out."

Arie returned to the first floor. Watching the stranger for a few minutes, Emerson decided to meet him. He carefully approached the man from the rear. Emerson couldn't make out his facial features. He saw the man's hand reach for his drink on the nearby table as he faced the ocean and enjoyed the full effect of the warm ocean breeze.

Walking in front of the man, Emerson looked down in surprise as he recognized him.

"What are you doing here?"

A hand reached up and took off the dark sunglasses. "The Cayman Islands are a great place to go diving, plus I would expect that there are a lot of fine looking female tourists here," he said in response.

"Sam!" Emerson said in mock exasperation to his Key West friend.

"Just get in line, E! I expect that the line of ladies vying for my romantic charms will be lining up right here," he boasted. "In fact, I'm surprised that the line hasn't started to form yet," he said as he looked around for single females.

Emerson shook his head from side to side. "You're incorrigible!"

"If that means I have sex appeal, I agree with what you just said," Duncan teased as he lifted his drink to his lips and sipped it. Two women in bikinis walked by as Duncan eyed them. "Whoa! Those babes speak two languages."

Emerson glanced at the two women. "How do you know that? Were you talking to them before I arrived?"

"Nope. I can just tell. They talk English and body. And I prefer their body language," he said as he peered over the top of his sunglasses and threw them a warm smile. "Going to do some technical diving?" Duncan asked.

Before Emerson could respond, Duncan continued. "The folks at DiveTech here are known for their technical dives. That's deep water diving at depths greater than 170 feet. You can't use air. You have to have special mixtures to go to those depths," Duncan explained.

Remembering his scuba lessons, Emerson responded, "Right. Sam, do you do technical dives?"

"Yes. Had to learn it for an assignment I was on. Check them out," Sam said as he pointed to the DiveTech office. "You can take lessons there and dive off the North Wall." He was now pointing to the ocean in front of them. "If you decide not to take the lessons, you can still shore dive from the end of the dock. Let's go say hello." The two walked around the far edge of the pool to DiveTech's operations.

DiveTech owners, Nancy and Jay Easterbrook, had founded the operation years ago and headquartered it at Cobalt Coast Dive Resort. They had assembled an international team of seasoned instructors and employees to teach a variety of scuba diving techniques and host offshore dive boat trips from two locations – Morgan's Harbour and across from the North Wall. They offered Trimix and Nitrox training as well as rebreather and technical training.

As Emerson and Duncan walked into the two-story building, which housed the dive shop on the ground level, they were greeted by a perky, attractive lady with short blondish hair.

"How can I help you?" she asked with a smile. "I'm Nancy and that's my husband, Jay, over there." She pointed to a tall, athletic man who was carrying tanks out the side door. He yelled a greeting as he exited.

Duncan opened the conversation. "I'm Sam Duncan and this little guppy is my good friend, Emerson Moore. He's interested in completing his advanced tech diving."

Nancy swung her eyes from Sam to Emerson. "We can certainly help you with that."

"That boy needs all the help he can get," Sam grinned.

"When can I start?" Emerson asked eagerly.

"We're filled up for tomorrow. How about the next day?" Nancy asked as she handed him a textbook on technical diving and mixed gases.

"Great. That'll give me a chance to dive tomorrow with my crazy friend, here. I'll warn you that he's rowdier than a sailor who puts into port after six months at sea."

Nancy's eyes flashed at the grinning Duncan. "Oh, I know how to handle his kind," Nancy kidded.

"And if she can't handle him, I can." They turned to see that her husband had reentered the shop.

"No worry here. I'm trolling for tourists," Duncan smiled.

They finalized their plans including registering Emerson for the advanced technical diving class and a morning dive trip. As they were leaving, Nancy handed Emerson more material to review before he started his technical diving class.

As they headed back to their rooms, Arie called to him, "So, you found your visitor?"

Emerson said, "Yes, although I'd say he found me. And, you were right. He's dangerous, but a dangerous friend."

"If he's your friend, he must be a nice fellow."

Emerson thought for a moment, and then responded. "I'm not sure how nice he is. That boy gets in trouble just by waking up each morning." Emerson followed the grinning Duncan into Duppies's Bar. They ordered their drinks and began to chat.

"Are you staying here, too?"

"No, I'm staying with a friend in town."

"Female?"

"Now, what would make you think that?" Duncan asked with a wink.

"I take it that you're not going to give me a yes or no?"

"Nah. I'll just keep you guessing."

"Going to be here long?"

"Hard to tell. I've got some business to conduct. So I'll be here and there," he said cryptically.

"Working, huh?"

Duncan was silent.

"Okay, you don't have to respond."

"I am looking forward to diving together."

"I am, too." Emerson sipped his Seven and Seven. "Mad Dog is going to join us."

They chatted for a few more minutes and then Duncan excused himself. "I need to head to my place."

Grinning, Emerson said, "Give her, whoever she is, my regards."

Sam didn't respond. He just waved as he walked through the entranceway and returned to his car for the drive back to town.

Emerson finished his drink and paid the bill before returning to his room to review his study material for the upcoming class. He wouldn't have too much time to study. He needed to change into his pirate costume and meet Mad Dog to ride the pirate ship into George Town Harbor.

Durty Reid's Bar and Grill
Red Bay

A burgundy Jeep with a thatched roof and the Kansas City Chief's logo on the hood was parked in front of the popular bar. The thatched tiki porch and entranceway, framed by ship figureheads of busty mermaids, combined to lure customers into Durty Reid's Bar and Grill. It was a must-see stop for tourists to the Cayman Islands and a favorite haunt of locals. They served up hefty drinks, reasonably priced island food and a host of colorful characters.

The bar and grill was owned by a red-haired, one-legged pirate, Reid Dennis. He had arrived on the island years ago after losing his leg in Vietnam and stints as a reporter for a number of newspapers in the United States. He had been a reporter for a newspaper in the Caymans before he switched careers and began running the bar. He often told people that he had worked for years developing the expertise to be a bar owner. After all, he'd been a serious drinker for a long time.

The 55-year-old had a quick wit and kept everyone laughing. Another smart move Dennis made was to hire unbelievably beautiful Caymanian barmaids like Keisha. With a twinkle in his eye, he would tell his clientele, "Nothing like having some great eye candy around. Keeps the customers coming back!"

The short, be-speckled and mustached Costa Rican bartender, Alberto, would disagree feebly that it wasn't the good-looking barmaids who brought customers in. He argued that is was his pleasant personality.

The bar's walls were decorated with photos of celebrities and sports figures, who had stopped in for a visit. A few of the football players had provided signed football jerseys, which were hung from the wall, or signed footballs, which were on display.

Navigating the narrow island roads and round-a-bouts, Emerson had driven to Red Bay, which was on the other side of George Town, to meet Mad Dog Adams at Durty Reid's. He parked his rented, white compact Daihatsu in front of the bar's front window and entered. He didn't realize that he would be walking into the middle of an argument.

In front of him were three individuals. They had surrounded a man in a wheel chair. One was Mad Dog. He was restraining the man in the wheelchair, Durty Reid. Mad Dog was assisted by Mark Rice, the owner of Rice Communications. In front of Reid was a tall and lean white-haired Caymanian. He was shouting at Reid.

"Reid, I've had enough of your bullshit! Now, I'm going to teach you a lesson," he spoke in a very direct and serious tone. "Hold him tight, boys!" The Caymanian produced a hammer and long nail.

Emerson's eyes widened as he saw the Caymanian quickly place the nail on Reid's shin and slammed the hammer down onto the nail. Reid screeched in pain.

Before the Caymanian could deliver the next blow to the nail, Emerson leaped at him, shoving him to one side. He then whirled to face Rice and Mad Dog. He was puzzled by Mad Dog's behavior. Emerson reached to free Rice's grip on Reid.

"Easy does it there, sport," the gray-bearded Rice cautioned as his face broke into a grin. In the background, Emerson heard Mad Dog's familiar laugh fill the air. Also laughing were Reid in the wheelchair and the Caymanian, who had been pushed aside.

"Welcome to Durty Reid's!" Reid Dennis said as he extended his hand to Emerson. As they shook hands, Dennis explained. "Mad Dog saw you pull into the parking lot and we decided to have a little fun with you. Of course, it was all Mad Dog's idea."

"Smile, Emerson. You're on Candid Camera. You should have seen the look on your face when Foster drove the nail in Reid's leg. It was classic," Mad Dog laughed.

"But the leg?" Emerson stammered.

"I'm wearing a wooden one today while my prosthesis is being repaired," Dennis grinned.

"We got you good!" the lean Caymanian said from behind Emerson.

Emerson turned to face the Caymanian, who was wiping tears from his eyes as he continued chuckling.

"Emerson, meet Steve Foster. He's one of my best friends and owner of the Foster Food stores on the islands," Dennis explained.

Shaking hands with Foster, Emerson apologized. "Hope I didn't hurt you when I shoved you out of the way."

"Not at all. With all the things I've been through, a little push is nothing, my brother." Foster turned to Dennis. "And Reid, you and I can't be best friends any more."

"Why not?" Reid asked.

"Reid, all my best friends are dying off. So, I'm taking you off my best friend list and you'll live longer," Foster kidded.

Turning to Emerson, Dennis added, "These guys tease me a lot about my wooden leg." He then quipped, "But one thing for sure, I don't have varicose veins like they do!"

With an impish grin, Rice remarked, "Don't forget to tell him about the time that Foster had a little bit too much to drink and we were playing darts. He took one of the darts and stuck it into Reid's leg."

"I remember that! The tourists began to scream when I did it!" Foster interjected.

"Yeah, so did I!" moaned Reid as he recalled it. "The only problem was it was my good leg! Foster had too much to drink that night and got my good leg and bad leg mixed up!"

"But I said I was sorry, my brother!" Foster commented reflectively.

Shaking his head at the group of rascals, Emerson stated, "You guys are something else! Is everyone in the Caymans like this?"

"Cayman Islands," Rice corrected.

Emerson looked at Rice.

"Caymans are a type of alligator. These are called the Cayman Islands and folks around here are a bit sensitive to it," Rice explained.

Thanking him, Emerson said, "I see. I'll be careful." He paused as he thought about a recent adventure in the Louisiana swamps and his deadly encounters with alligators. He looked at Rice and asked, "You still have alligators around here?"

"Oh, you might see some from time to time," Rice answered. "But they're small ones." He continued, "The ones you really want to watch out for are saltwater crocodiles."

"You've got them around here?"

"Not really. But you never know when one might lose his way and accidentally pay a visit."

"And if he did, I'd find him and we'd have crocodile stew," Reid grinned. "Alberto, you know how to cook crocodile, don't you?" he called back to his busy bartender and sometime cook.

"Reid, for you, I can cook anything," he smiled as he served beers to several locals seated at the bar.

"Seriously," Reid began, "you wouldn't normally find them around here."

Mad Dog interjected his comments at this point. "Yeah, I went diving off of Darwin, Australia, once. I was looking for Great White Sharks. I couldn't find any. One of the locals told me that the crocs ate them all. I'd rather swim with a Great White any day rather than one of them big bad boys, by crocky!"

Rice continued, "They're pretty aggressive compared to alligators."

"And very territorial," Mad Dog added.

"I certainly don't want to be on top of their food chain list," Emerson stated firmly.

Mad Dog changed the topic. "What do you think, Emerson? Isn't this a great place?"

"Yeah, filled with pranksters," Emerson observed.

"Did you see the building next door?" Mad Dog asked.

"I didn't notice."

"It's a funeral home." Mad Dog had an impish look on his face. "They've got a nickname for these two establishments being side by side."

"Oh?"

"Stab Em & Slab Em!" Mad Dog howled as he set up Emerson.

Emerson just shook his head at his friend's comments.

The serious looking Rice leaned toward Emerson and commented, "Your friend thinks he's funny. It's not really that way here."

Before he could respond, a sweet voice purred in Emerson's ear. "Like a drink?"

Turning he saw a tall Caymanian female waitress. She had beautiful skin tones, large brown eyes and full lips. "Seven and Seven," Emerson responded as the girl turned and walked away, wiggling her hips seductively in her tight jeans. "Reid?"

"Yes?" Dennis asked.

"How in the world do these women here get into those tight jeans? I've never seen women poured into jeans like down here."

Reid smiled as Rice answered. "It's part of their heritage. Women in the Caribbean are very comfortable with their sexuality. It's as comfortable and natural to them as women in the states wearing those short mini skirts."

Emerson nodded as Mad Dog quipped, "And let's be honest here, they all look great!"

Keisha returned and the group chatted away the rest of the afternoon; telling tall tales, sharing their experiences in the Caribbean and talking about the movie, "The Cayman Triangle," which had been filmed on the island. It had featured Reid as a one-legged pirate captain and Steve Foster, the island food chain magnate, as Nazrat (Tarzan spelled backward.)

A portion of the film included scenes with Nazrat and Yob (Boy spelled backward). The film showed Foster swinging through the jungle on a vine and wearing a brief loincloth. The lean and muscular Foster could probably replicate the scenes today, even though he was in his 60's.

"We had an argument about me wearing the loin cloth," Foster said as he sipped his beer.

"Yeah, we all wanted him to wear a bigger one," Reid teased.

Foster turned his head and looked Emerson straight in the eyes. "No, that wasn't it at all, my brother. I told them that I wasn't going to wear one."

"Yeah and he didn't on the first take. He came swinging out on the vine with no loincloth on. He was buck ass naked," Reid chortled as he recalled the scene.

Laughing, Emerson responded, "Bet you surprised everyone!"

Reid and Rice were chuckling, but didn't comment. They were waiting for Foster to finish the story.

"The surprise was really on me." He went on to explain, "My good friends here set me up. They knew me well enough that I'd come out naked. What I didn't know was that they had wrapped itch weed around the vine. I was in such a damn hurry to swing out and surprise everyone that I didn't notice it."

"Itch weed?"

"Yeah, it's called Cow itch. It would be like putting fiberglass on a vine. As soon as I grabbed the vine and swung out, I knew I was in trouble."

"He itched for a long time. You should have seen him walking around and squirming from that Cow itch," Reid laughed as he recalled that day's shooting.

"On that note, I need to find the men's room." Emerson stood as Reid pointed to a back hallway.

As he walked down the hallway, Emerson chuckled at a sign, which hung from the ceiling over the doorway to the small men's room. It had been painted and placed there in December 2005 on a piece of driftwood by a visiting author. The sign read "Occupancy Limit: One." It was crafted after the author heard the story of two inebriated patrons, one female and one male, who had a romantic encounter in the small men's room.

East End
Cayman Islands

The East End was the second largest district on Grand Cayman and encompassed 20 square miles. While it was known for being one of the top food-producing districts, it also had a reputation for being the highest drug-producing district on the island. Being the island's closest point to Jamaica, it was a natural port of entry for illegal drugs.

Ten miles offshore, two Caymanian fishing boats rode silently at anchor under a night sky filled with sparkling stars. The roar of an approaching high-powered motor interrupted the night's peaceful tranquility. It was one of the Jamaican drug running boats, the Jamaican canoes. These twin-engine, low profile vessels delivered drugs throughout the Caribbean, and tonight would be no exception.

Slowing its engines as it approached the anchored fishing boats, the canoe's crew watched for the recognition signal as they cautiously approached. Signals were flashed from both fishing boats using hooded flashlights and a return signal was flashed from the canoe.

The distance between the three boats closed and the canoe pulled between the two boats, but left its twin-engines idling. Quickly, the three boats were lashed together and the transfer of drugs between the vessels commenced. While the bales of ganja were being hidden in the bait wells, a lookout on each of the fishing boats scanned the horizon for any evidence of approaching drug interdiction boats.

Once the canoe was emptied, the crews quickly unlashed the boats and the canoe sped off to return to Jamaica. One of the fishing boats headed toward East End where it would unload its valuable cargo. The other set a course around the north side of the island to Morgan's Harbour where it would dispense its goods.

Near the North Wall
West Bay

∾

A series of splashes announced the invasion of eight divers into an underwater realm filled with magical experiences. The water temperature was comfortably in the low 80's and visibility stretched over 100 feet. This was normal for Caymanian waters in early winter.

The eight divers dropped slowly to the reef at the top of the North Wall at around 50 feet. Here, the divers enjoyed seeing yellowtail snappers, parrotfish, yellow goatfish, and angelfish. As a Queen Angelfish with its well-recognized blue ring crown atop its head swam nearby, Emerson shot a photo of it with his new Canon D-200 camera in a waterproof Ikelite housing.

After he took his shot, he reviewed the picture on his LCD to be sure he had gotten the shot he wanted. He turned his head and gave his dive buddy, Duncan, an "okay" sign with his thumb and forefinger to communicate that he was happy with the photo he had just taken. Duncan nodded his head and smiled. He knew Emerson was just learning his new camera and that it would take time and a lot of practice for him to become better with it.

The North Wall is part of an underwater mountain range that bottoms out at 24,000 feet. As the divers weightlessly drifted out over the edge of the wall to begin their descent to their planned maximum 60-foot depth, each diver thought about where the bottom of this wall really was and decided to monitor their buoyancy and depth gauges carefully. If there was an accident on this dive, it would be one in which the divers would probably not return. Their bodies would never be recovered.

As the wet-suited divers went over the edge and began to sink through the watery wonderland, they absorbed the beauty of the wall populated by a wide variety of fish darting about. Four of the divers took turns snapping photos of the yellow Elkhorn Coral with its spreading branches like some miniature underwater oak tree. Deeper down, the sides of the wall displayed bright yellow tube sponges, red rope sponges, white Brain Coral, finger coral and wondrous sea fans.

From time to time, Emerson turned his head away from the wall to see if there were any pelagics swimming by in the blue water beyond the wall. On one glance, he caught sight of a Great Barracuda only about 6 feet away with its long, cylindrical body and large under slung jaw filled with sharp, lethal teeth. As Emerson swam horizontally, the barracuda swam parallel to him and watched him from its large, beady eye. When Emerson slowed, it slowed too as it maintained the same distance from Emerson and carefully studied this underwater intruder.

Emerson thought quickly as to whether he might be wearing any flashy jewelry or anything else, that might encourage the dangerous barracuda to strike. He breathed a sigh of relief that he had remembered not to wear his favorite gold ring. He had heard stories about barracuda striking at the fingers of divers wearing flashy rings, thinking it might be a glistening, darting fish. When barracudas struck, they would move so fast through the water that the diver wouldn't have a chance to dodge. It was easier to take the precaution than have to worry about it once you were down, especially since the Cayman Islands prohibited the wearing of gloves while diving. With gloves, divers are more likely to touch a reef or fragile underwater growth and damage it.

Emerson looked around for Duncan and spotted him near the wall. Duncan was looking perilously close into a number of openings and small nooks. Better be careful of any Moray eels, Emerson thought to himself as he watched his friend flash a light into a number of openings.

As Duncan peered into one opening, his head pulled back suddenly and he recoiled backwards from the wall as a large green moray emerged suddenly from the opening. Duncan looked for Emerson and gave him an "okay sign".

Emerson shook his head from side to side at his friend's dangerous folly then turned and pointed his camera at a blue-striped grunt, a fish with alternating blue and yellow stripes.

As the dive progressed, he spotted a large black grouper and began snapping pictures of it. The 2-foot long grouper was very accommodating and even seemed to enjoy having its picture taken. After each shot, it would start to slowly swim away then stop and seemingly pose in front of spreading sea fans or a small barrel sponge. Then it would swim toward Emerson, only to start the process over again.

Farther across the wall, Emerson noticed a huge stand of black coral, measuring almost 4 feet across and hanging from the ceiling of a small cavern. Its feathery appearance almost looked like cotton candy. As Emerson framed his shots, he thought about the illegal black coral market and how it was supported by anyone who purchased black coral jewelry. When one piece was purchased, another would have to be harvested to take its place.

Emerson was so immersed in his photography that he lost awareness of the time that had elapsed. As he focused on a small sea snail crawling around a large Corky Sea Fingers, he felt someone grab at his elbow. He turned and saw Duncan pointing at his watch and then giving a thumbs-up toward the surface. When Emerson looked around he saw the other six divers had already started their ascents. He looked at his dive computer and nodded his agreement to Duncan that it was time for them to ascend also.

Prior to boarding the dive boat that morning, the divers had prepared their dive profiles, using the dive tables, and then compared them to the dive computers, which they would take with them. The advance dive table planning was critical in the event that their computers failed while the divers were at their planned maximum depth level. They had planned a square profile, which would permit them to drop to the 60-foot level and spend about 40 minutes there before ascending to their safety stop at 15 feet.

Their ABT (actual bottom time) at 60 feet had been 40 minutes and they had allotted five minutes for their safety stop. Safety stops were a precautionary decompression stop during the ascent process at a depth around 15 feet. Safety stops were designed to reduce the risk for decompression sickness (DCS), or the bends.

Divers' bodies absorbed excess nitrogen as they spent time under water breathing compressed air and this excess nitrogen needed to be eliminated as the diver ascended. Too fast of an ascent could cause the nitrogen to form bubbles in a diver's body, which then resulted in an air embolism or decompression sickness. This typically happened within one hour after diving. Decompression sickness could be as minor as a mottled skin rash and joint pain, or as serious as permanent injury such as paralysis, or even death.

When Emerson nodded at Duncan, the two began to work their way upward to their 15-foot safety stop. They were the last two to finish their safety stops and break the water's surface to board the DiveTech boat. Dropping the mouthpiece from their mouths and pushing their facemasks down around their necks so as to not lose them to an errant wave, the two took off their fins and handed them to a waiting crew member.

Then, Emerson pulled himself up the hanging ladder and onto the dive platform at the boat's stern. He stepped onto the deck where willing hands assisted him in taking off his Buoyancy Compensation Device (BCD). The crew member dismantled the used tank from the BCD and slid it into the tank rack on the port side.

Grabbing his fins, BCD and mask, Emerson threw them in his dive bag as Duncan joined him on deck. Then, he grabbed his camera rig from the fresh water rinse tank where the crew had carefully placed it.   In a few short minutes, the two joined the other divers who were eating fresh orange slices and downing ice cold bottled water as they excitedly talked about the marine encounters from their dive.

A crew member checked to be sure that all the divers were on board, then signaled the pilothouse so that the boat could move on to the next dive spot.

Ocho Rios
Jamaica

Two dark, hairy legs extended from underneath the old Chevrolet Impala, which looked like it belonged in the scrap yard. The car had seen much better days. The beat up Impala was missing its four wheels and was precariously perched on four concrete blocks, set on their ends. They didn't provide a very stable perch for the mechanic to work under.

As the mechanic wrestled with an unmovable bolt, the car wobbled. Between the mechanic's focus on his work and the reggae music playing from a worn radio, the mechanic didn't hear the approaching footsteps.

"Problem with your car, Hernado?" the steely cold voice asked.

"What?" the voice called from underneath the behemoth. Hernado hadn't heard the three men walk around his house to the backyard where he worked. "Who is it?"

A deep guttural laugh was the only response he got – and it sent a chill through his spine as he recognized it. He anguished as to whether he should stay under the car or slide out to greet his unexpected visitor. He chose to slide out. "I'd recognize that laugh anywhere," he said nervously as he slid out from underneath. Shading his eyes in the bright sunlight, he looked up at Pryce Clarke. "I didn't know you were coming over for a visit."

"It's better that way. Too many people are interested in my whereabouts," Clarke said sternly. "Besides, I like to surprise people when I visit. Does my visit surprise you?" Clarke asked with a sneer.

"Yes. But then nothing surprises me about you," Hernado said.

"That is good and bad," Clarke said icily.

The cold look on Clarke's face was not lost upon Hernado. "What can I do for you?"

"Talk to me about Friday's shipment."

"What's there to talk about?" Hernado searched his memory for any problems from running his Jamaican canoe to rendezvous with two fishing boats off Grand Cayman's East End.

"It was light ten bales."

"I don't know nothing about that."

"This is the third time."

Hernado paused before answering. "I understand that. But I told you on the phone the first two times that I don't know anything about it."

"That's why I decided to come here in person."

"That's why? I don't understand."

"Yes. So I could look you in the eyes and tell if you're lying to me."

"I'm not."

"I'm not so sure about that." Clarke's sixth sense, which had helped keep him one step ahead of the drug interdiction boys most of the time, told him that Hernado was lying. It was a shame too, since he had been one of his best boat captains and mechanics. He decided to give him another chance. "Let me ask you one more time. Do you know anything about the missing weed?"

Hernado straightened himself and stared squarely in Clarke's eyes. "No!"

Clarke began to turn and walk away, closely followed by his two men. He stopped abruptly and looked back at Hernado. "Okay then, let's see what happens with the next delivery."

"There won't be any more problems. You can count on that."

"I am."

Hernado couldn't see the evil grin on Clarke's face, which was now turned away from him. Hernado breathed a sigh of relief as he watched the three walk around the corner of the house. With his reggae music blaring, Hernado sipped on his now warm beer, and then crawled back under the car.

He had been working for only a few minutes when the car wobbled on its shaky perch and an ominous voice said, "One more thing."

Hernado cringed when he heard Clarke's voice above him as the car wobbled again. Clarke was leaning on the car and staring through the engine compartment at Hernado. "Sometimes, you just have to lean on people when they lie to you. Good-bye Hernado." Clarke and his two associates leaned on the car, pushing it off its perch. Hernado knew what was coming and opened his mouth to scream, but nothing came out as the car dropped, crushing Hernado's chest and killing him.

Clarke smiled as he saw Hernado's feet cease twitching.

"Ready to go, boss?" one of his thugs asked.

"Not quite. I want to listen to the end of this song and enjoy the beauty of what we just did." Clarke tilted his ear toward the radio and listened as he stared at the lifeless body trapped under the Impala. When the song ended, the three men walked back to their vehicle and headed to their waiting boat for the return ride to the Cayman Islands.

Durty Reid's
Red Bay

This popular watering hole was packed with locals and tourists crowding to enjoy the antics of the two performers on stage, Mad Dog Adams and legendary Grand Cayman Island singer, Barefoot Man.

The Barefoot Man, George Nowacki, had arrived at the Caymans from his native Germany many years ago and had quickly adopted the Cayman Islands as his new home. He was the *Jimmy Buffet of the Cayman Islands* and wrote a song for and appeared in the film *"The Firm,"* which featured Tom Cruise.

Just seated at a small table in the corner, Emerson had ordered drinks and was preparing to enjoy the evening's entertainment when Ben "Mongo" Marich spotted them. Marich was a well-known treasure hunter and scuba diver throughout the Caribbean. He had been featured several times on the Discovery Channel on his treasure hunting expeditions and had been interviewed in Key West two years ago by Emerson.

"Come and sit with us," the lean, muscular treasure hunter called to Emerson.

Standing, Emerson walked to Marich's larger table where he was seated with a bearded gentleman with a small but muscular frame. "Emerson, you've got to meet this diver friend of mine. This is Roger Rothman."

The two shook hands.

"You're a diver, too?" Emerson quizzed.

"Yeah. I do a little underwater videography," Rothman stated quietly.

"It's much more than that," Marich chimed. "Rothman shoots for *National Geographic* and the *Discovery Channel*. He's a nationally recognized, award-winning underwater videographer."

Rothman took a drink of his Long Island Iced Tea, but said nothing.

Marich continued. "He's also done work with the Cousteau family and..."

Rothman interrupted. "He means Inspector Clouseau," he grinned.

"No really, he's been on a number of dive expeditions." Turning to Rothman, Marich urged him, "Tell him about the two Russian frigates which have been sunk here."

"I'd be interested in hearing about it," Emerson encouraged.

"Okay, then. With the break up of the Soviet Union and downsizing of its navy, there were two Russian frigates stationed in Havana. They both were put up for sale and the Cayman government bought them at fire sale prices."

"To sink here?" Emerson queried.

"Exactly. After they were stripped and their ship-to-ship and ship-to-air missiles as well as munitions removed, the Cayman government brought them here to sink them as artificial reefs. The one, which was renamed the *MV Capt. Keith Tibbetts*, was sunk on the North Wall off of Cayman Brac. The other sunk off of Boatswain's Bay, close to West Bay."

"I'm staying out there," Emerson interrupted as he realized that he might be able to dive it.

"Where?"

"Cobalt Coast Dive Resort. Right by DiveTech."

"Great folks at both places," Rothman commented knowingly. "You've been through Hell on the way?" he asked with a grin.

Emerson nodded his head affirmatively as he smiled. "Yeah, drove through it. I've never seen a village like that, with all of the strange rock formations."

"That's why they call it Hell," Marich interjected.

"And the good news is that I'm staying on the other side of Hell," Emerson teased. "At a touch of paradise called Cobalt Coast Dive Resort."

Rothman and Marich chuckled softly.

"Arie is the best," Rothman added as he thought about the resort's affable Dutch owner.

"So is Dora," added Marich, referring to Arie's assistant. Then, Marich urged Rothman to continue, "Tell him what you did during the sinkings."

"Jean-Michel Cousteau dressed in his scuba gear and took a position in the bow of the *Tibbetts* where he rode the ship down as it was sunk. I was in the foredeck with my video equipment.

I filmed the sinking and Jean-Michel as the water cascaded over the decks and we sunk to the bottom."

"That must have been exciting!" Emerson commented.

"Nothing like it! To be on board a sinking vessel when you're in a controlled environment and it is being done to advance underwater life is very rewarding," Rothman said.

"Did you film Jean-Michel on the one off Boatswain's Bay?"

"No, I didn't."

"Go ahead and tell him what happened," Marich pushed.

"I filmed it, but it wasn't what I expected."

"How's that?"

"I was on board the tug, towing her from Havana. We were just coming around the north side and off Boatswain's Bay when a storm caught us by surprise. It was a big one. We had a tough time trying to tow her and the line snapped."

With widening eyes, Emerson asked, "What happened?"

"We were okay, but the ship, which by the way, had been re-named the *Reid Foster*..."

Interrupting, Emerson observed good-naturedly, "After those two scoundrels?" He was pointing to Durty Reid and Steve Foster.

"It's hard to believe, isn't it?" Marich replied.

Rothman continued with his story. "We were in heavy seas. She drifted toward the reef and struck it hard. It ripped a long gash in her hull and seawater rushed in and began filling her. After she was carried across the reef, she slid down the backside and sunk to a position tight against the base of the reef."

"And they left her there?"

"Yes. Because of the cost to attempt to raise her, the Caymanian government decided that she would have to serve as a dive site where she sunk. But she's a dangerous dive."

"Why's that?"

"Unlike her sister ship and due to her sudden sinking, the unsafe areas were not closed off by welded bars and gates."

"So you could become disoriented if you're deep in her hull?"

"Yes, or you could get equipment tangled on broken pieces of metal or forget about your bottom time and stay down too long. Then you'd have trouble with having enough air and making your decompression stops on the way up."

Emerson nodded his head in understanding.

"There's another interesting twist," Rothman said.

"Oh?"

"I know what you're going to tell him," Marich grinned.

"She sunk off of Cobalt Coast Dive Resort and DiveTech. Right where you're staying."

"In my backyard. We'll have to dive it. Interested in going together?"

Sipping his drink, Rothman looked over the edge of the glass at Emerson. "Let's plan on it."

"Great!" Emerson said without a moment's hesitation.

"Let's see what we can do in the next few days. Mongo, you want to join us?"

"I can't. I'm flying to London. We've got a lead on the *S.S. Wernecke*. She was a side-wheeler, that sunk in 1865 in the English Channel."

"Sounds like some tough diving in even tougher conditions to me," Emerson volunteered.

"That it will be," Marich said as he beamed at the challenge. "She was one of the largest ships in the Collins Line of steamships."

"What caused her to sink?" Emerson probed.

"French ship ran into her, putting three holes in her. One was as big as a car! This could be bigger than the *Atocha* with the treasure it was carrying when she sunk."

As Mad Dog and Barefoot Man began to sing, the three of them turned their attention to the stage and to enjoying the entertainment.

DiveTech
Cobalt Coast Dive Resort

The morning's Advanced Trimix class was filled with instructions on the aspects of technical diving from nationally recognized technical diver, Nancy Easterbrook. Once she completed teaching the four-day class, the two students would be able to dive as deep as 330 feet.

Emerson and his one classmate, a diver from Seattle, Washington, had completed coursework in rebreathers, advance Nitrox and Normoxic Trimix as well as earning their full cave diver certification. The prior year, Emerson had completed his coursework at Port Clinton's New Wave Dive Shop and had gone on several Lake Erie dive trips with BAD (Bay Area Divers) and LEWD (Lake Erie Wreck Divers).

After Nancy stepped out of the small classroom to allow the two students to complete an assignment, Emerson found himself gazing out the open window at the azure waters. They seemed to beckon him to discover their hidden treasures. He smiled as he thought about diving deeper along the North Wall and recalled several of his Lake Erie diving adventures.

In Eastern Lake Erie, he had dived on the *Dean Richmond*, a 238-foot long wooden ore carrier that sank on Halloween in 1893. The ship's rudder had been damaged and she was helplessly caught in a gale, sinking to 150 feet where she settled on her starboard side. He also had dived on the *Oxford*, a 114-foot long schooner that sank in 1856 in 160 feet of water off the Erie, Pennsylvania, harbor entrance after a collision with a steamer. The well-preserved schooner still had it masts, rigging, winches, windlass and bilge pumps in place.

Glancing at his assignment, Emerson recalled the inherent dangers and risk, which deep-water technical divers faced if they didn't follow certain safety precautions.

Breathing regular air at lower depths while experiencing increased pressure could lead to nitrogen narcosis, a state similar to alcohol intoxication. Jacques Cousteau had called it the "rapture of the deep." This dangerous condition could impair decision-making, focus, judgment and coordination as well as cause hallucinations and unconsciousness. It could induce panic or strange behaviors like an affected diver offering his regulator to fish or removing the facemask at deep depths, then ascending quickly. The end result could be fatal from its own toxic effect or illogical behavior caused in a dangerous environment.

As a diver descended and pressure increased, nitrogen dissolved more slowly than other gases in the diver's blood. The gas could build up and penetrate the lipids of the brain's nerve cells and interfere with signal transmission between cells. One way to reduce the possibility of nitrogen narcosis was to reduce the amount of nitrogen in a diver's tank, replacing some of the nitrogen with helium.

Trimix was a mixture of oxygen, helium and nitrogen, which effectively reduced the proportions of oxygen and nitrogen. Oxygen needed to be reduced so that oxygen toxicity didn't take place during deep dives. Oxygen toxicity caused free radicals to form, and could manifest itself as dizziness, nausea or convulsions. This, in turn, could cause drowning or lethal pressure damage during a rapid ascent.

A mix named "Trimix 10/70 consisted of 10% oxygen, 70% helium and 20% nitrogen and allowed a diver to dive to 330 feet. Many technical divers would carry multiple high capacity diving tanks and stage bottles to ensure adequate breathing gas supply as they went through their decompression stops. Some divers utilized rebreathers; a breathing set that recycled exhaled gas and augmented times that could be spent underwater.

Technical dives were carefully planned as far as depth and duration of the dive as well as mandatory decompression stops as the diver ascended to the surface at the dive's completion.

Emerson refocused his attention on completing the assignment before Nancy returned to conduct the balance of the class. He was anxiously looking forward to technical diving in the islands.

"Beautiful! This is one of the most beautiful places on this planet!" Emerson gushed as he rounded the building and saw the dreamlike setting before his eyes. "If I didn't know any better, I'd think that I died and ended up in paradise!"

"This is the other side of Hell," Mad Dog mused aloud.

Late that afternoon, Emerson, Duncan and Mad Dog had met at Durty Reid's and crammed themselves into Emerson's small rental car. They then headed to Rum Point, located on the picturesque north side of the island. Its name dated back to a number of rum barrels that had washed ashore from a wrecked schooner. Mad Dog provided the directions for the 20-minute ride that took them across the middle of the island to the north shore.

An L-shaped dock stretched out through the crystal clear blue water, which seemed to merge with the sky on the horizon - the only differentiator being that the sky had large white cumulus clouds. The shallow, clear water and white sandy beach partially shaded by casuarinas trees epitomized an island paradise. The wispy Australian pines had hammocks strung between them and lured visitors to a shaded respite as fresh island breezes provided a cooling effect.

Colorfully painted yellow and green picnic tables were set throughout the uncrowded beach area, which featured a raised wooden walkway. It led by the lizard cage and the parrots perched on tree limbs, squawking at passers-by. Several weathered, gaily-painted signposts were located throughout the beach area with their signs pointing toward their various destinations. They showed the number of miles to Havana, Miami, London and others. Emerson was surprised when he saw one of the signs pointing north and labeled "Put-in-Bay 1,542 Miles."

Mad Dog grinned. "I had them put that one up a few years ago. Let's go see Tammy and grab a few drinks."

"I'd rather grab Tammy and see a few drinks if you don't mind," Duncan chimed in.

"It's not me who would be minding. Tammy's husband is a black belt karate instructor in George Town," Mad Dog cautioned.

"Like I said, let's go see Tammy and grab a few drinks, then," Duncan reacted.

"Some things just don't change," Emerson said as he eyed his impish friend.

"E, it wouldn't be me, otherwise!" Duncan retorted with a grin.

"Sam, you're still incorrigible!"

"Count on it!"

The three walked toward a yellow-painted building with large open windows and a high peaked tin roof. Above the doorway hung a sign that read "Wreck Bar."

Entering the bar, they saw a variety of shipwreck remains. A ship's mast stretched to the center of its high ceiling from which hung ship rigging and fish nets, wooden deadeyes and a couple of lobster traps. Below each opened window with its wide ledge were high backed chairs from which the occupants could enjoy a refreshing drink as they gazed at the beach scenery.

Scattered through the bar were large barrels, serving as tall tables. The planked bar was painted a bright green and topped with dark walnut. Behind the bar were three shelves and another sign, announcing the name of the bar as "The Wreck Bar." The bar area was covered by a thatched roof which provided an additional tropical dimension to the inviting bar and grill.

"Tammy!" Mad Dog called to an attractive blue-eyed blonde working behind the bar.

She looked up and her face broke into a large, warm smile. "Mad Dog! I heard you were on the island!" She stepped from around the bar and hugged the singer.

Returning the hug, Mad Dog introduced his two friends. "Meet a couple of my rowdy friends, Emerson Moore reporter extraordinaire and Sam the Man Duncan. You got to be careful with Mr. Sam. He's got an eye for the ladies!"

With a twinkle in his eyes, Duncan started to give her a hug. "I'm a hugger, Tammy."

"And I'm married, Mr. Sam the man!" Tammy said as she hugged him and displayed her wedding ring. "Mad Dog was in my wedding."

"Just my luck. All the pretty ones are married."

It was Emerson's turn to step into Tammy's open arms. "Nice meeting you, Tammy. You've got to have one of the best jobs on this earth. I've never seen a place like this!"

Tammy stepped back and smiled at Emerson. "I'm very fortunate to work here." She gazed out the open windows at the tranquil sea and peaceful surroundings, then looked at her three visitors. "It's a touch of paradise."

"My exact words," Emerson said warmly.

"What can I get you, boys?"

The guys placed their orders and settled on the bar stools, watching her as she quickly prepared their drinks. Once she had served them, Duncan said, "I think I'll drink my drink by the beach." He stood and followed two bikini-clad women out of the bar.

"You go right ahead," Tammy called. "And those two are single," she added.

Turning his head back to Tammy, Duncan winked, flashed her a smile, and continued following the two women.

"Like I said before, Mad Dog, some things do not change," Emerson repeated.

"Yeah, like this good-looking Tammy and Rum Point's beauty!" Mad Dog commented.

For the next 20 minutes, the three of them chatted about Mad Dog's early career on the island and his days singing at the old Holiday Inn's The Wreck of The Ten Sails Pub with Barefoot Man.

Chuckling, Tammy recalled a few of the questions she had been asked by visitors to the Wreck Bar. "Once, a customer asked me if you could swim under the island. I said he could give it a try, but he had to pay his bar tab first. One guy asked me where the best place to snorkel was and I told him that the water would be a good place to start."

Mad Dog and Emerson chortled at her comments.

"One customer wanted to know if we imported all of our beer and I told him that not only did we import the beer, but we also imported all the help. Then, there was the lady who wanted to know if you could go shopping at Stingray City."

Sting Ray City was on the edge of the North Sound, next to the reef. It offered divers a chance to swim with sting rays and feed them.

"It's amazing what people ask without thinking," Mad Dog commented.

"Yeah," Emerson agreed. "I've had tourists stop me on the street in Put-in-Bay and ask me where Perry's Monument is stored during the winter months. I just tell them that it's lowered underground," he said, chuckling.

Late Afternoon
Off the North Shore

Despite the reduced visibility, the four divers saw the sunken Soviet frigate, the *Reid Foster*. It was listing 30 degrees to starboard and had settled in 85 feet of water. According to the Navy dive tables, this would mean the divers would only have 21 minutes to explore the ship without entering decompression if they remained in the deeper parts of the ship.

The wall to which the ship abutted was dotted with barrel sponges large enough to hold a 55-gallon drum. Nooks in the wall were filled with big eye squirrelfish and lobsters the size of Shaquille O'Neal's feet. The abundant marine life around the vessel included surgeonfish, parrotfish, stingrays, and even a juvenile batfish. As the years passed, the *Reid Foster* had become encrusted with algae and coral.

Because of the cost to attempt to raise her, the Caymanian government decided that she would have to serve as a dive site where she sunk. Unlike her sister ship, and due to her sudden sinking, the unsafe areas were not closed off by welded bars and gates. Caymanian dive operators have been carefully coordinating dives on her ever since and warning divers about her unsafe areas.

Emerson was paired with underwater videographer Roger Rothman, while Mad Dog and Duncan buddied up. They slowly approached the ship, whose breathtaking view emerged as they closed the distance to it. Its massive anchor could be seen dangling from the bow. The forward gun turret had its long barrels pointing straight ahead at some imaginary underwater threat. Emerson swam up to one of the gun barrels where he paused to peer into it while Rothman worked his camera. In a burst of bubbles, Emerson abruptly shot backwards from the gun barrel opening as an adult Bluehead Wrasse darted quickly from its opening, startling him.

Emerson swung around and sheepishly gave Rothman an okay sign with his finger and thumb. He could tell by the twinkle in Rothman's eyes that Emerson's reaction to the fish swimming out of the gun barrel must have been quite comical. But all divers know that they need to be acutely aware of everything around them and sometimes that did tend to make them a little jumpy.

Then, Emerson began swimming toward the entrance door of the forward gun turret with his head down, studying the deck below him. He was pleased to recognize small coral polyps that had attached themselves to the deck, knowing that these would someday grow to be large, beautiful corals. As he neared the door, he heard Rothman tapping his tank frantically with his dive knife and looked back. Rothman was distinctly shaking his head and pointing toward the top of the door. It was then that Emerson saw the Great Barracuda hovering, as if guarding the turret.

Emerson nodded back, swam away from the entranceway, and headed toward the bridge. He knew how territorial barracuda could be and didn't want a close encounter with one. Rothman followed him and saw that the other two divers were already entering the bridge.

When they were all together, Mad Dog indicated that he wanted to go into the officers' quarters and turned with Duncan close on his fins. They swam down a companionway and disappeared from view. Rothman was already filming a sergeant major damselfish guarding and fanning his nest of roe that had been laid on a wall of the wheelhouse. Females lay these eggs then leave the male to guard them. If he didn't guard this nest, the roe would instantly become a feast for other fish.

Emerson was standing at the wheel, imagining how it would have been to man the wheel while it was on active duty. Rothman recognized this shot opportunity and turned his camera on Emerson. When Rothman kept the camera perfectly level, Emerson would appear standing crooked and when Rothman turned the camera to match the 30 degree list of the ship, Emerson's bubbles seemed to flow sideways.

When Rothman finished his shots, he and Emerson descended back down to the main deck where they noticed that a hold cover was missing. When Emerson got to it, he looked in and thought about the sailors that lived in this ship. As he saluted the hold, he took solace in the fact that no one had died on this ship.

Then Emerson signaled to Rothman that the opening was too small for a diver to penetrate with his gear on. Rothman began removing his gear knowing what Emerson was thinking. Emerson removed his gear as well and eased his gear into the hold carefully, being sure to keep a tight grip on the regulator with his teeth. Then he carefully squeezed his body through the hold head first, with Rothman following suit after handing his video camera through.

They had dropped into a control room filled with dials and gauges, all labeled in Russian. There were shelves and cabinets on every wall from floor to ceiling. The room had little ambient light so Rothman switched on his video lights and began filming.

While looking around, both divers quickly realized that they needed to be very careful in this closed environment. It was obvious that this was one of many areas of the ship that were not meant for divers to visit. Wires hung from the ceiling in tangles and jagged edges of metal were everywhere just waiting to cut a dangling air hose or penetrate a careless diver's skin.

An open door at one end of the room led to a hallway with bunks tightly tucked into the walls. Emerson climbed into one of the bunks and posed as if sleeping. Rothman slowly started panning the hallway and bunks with his camera, purposely ending his pan at Emerson.

After swimming through a number of passageways, they found themselves in the Captain's quarters which Rothman filmed while Emerson explored it.

Meanwhile, Mad Dog and Duncan had begun their own exploration. They searched the officers' quarters for anything that might have been left behind. They figured that there would be no logbook or uniforms, but maybe they could find a loose button or medal. Being careful to not stir up any sediment that would impair visibility, they began opening all the drawers and cabinets they could find.

Then Duncan heard a squeal that sounded like, "Wahoo!" and he knew Mad Dog had found something. As he turned around, Mad Dog showed him a two-inch pin in the shape of the ship. It was a pin that Russian officers wore on their uniforms.

Excited about their find, the pair signaled each other that it was probably time to start heading out and up to avoid going into decompression. They made their way back to the wheelhouse and carefully swam out through one of the large windows that had broken when the ship sunk.

As they emerged into open water, they looked up to see that Emerson and Rothman were already on a hang line at 15 feet, doing their safety stop. This stop would allow their bodies to purge the built-up nitrogen that all divers get when breathing compressed air. If this nitrogen isn't purged enough, divers will get decompression sickness, otherwise known as the bends.

Mad Dog calculated that since the other two divers were already on the hang line, they must have studied areas of the ship that were deeper than where he and Duncan had been. He could see both divers intently studying their gauges, keeping track of the time they were hanging and making sure they remained at the 15-foot depth. That's when Rothman handed his camera to Emerson and showed Emerson that some of his hoses were tangled.

When he had exited the hold and donned his gear, he had inadvertently allowed one hose to end up through an armhole of his buoyancy vest. Rather than take time at the deeper depth to resolve this problem, Rothman knew it would be safer for him to fix it while doing his safety stop. But while Rothman concentrated on his gear, Mad Dog saw a shadow emerging from deeper water. It was heading toward Emerson and Rothman.

With their attention focused on their gear, the two divers were unaware that a predator was circling them. It was an 8-foot long Caribbean Reef shark. When the circles got noticeably smaller, Mad Dog realized that the shark was thinking of an attack. This was one behavior he had seen numerous times before on previous shark dives. Then the shark lowered it pectoral fins, arched its back, and began its swim directly toward Emerson.

Mad Dog quickly pulled out his dive knife and frantically tapped it on his tank to get their attention. As Emerson turned to find out what was up, he saw the shark heading straight toward him. He knew he would only have one chance at deterring this attack.

He quickly raised the camera and pushed it toward the open jaws of the shark. The camera struck the shark's snout severely. The punch of the camera housing's hard aluminum on the shark's snout was enough to make the shark peel away.

Sharks prefer to be the aggressor and aren't fond of being the aggressee. This blow was enough to send the shark on its way to look for easier prey.

Back on the dive boat, Mad Dog was heralded as a hero for having saved Emerson and Rothman some serious grief. Since most sharks don't like the taste of human flesh, it probably wouldn't have killed either diver, but it would have taken a bite. That bite would have at least been enough to draw blood, which would have quickly attracted other sharks to the area.

After dinner in the salon, Rothman hooked his camera up to the TV to review and catalog the day's footage while Mad Dog showed off his newly discovered officer's pin. Everyone gathered around the TV knowing that Rothman always came up with some great marine behavior sequences, like the sergeant major damselfish guarding its nest. When Rothman played the sequence of Emerson steering the ship, everyone laughed at the different perspectives.

When he got to the sequence of Emerson sleeping in the bunk, Mad Dog teased Emerson about not getting enough sleep the night before. Duncan chimed in by asking Emerson who he might have been with the night before. As the divers joked with each other about this shot, Rothman played the shot over and over to keep the good-natured teasing going.

The teasing continued as the dive boat headed back to its dockage.

Sipping his Seven and Seven, Emerson stood on the dock and gazed at the starlit night.

"Beautiful evening, isn't it, E?" Duncan observed, then took a swig of his beer.

"I'll say," Emerson responded as he enjoyed the evening's tranquility. The sound of the waves breaking on the beach mingled with the rhythmic music, which drifted from Duppies, the resort's bar and grill. The fresh ocean breeze invigorated Emerson. "There's nothing like being near the ocean on a star-studded night."

"Oh, I can think of a few things I'd rather be doing," Duncan dreamed aloud.

Emerson ignored his friend's comment. "I've enjoyed walking out here at night and veggin' out. It's so serene with the waves splashing against the dock and watching the passing boats."

"I'd rather be watching the passing girls," Duncan leered.

"Always in the hunt, aren't you?"

"Never know when I'll find that right one," Duncan grinned.

"I'm not sure that you're really trying to find the right one. I seem to recall you telling me once that you couldn't settle down with one woman because of your profession." Emerson was positive that Duncan was a contractor to various government agencies, including the CIA, but Duncan was very elusive in confirming Emerson's suspicions.

"Probing again? Using leading questions?"

"Not really."

"E, you know I can't officially tell you what I'm involved with. I'm sworn to secrecy. Besides, you might print it."

"I wouldn't do that. Not to you."

"It's better that I just let you draw your own conclusions on some of this stuff. It's safer for you and me."

The light from an anchored boat caught Emerson's eye. "That boat's been out there every night."

"Probably setting lobster traps," Duncan guessed.

"But they don't move. It seems like they're in the same spot every night. I don't see them moving. Some nights, I've been out here for hours and they haven't moved."

"Hard to say," Duncan dismissed Emerson's comments.

"Curious. Curious," Emerson deliberated.

"Shall we head over to Durty Reid's?"

"Sure," Emerson said as he finished the rest of his drink and turned to follow Duncan. As he walked, he again looked at the mysterious boat at anchor. He had a growing suspicion that there was more there than met the eye. A plan was forming in the back of Emerson's mind. He would take action on it later that evening after visiting with his friends and grabbing a bite to eat at Durty Reid's.

Later That Night
Off Cobalt Coast Dive Resort

Dimmed lights shone from the fishing boat, which was riding gently at anchor. One of her crew cocked his head as he heard the approaching jet ski. "Looks like we may have a visitor."

The other crew member cackled, "It'll be like shooting ducks in a barrel." He walked into the pilothouse and emerged with a rifle as the other crew member positioned himself next to the searchlight.

"When I yell, you turn on the searchlight," he called.

"Got it, man!"

The jet ski was 100 yards away when the rider switched on a powerful hand held light. It illuminated the fishing boat and the figure holding the rifle. Just as quickly, the jet ski's rider switched off the light. He spun the jet ski into a tight turn and headed toward shore.

"Now!"

The brilliant light from the fishing boat's searchlight quickly found its fleeing target and the rifleman took aim. His first shot flew over the jet ski rider's right shoulder.

Hearing the shot, the jet ski rider began zig zagging to make himself a more difficult target. Two more rifle shots followed. Both missed the rider.

"Aw, you missed him."

"Sure. Remember what the boss said. We're just to run them off. He doesn't want us to kill anyone. We don't need to get any police involved in a murder."

On shore, the jet ski ran up on the beach at the Cobalt Coast Dive Resort. Emerson Moore made sure it was beyond the high tide level and secured it. He then sat on one of the large rock formations and looked toward the fishing boat still at anchor in the distance. A smile crept across his face.

He had accomplished his objective. The name of the fishing boat was *Turtle Dancer*. Now, he could run down the ownership of the boat. He also had the boat's GPS position from the unit, which he had affixed to the jet ski, so that he could return to the site during the daytime. And he would be equipped for a tech dive. When he had flashed his light on the boat, he had noticed that there were a number of Trimix tanks on board. Someone or multiple people were diving and diving deep. He was curious as to what they were after, especially after what he had seen dangling from the boat's overhead winch.

Emerson stood and walked to his room. It had been a very productive evening, and his curiosity was growing.

Durty Reid's Bar & Grille
Red Bay

The next evening, Emerson climbed into his little rental car and made his way along West Shore to Durty Reid's. As he drove, he thought about the prior evening's discovery and how he was going to identify the boat's owner. He also realized that he hadn't seen or heard from Duncan that day.

Duncan had said that he was taking a number of day dive trips, but Emerson was suspicious. He wasn't using the DiveTech boats for his dives. Duncan had also indicated that he was planning a dive trip off of Cayman Brac, the outermost island in the Cayman Islands.

Putting his concern for Duncan aside, Emerson wheeled the rental car into the parking lot at Durty Reid's and entered the tropical-designed building. Even though it was early evening, the place was already crowded. Emerson spotted the bar's owner and made his way over to him. "Hey, Reid," he called, "mind if I join you?"

"Hell, no," Dennis replied. "Pull up a chair."

As Emerson sat down, Keisha appeared. "Seven and Seven?" she asked with a warm smile.

"Good memory," he nodded. "Reid, I need your help."

"Sure. What can I do?"

"I want to find out who owns a certain fishing boat that I've seen."

"In the West Bay district?"

"Yes. It was offshore Cobalt Coast Dive Resort."

"Go talk to Ratty Blackwell."

"Ratty?"

"Like the name, huh?" Dennis grinned at Emerson's perplexed look.

"Different."

"Yeah, so is Ratty. Picked up the nickname for his ability to kill rats.

Emerson grimaced.

"He knows the water and the boats around here like no one else. I thought I knew what was going on the island, but it doesn't compare to this Caymanian's contacts."

"Where do I find him? Does he come in here?"

"Sometimes. You can find him usually at one or two places. Harbour House Marina over on North Sound. He may be working on the *Southwind*. You can't miss her. She's a treasure hunting ship with two huge mailboxes at the stern."

Emerson knew about mailboxes. They used prop wash to blow away sand underwater when treasure hunting.

"But, it's probably too late to catch him there," Dennis said as he looked at his watch. "You can probably find him over in West Bay." Dennis paused as he grinned. He looked Emerson in the eyes. "You ready for an adventure?"

"How's that?"

"You'll probably find him settled in at the Green Parrot Bar," Dennis suggested. "It's a place where the locals hang out. It's a tough joint. You need to watch your back and don't get pushy with anybody over there. You won't like the results. They play rougher than you'd expect."

"It does sound like an adventure," Emerson mused.

"Oh, that's not the real adventure there. It's the dining experience that's the real adventure!"

"Oh?"

"I was in there one day and saw the bartender ask a female customer what she wanted to drink. She said that she wanted a vodka tonic. When the bartender picked up a glass off the back of the bar, a cockroach ran out. He smashed it with his thumb, and then, without wiping off his thumb, he reached into the ice

– 116 –

bin and grabbed a handful of ice and threw the ice in the lady's glass. She saw the whole thing!"

"What did she do?" Emerson asked as he shook his head in disbelief.

"Passed out. Good thing I was sitting next to her because I caught her." Reid paused and smiled. "It's not every day that I have beautiful females swooning and falling into my lap!" he grinned as he gave Emerson a mischievous wink.

"The place also has another distinction," Dennis offered.

"What's that?"

"It's their quality control program for food."

"How's that?"

"It's the only place where the cook takes a bite out of every sandwich to make sure it tastes good."

"You're kidding!"

"I wish I was, but it's a local tradition. And if you saw the cook, you wouldn't want to eat there. I don't think the guy ever takes a bath. His body odor is overpowering!"

"My kind of place," Emerson joked. Switching gears, he asked, "What's this Ratty look like?"

"Just ask for him. Everyone knows him. I first met him when he was in his 30's and he looked like he was in his late 60's," Dennis smiled as he took a swig of his beer. "He'll be easy to spot. He always has a corncob pipe in his mouth. He'd probably be wearing a soiled tee shirt and khaki colored slacks. He won't have any socks on and, if you get close enough, you'll learn he doesn't wear any underwear," Dennis grinned.

"Information overload! I don't need to know the no underwear part," Emerson grimaced.

Dennis was chuckling at the strained look on Emerson face.

"I think I'll head out there right now."

"To check out the no underwear part?" Dennis couldn't help himself. "Gee, as soon as I mentioned that, you want to leave and check out this guy." Dennis knew better but couldn't resist poking fun at nice guy Emerson.

"No, I need to create some space between us."

"I don't mind that at all. Just be sure to create space between you and Ratty." Dennis threw in another jab.

Emerson got directions from Dennis and headed toward the door.

More seriously, Dennis cautioned, "Watch yourself when you go in there. You might want to take your buddy, Duncan, with you."

"Nothing I can't handle. I just want to meet the guy. Besides, I haven't seen Sam. He disappeared on me today."

Emerson walked through the door and drove to West Bay and the Green Parrot.

The Green Parrot Bar
West Bay

The pool cue broke across the Jamaican's head with a loud crack, leaving the cue stick with a jagged point. Wielding the cue was a short Caymanian. Between his teeth, he clenched a corncob pipe.

Pointing the jagged end of the broken pool cue at three other Jamaicans, he asked, "Which one of yous wants to be next?"

The three Jamaicans stared at the old banty rooster holding the cue. They also took in the 10 Caymanians who stood behind him, ready to participate in a melee. They decided not to take him up on his offer.

"Pick up yous friend and be off with yous!"

The fallen Jamaican was rubbing a bloody bruise on his head as he struggled to stand. His friends assisted him to his feet and escorted him to the doorway and safety.

As they walked through the doorway, one of them bumped into Emerson, who had arrived just in time to see the Jamaican struck with the cue. The Jamaican eyed Emerson as if he recognized him, but put it aside as he hurried out the door.

From the outside, the low concrete block building was unappealing. It needed a coat of paint to freshen its green exterior, and its tin roof appeared to be sagging. The inside was not much better. Worn tables and chairs were scattered around the inside. Faded and out-of-date posters dotted the walls along with beer signs. A blue haze seemed to hover at just the right level for people to breathe second-hand smoke. The small bar was in the shape of an "L" and the rickety bar stools were occupied. Someone replugged the jukebox and island music filled the air.

The man, holding the cue, handed it to the bartender and said, "Put it on my tab."

Emerson approached the man and asked, "Ratty?"

The man whirled around to face him. In his hand, a knife had magically appeared and it was pointed toward Emerson. Eyeing Emerson up and down carefully, the man asked, "And who wants to know?"

"I'm Emerson Moore."

"So?" he asked as he evaluated Emerson as a foe or friend.

"Reid Dennis suggested I talk to Ratty."

"And why would yous be wanting to talk to this Ratty fellow?"

"It's about the ownership of a boat that I saw."

"I'm not saying whether I'm Ratty or not."

Before he could continue, the sirens of police cars rushing to the bar from the West Bay District Station grew nearer.

"We'd better step out back," he suggested as he took a fresh beer from the bartender and began to walk with Emerson to the outside patio that overlooked the beach. "It's going to get a little bit too crowded in here."

"They'll pick you up?"

"No. Ain't no one inside who saw anything. And no one is going to point me out, that's for damn sure." He settled on top of one of the picnic benches and gazed at the ocean.

"Nice view," Emerson commented.

"Yeah, but I don't think Reid sent yous to see me to talk about the view."

"No, he didn't." Emerson smiled to himself as he realized that the man he was talking to just acknowledged that he was Ratty.

"So, what is it that yous want from me? I don't come cheap."

"Reid said that you knew everything that goes on around the island."

"At the lower level, that would be right. I don't know what goes on with the high muckety mucks."

"I'm not sure that I'm interested in them."

"What is it then?"

"I'm trying to find out who owns a certain fishing boat."

"Why do yous want to do that?"

"Curiosity."

"Yous with the law?"

"No. I'm an investigative reporter for *The Washington Post*."

Ratty was silent as he sipped his beer. Then he spoke. "A reporter?"

"Yes."

"I don't talk to reporters. All yous going to do is to write bad things about me."

"No. No. I'm not writing anything about anybody. I'm here on vacation. Not writing a story." Emerson was being truthful, but then again he never knew when he'd discover something, which would be story worthy.

Ratty stared at Emerson briefly and he pondered whether he was going to help the likable man standing near him. He decided to help him. "What's the name of the boat?"

"*Turtle Dancer.*"

Ratty took another sip of his beer and looked out to the sea.

"You know the boat?"

Ratty didn't reply. He continued to stare at the sea.

Emerson asked again. "Do you know the boat?"

Slowly, Ratty turned his head to look at Emerson. He took another sip from his beer bottle. "Yes," he said in a low voice as his body tensed.

Emerson read Ratty's body language. "Is there something wrong?"

"I'd drop it if I was yous."

That comment only fueled Emerson's curiosity.

"Yous don't want to mess with these guys. They are bad ass people. I can mess with them. I know them and how to do the dance with them. Yous an outsider. It would not go well for yous."

"Listen, Ratty, I appreciate your concern, but I've dealt with all kinds before. I'm good at handling myself."

Ratty thought for a moment before answering his persistent visitor. "These boys like to cut people. People disappear when they don't like them. I hear that they cut them three ways. Let me remember how they say." He took a long pull on his bottle. "Yeah, I remember. They cuts them long, deep and continuous. Then, they weigh them down and drop them overboard into the trench. Nobody going to find your body."

"I'm not worried about that."

"Yous should be!"

Ignoring the comment, Emerson continued, "I'm just curious as to what they're up to."

"No good, that's for sure. Yous go write a story on tourism here in the islands. Much safer for yous."

"Does that mean you won't tell me who owns the boat?"

"If yous a true friend of Reid's, I shouldn't tell yous." He paused as a police officer walked out of the bar and surveyed the picnic table area before returning inside. "Yous saw some of the *Turtle Dancer*'s crew when yous walked in."

Emerson recalled the Jamaicans leaving the bar when he arrived. "The Jamaicans?"

"Yes. The ones I kicked butt with."

"And they work for?"

"Pryce Clarke."

"Pryce Clarke," Emerson repeated the name. "So, who is he?"

"He's a Jamaican bad ass. He's got a big house over on Morgan's Harbour."

"Sounds like he has money."

"He has lots of money," Ratty confirmed.

"What's he do?"

"Runs fishing boats."

Ratty's answer seemed evasive to Emerson. "And what else does he do?"

Ratty didn't respond.

"Does he run Jamaican canoes?"

"Don't even go there. We done talking. Yous tell Reid that I helped yous, but I did it reluctantly." Ratty stood and turned his back to Emerson to signify that the conversation was over.

"Thank you, Ratty," Emerson said as he spoke to Ratty's backside. Ratty responded with silence. Shrugging his shoulders, Emerson turned and walked back through the bar to where he had parked his car.

Leaning against the car and looking toward the worn bar, Emerson replayed the exchange with Ratty. He made a decision. He was going to learn more about Pryce Clarke. He opened the car door, entered the vehicle and drove back to Cobalt Coast Dive Resort.

On the Phone
Cobalt Coast Dive Resort

"No! No! No! You don't want anything to do with that man!" Dennis anguished when Emerson called and told him that he wanted directions to Pryce Clarke's home.

"Why?"

"Didn't Ratty tell you anything about him?"

"Yes. In his words, 'He's bad ass people'."

"There you go. That sums it up in a neat package!"

"Come on, Reid. Stuff like that doesn't hold me back. I know there's something big here. I feel it in my bones."

"If you want those bones to remain unbroken, I'd drop pursuing this further," Dennis cautioned.

"Don't worry. I've always been careful – and I've always gotten my story."

"Pryce Clarke would cut off your testicles while dining with his mother and not think twice about it."

"Yeah, yeah. I've run into his kind before and lived to write about it. Come on Reid; help me out with the directions. I can always get them from someone else, I'm sure," Emerson pleaded.

Silence greeted Emerson from the other end of the phone. "Reid, are you there?"

"Listen, I'll get directions to Clarke's house for you, but under one condition."

"What's that?"

"I want you to go meet with Superintendent Derek Fleming."

"Who's he?"

"He's the head of the Royal Cayman Police."

"Why do I need to talk to him?"

"What's your life worth to you?"

"Reid, you're being melodramatic!"

"Humor me and talk to him, okay?"

"And you'll give me the directions to Clarke's house?"

"Yeah. I'll get them. He lives on the other side of Hell."

"That's interesting. Just a few months ago, I was in the Promised Land." Emerson said as he thought about his recent adventure in New Orleans and Hurricane Katrina.

"I'm serious. You need to talk to Fleming or you'll be seeing the real Promised Land sooner than you'd expect. Deal?"

"I guess," Emerson reluctantly responded.

"Good. I'll call you back in a few minutes with the directions to Clarke's house."

Five minutes later, Dennis called back. "Here's the directions." He gave Emerson the directions.

"Hey Reid, before you hang up, have you seen my buddy, Sam Duncan?"

"No, why?"

"He said he was going out diving, but I haven't seen him in a couple of days. Nor has any of the staff here."

"He hasn't been here if that's what you're asking."

"Okay, then." Emerson wondered where he friend was. "Thanks for your help, Reid."

"Go and see Derek Fleming first. You promised."

"I will. I always do what I say I'll do."

Emerson hung up and called the police station where he was able to secure an appointment with Fleming. They could see him in an hour and a half. Emerson quickly left his room and walked to his car for the drive into George Town for the meeting.

Royal Cayman Islands Police
George Town Headquarters

"I have an appointment to see Superintendent Fleming," Emerson spoke to the receptionist in the first floor lobby of the Royal Cayman Islands Police Headquarters.

"Could you please sign in?" the cheery receptionist asked as she pushed the sign-in card through the slot below the security window.

Emerson completed the registration card and slid it back. Picking up the card and reading the visitor's name, the receptionist telephoned Fleming's assistant. "I have a Mr. Emerson Moore here to see Superintendent Fleming," the receptionist said. She listened to the voice on the other end of the line and nodded her head, "Why yes, you've described him very well," she said with a look of astonishment.

The voice on the line made several more comments and a smile crossed the receptionist's face. "His assistant will be down momentarily. Please take a seat over there." She was pointing to two chairs in the small reception area.

Emerson's curiosity was rising as he tried to understand the phone conversation.

A few minutes later, Emerson heard a voice greet him from the open door to police operations. "It's been a while since I've seen my favorite pirate."

His head whipped around and he was looking at Denise Roberts, the lady whose purse he had rescued from the-would-be-purse-snatcher. Emerson smiled. "Aaargh! I've been busy capturing Spanish treasure ships," he teased.

"Once a pirate, always a pirate," she responded with a smile.

"You work here?"

"Yes. For the Superintendent."

"What a surprise!"

"If you'll follow me, I'll take you to his office."

I'd follow you anywhere, Emerson thought to himself as he walked through the open door and followed the good-looking assistant up the stairs to the second floor.

"How has your stay been?" she asked over her shoulder as they climbed the stairwell.

"Good."

"Get any diving in?"

"Yeah, my friends and I dove the *Reid Foster* a couple of days ago."

Her body tensed when she heard his comment, but Emerson didn't notice it. "Find anything interesting?" she asked.

"Not really. Ran into a barracuda guarding the forward gun turret, though."

She stopped in the stairwell and turned to look at him. "Stay away from that barracuda. I've heard stories about her. She's severely injured tourist divers, who crossed into her domain."

Grinning, Emerson said, "I've been warned. I know how territorial barracudas can be."

"Didn't you tell me that you were taking advanced technical diving classes at DiveTech in West Bay?"

"Yes. I've completed them and have my certification."

"Great." She paused. "I don't think I mentioned that I live in West Bay, not far from DiveTech."

"Really? Small world." Emerson eyed the attractive woman for a moment, then asked, "Would you be interested in getting together for a drink sometime?"

As they emerged onto the second floor, she nodded. "That would be nice. Do you know where the Calypso Grill is in Morgan's Harbour?"

"Yes. DiveTech's boats are docked there."

"Right. I could meet you there."

"I'd love to."

"When would you like to meet?"

"Tonight?"

"Can't tonight. I've got plans. I could meet you tomorrow night," she said as she walked by her desk.

"Good. About seven o'clock?"

"I'll be there. Here's the Superintendent's office." She held up her hand for Emerson to remain outside while she stuck her head into his office. "Mr. Fleming, I have Emerson Moore to see you."

"Please send him in." Unlike the white-shirted and dark-trousered uniformed police officers in the building, the senior staff was smartly attired in sport coats. Fleming was wearing khaki slacks, a white shirt with a blue and gold regimental striped tie and a navy blazer. As Emerson walked into the office, the lanky, gray-haired superintendent stood and extended his hand to Emerson.

"I had a call from Reid Dennis that you'd like to see me," he said as they shook hands and he motioned to Emerson to sit in a nearby chair. "What can I do for you, Mr. Moore? Working on a story about our beautiful Cayman Islands?"

"So, Reid told you I'm a reporter?"

"Yes, with *The Washington Post*, if I recall correctly." The shrewd Fleming knew exactly who Emerson was. After Reid had called him, he had a background check run on Emerson. "You're in the Cayman Islands on vacation. Too much snow and ice for you in Ohio."

Sitting back in his chair in amazement, Emerson commented, "You do your homework."

"That I do. Very little gets by me on this island. Sort of like your little island and Put-in-Bay."

"Very good. Very good indeed." Emerson was impressed with the likable Fleming.

"Snow and ice versus paradise. I'd gather it wasn't a difficult decision to make to escape that for what we have here."

"It wasn't. I traded the ice for advanced technical diving classes at DiveTech in West Bay."

Fleming nodded his head as he listened skeptically to Emerson. He didn't trust reporters, but Emerson seemed to be very affable.

It was at this point that Emerson decided to be a bit cagey with his story. "I've heard about a fellow named Pryce Clarke."

"That's what Reid told me. You have some particular interest in our Mr. Clarke?"

"From what I can gather, he might be someone I'd be interested in meeting and doing a story on him, if it was warranted."

Fleming's face grew serious. "Pryce Clarke is dangerous. The best piece of advice I can give you is to stay away from him."

"I hear you, but it seems like he's a model citizen based on what I found out about him this morning on my Internet search."

Fleming paused before answering. "You, of all people, should know that appearances can be deceiving."

"So, are you saying he's a wolf in sheep's clothing?"

"I'm not saying anything and don't try to twist my words. And don't quote me, whatever you do. This is an off-the-record conversation, Mr. Moore. The only reason I'm even talking to you is because my good friend, Reid Dennis, asked me to talk to you as a favor to him."

"You can count on it. I'm not even taking notes," Emerson responded.

"Good. I'll share with you what is known about him publicly, but I can't share any information which we might have in our police files."

"I'd assume that you couldn't and wouldn't." Interesting, Emerson thought to himself, that Fleming let slip that they had police files on Clarke.

"I gather that you've already talked to other people about Clarke."

"Yes."

"Not a good thing when he finds out you're asking about him."

"Why's that?"

"A year ago, there was a reporter down here from London. Nice chap. Very intelligent. Always wore a bright green cap. He decided to write about Clarke when he heard some of the rumors floating around about him."

"And?"

"Disappeared."

"Disappeared?"

"Yes. No one could find him. Not a trace."

"Diving accident?" Emerson suggested.

"Didn't dive. When the resort reported him as missing and we checked his hotel room, his clothes and bags weren't packed. His laptop was still on his desk."

Emerson's eyes widened. "Do you have his laptop?"

Chuckling, Fleming responded, "I suppose you'd like to take a peek at his notes?"

Emerson's head bobbed affirmatively.

"We've already reviewed his notes. Good notes. But nothing in there that we didn't already know about Clarke. After our computer experts were finished dumping his data, we shipped the laptop to his family in London. I'd be very careful of asking questions about Clarke."

"So, you think Clarke was responsible for this reporter's disappearance?"

"Of course. But, Mr. Moore, we don't have any proof."

Emerson pushed. "Did you search Clarke's residence for any evidence?"

"No. We didn't have any basis for securing the appropriate legal document from the court to inspect his premises."

A number of ideas surged through Emerson's mind.

"Mr. Moore, I suspect your mind is racing, but again let me caution you about pursuing any interest in Clarke. The Royal Cayman Police Department does not need you mucking up any investigations under way on Mr. Clarke. Do I make myself clear?" Fleming asked with a very serious tone in his voice.

"But, I may be able to help...," Emerson started.

Fleming interrupted. "You wouldn't be helping. You just fancy doing a breaking news story on Clarke, just like you have with your other stories, Mr. Pulitzer Prize winner."

Fleming had certainly done his homework, Emerson thought to himself. "Okay, I'll stay away from Clarke."

"Good. Now, I have other pressing matters, that I must attend to." Fleming called out, "Denise, could you escort Mr. Moore downstairs to the lobby?"

Denise quickly appeared in the doorway as both men stood.

"Thank you for your time and help, Superintendent." Emerson said as they shook hands.

"I'm not sure that I was helpful. Have a good day, Mr. Moore, and touch wood." Fleming settled back into his chair as Denise and Emerson exited his office. Not for one second did Fleming believe that Emerson would back off of his interest in Clarke. And Fleming's observation would prove to be true.

A plan began to form in Fleming's mind as he recognized that opportunity was knocking at his door. He smiled to himself as he thought how clever he was. He reached for the phone and placed a call.

Pryce Clarke's House
Morgan's Harbour
The Next Day

The Toyota Corolla flew out of Clarke's drive, nearly hitting Emerson's car. Swerving to avoid a collision, Emerson stole a fleeting glance at the female driver. She was a black woman and wore a blue-green scarf on her head and oversized sunglasses.

As he pulled up to the pastel painted two-story waterfront house surrounded by lush landscaping and an 8-foot high coral stone wall, Emerson wondered what had triggered the woman's erratic driving. He parked the rental car on the brick, semi-circular driveway in front of the main entrance.

To the right of the house, he saw a guest house with a terra-cotta tiled roof perched above the three-car garage. Through one of the open garage doors, he saw a silver Bentley. On the other side of the garage, he saw a man lounging in the shade of a tree. He was armed. Probably a guard, Emerson thought to himself.

After meeting with the dive instructors at DiveTech that morning, Emerson had driven the winding roads to Clarke's home. As he drove, he wondered how Duncan's dive trip to Cayman Brac was going. He hadn't heard from him in a while and neither had anyone at Cobalt Coast or DiveTech. Emerson had thought that Duncan may have disappeared on another of his clandestine assignments as he had from time to time in the past. Those were the kind of assignments, which he would not discuss with Emerson.

Emerson walked to the entranceway and knocked on the massive mahogany door. A serious-looking, tall, young Jamaican answered his knock quickly. "May I help you?" he inquired.

"Yes. My name is Emerson Moore. I'm a writer doing a series on unique, island homes in the Cayman Islands. I was driving by and was captivated by how inviting yours is."

"Thank you."

"I wondered if I might take a tour of the home and include it in my newspaper story back home." Emerson had planned this approach to gain entrance to the house and came equipped with a camera as part of his ploy. He handed the young man his business card.

Taking the card, he looked at it quickly. "This is not my home. Wait a moment while I check with the owner, although I doubt that it would be possible without a prior appointment."

"I understand." Emerson didn't get to finish as the door closed abruptly in his face and with a loud click as it was locked.

While he waited, Emerson took in the green foliage and flowering plants, which filled the front portion of the lot. A few minutes later, the door opened.

"Mr. Clarke has agreed to allow you to interrupt his busy afternoon and will meet with you. Please come in." The Jamaican gave Emerson a cold stare as he spoke.

Emerson entered the massive home and followed the young man through the main hallway and into a mahogany-lined study. A Jamaican man with a shaven head and a large diamond earring in one ear stood from the leather chair behind the large wooden mahogany desk.

"I'm Pryce Clarke," he said as he walked around the desk to greet Emerson.

"Emerson Moore."

"I understand that you are interested in my home for some sort of story you're writing."

"Yes, I apologize for dropping in unannounced, but I was driving by and was quite taken by your beautiful home. I thought I'd stop in and take a chance that I might intrude. I'd like to include it and several photos in my story about luxurious Cayman Island homes. I wasn't sure whether you'd be interested." Emerson paused to see if the bait would be taken.

"And who do you write for?"

"*The Washington Post.*" Emerson wanted to ask if he could read since he had presented his card to the man who had greeted him at the door.

"I see."

What Emerson didn't see was that the young man, who had greeted him at the door, left the immediate area and went to a small anteroom where he began to Google Emerson on the Internet.

Clarke decided to commence a tour of his palatial residence. "I'd be more than happy to show you around, Mr. Moore," he said with deep pride as he motioned Emerson to follow him. "The house was constructed in 1996 and has 8,000 square feet."

"8,000 square feet! This is a big house!"

"Thank you. I like to think so," Clarke smiled to himself as he began the house tour. It was always Clarke's intention to overpower people with his home's grandeur just like he enjoyed overpowering people with his bigger-than-life personality.

They walked through an open kitchen with a breakfast bar into a bright and airy dining room with a wall of windows overlooking Morgan's Harbour. The adjoining living room was spacious and also had a wall of sliding glass doors overlooking the harbour. Tasteful tropical furnishings added to the elegant, yet casual décor. The floors were a combination of luxurious marble and wood while the ceilings were 18 feet high throughout.

They walked up the teak stairs to the second floor and toured the five large bedrooms with king-sized beds. Each bedroom was hand-painted in a variety of pastel colors and had large windows, which provided unobstructed harbour views. The sixth bedroom was the master suite and was painted in red tones. It contained a plush round bed and a built-in Jacuzzi for four. Sliding glass doors opened onto a large balcony, which overlooked the large stone patio and deep pool.

"Impressive! " Emerson said unabashedly as he jotted notes in the small notebook he had retrieved from his pocket. He had taken several photos as they toured. "This will be very interesting to our readers."

Clarke smiled smugly as they returned to the main floor, "I thought it would." As they stepped through one of the sliding glass doors onto the patio, Clarke's cell phone rang.

"Yes, one moment please." Turning to Emerson, he asked with a sly look, "Could you please excuse me for a moment?"

"Sure. I'll just look around the pool."

Clarke stepped back into the living room, pulling the sliding glass door closed. Watching Emerson walk toward the pool, he spoke into the cell phone, "What did you learn?"

In the anteroom, the young man on the other end of the cell phone call explained what his Internet search revealed. "Moore isn't an island home writer. He's an investigative reporter. Looks like he snoops around looking for stories. You'll want to be careful with him, Boss."

Clarke's eyes narrowed as he watched Emerson walk to the far side of the pool where he could look down on the boat docks. There were three boats tied there; a go fast boat and two large identical fishing boats. One was named *Turtle Dancer*; the other was named *Turtle Chaser*. Both were equipped with winches.

At the end of the dock, which extended 80 feet from the shore, was a thatched-roof shelter with two wooden benches. Below it was tied an inflatable Zodiac with an outboard engine.

"Thank you." He noticed Emerson looking back at him and smiled sinisterly at him. Closing the cell phone and depositing it in his pocket, he opened the sliding glass and walked across the patio to where Emerson was standing.

"Please excuse the interruption."

"Oh, no problem. You remember I'm the one who dropped in unannounced," Emerson responded. Looking at the dock and the boats, Emerson asked, "Yours?"

"Yes."

Seeing the dive gear and tanks aboard the *Turtle Dancer*, Emerson probed, "You do much diving?"

"I enjoy it."

"Do you dive at night?"

"Sometimes."

"You know, I believe I've seen the *Turtle Dancer* off of Cobalt Coast Dive Resort. It seems that they've been out there every night since I've been on the island," Emerson pushed for a reaction.

"Some of my employees borrow the boat and go lobstering."

"Every night and in the same place?"

"Must be a good spot then. Wouldn't you agree?"

"Just seems strange to me."

Clarke was tiring of the game Emerson was playing. "I don't know where they go lobstering. I lend them my boat and they go where they wish." He glanced at his watch. "I must hurry along so that I'm not late for an appointment."

They turned and walked between the pool and the built-in aquarium. "That's interesting," Emerson said as he brought up the camera for a quick shot. He noticed a few drops of dried blood at the edge of the aquarium, but wasn't sure if it was human or not.

"It's salt water. I keep it well stocked with a number of species. I really must go." It was Clarke's turn to push.

Seeing an area enclosed by a high fence with a danger sign affixed and at the far edge of the patio, Emerson asked, "What's over there?"

"Chickens," Clarke lied wearily.

"You need a danger sign for chickens?" Emerson wasn't buying that answer for one second.

Realizing that he needed a more plausible answer, Clarke replied, "They're Caymanian fighting roosters. I use them for cock fights on the island. I am truly sorry, but I must ask you to go." Clarke escorted Emerson into the house and to the front door.

As he walked out the door, Emerson suggested, "Perhaps, we could go diving some time."

"Perhaps. Good-bye Mr. Moore." Clarke closed the door and stood on the other side, thinking. Yes, perhaps they could go diving some time. Two go down, but only one comes up, Clarke thought sinisterly as he heard the rental car's engine start and drive out of his driveway.

Calypso Grill
Morgan's Harbour

"Seven and Seven," Emerson ordered as he sat back from the bright blue-tiled table and relaxed in the bamboo-framed chair. The chair had blue and red plastic woven through it. As classic string music played in the background, Emerson gazed across the water from his seat on the patio deck overlooking the harbour.

When Emerson arrived for his meeting, he scanned the restaurant, but didn't see Denise. He had chosen the less formal outside patio, which had palm trees growing through its wooden floor. As he walked to his table, he took in the tables with their white tablecloths. The walls of the restaurant's interior were painted in a variety of peach, yellow and rose hues. The French doors were painted in a deep Caribbean blue.

"Been waiting long?"

The voice startled Emerson. He looked around and stood to his feet. "Here, let me pull out your chair."

"Thank you," Denise purred.

"Beautiful view," Emerson said as he sat down.

"It is. This is one of my favorite places on the islands."

Emerson raised his eyebrows. "I wasn't talking about the island."

"Oh," she responded with surprise. "I guess, I should say thank you."

"And I should apologize. I'm not usually this forward." Emerson was truly surprised at himself. This was not his normal style of talking with women.

The waitress appeared and took their drink orders.

"So you work for Superintendent Fleming?"

"Yes. I've been at police headquarters for the last three years."

"And before that?"

"I was a secretary in Ocho Rios."

"Are you Caymanian or Jamaican?"

"Jamaican."

Emerson nodded and waited for her to continue.

"When I lost my job in Ocho Rios, I started looking for work. A friend of mine told me that there were plenty of openings in the Cayman Islands. So, I decided to check it out. I was able to obtain a work visa and applied at police headquarters."

"For Superintendent Fleming?"

"No. I was working for one of the inspectors when Mr. Fleming's secretary was killed in an auto accident. Next thing I knew, I was reassigned to work for Mr. Fleming."

Interesting, Emerson thought to himself with a growing suspicion. Perhaps Fleming wasn't who he appeared to be. Emerson thought about how quick Fleming had been to try to dissuade Emerson from following up on Clarke. He put his thoughts in the back of his mind and concentrated on Denise. "How do you like working there?"

"I enjoy it. There's always some sort of crisis breaking each day. You certainly don't have time to be bored," she smiled. Changing the direction of the conversation, she asked, "And what about you? When we first met, you told me you're a reporter."

"That's correct. I'm an investigative reporter for *The Washington Post*."

"But you do not live in Washington, you live on an island, right?"

"Good memory. I live in the Lake Erie islands. There's a small resort town on South Bass Island named Put-in-Bay. Since I travel so much on stories, it doesn't matter much as to where my residence is located. What matters is that I file stories."

"And you're working on a story now? That's what brought you to see Superintendent Fleming yesterday?"

"Maybe. I was running down some leads and trying to flesh out my thoughts. We will see where it takes me."

"The superintendent is a good man. He could be very helpful for you."

"I'm not sure that he will be." Emerson paused, "But maybe you could help me. If I need some information, maybe you could assist me."

"Certainly, I'd be glad to place your requests to Mr. Fleming."

"That's not what I was thinking."

"Oh?"

"Maybe, you could quietly look in some files for me," Emerson pushed.

Repressing her shock, Denise responded quietly, "I couldn't do that, Emerson. Not without Mr. Fleming's approval."

Disappointed, Emerson sat back in his chair. "Tell me about Fleming. Has he been in the Cayman Islands for very long?"

"About five years."

"Where was he before?"

"Hong Kong."

"Police work there?"

"Yes."

Emerson wondered if Fleming might be tied in with the Southeast Asia drug cartels and now here in the Cayman Islands with Clarke and drug running. His thoughts were searching for the pieces to the puzzle.

The waitress returned with Emerson's Seven and Seven and Denise's Daiquiri.

Changing the subject, Emerson pointed to a passing sailboat and said, "Wish I was aboard her."

"That would be fun," Denise commented as she sipped her drink. "How are your diving classes going?"

"Good. I just completed my technical diving lessons at Dive-Tech. I think I told you I was staying there at Cobalt Coast Dive Resort."

"Yes, I remember. When you drive to Cobalt Coast and you turn left at the West Bay Police Station?"

"Yes?"

"If you didn't turn and drove past the station, you'd find my house. At least, it's where I'm staying with several of my friends."

Emerson glanced at her fingers and saw that she wasn't wearing a wedding ring. She reminded him a bit of Melaudra Drencheau, the New Orleans police detective with whom he had been infatuated.

The waitress reappeared and took their dinner order. The two continued chatting and dined while the sun set. At the end of the dinner, Emerson walked Denise to her car.

"It was kind of you to invite me to dinner," she said appreciatively.

"My pleasure. I enjoyed your company."

Denise had found the reporter interesting and charming. He was the kind of guy that she could get serious over, but she also realized that it wouldn't be long before he returned to the states. No long-term relationship here, she thought to herself, but he was fun to be with.

"I'd enjoy getting together with you again," she said demurely.

"I would, too." Emerson grinned.

She produced a pad of paper and pen from her purse. After writing down her cell phone number, she handed it to Emerson. "Here's my number. Thank you again."

She hugged Emerson and stepped into her car. "Hope to see you soon," she called as she started the car, put it in gear and began to drive away.

"Likewise," Emerson called as he watched the departing car. He was smiling to himself. It had been a somewhat productive evening in that he had a growing suspicion about Superintendent Fleming and his relationship with Pryce Clarke. On top of that, he had enjoyed spending time with Denise. He walked toward his car to begin the return trip to his hotel.

Harbour House Marina
North Sound

Harbour House Marina sat on the southern edge of the North Sound, a large harbour that virtually divided Grand Cayman Island in half. The marina was filled with a variety of boats floating gently at their dockage and a number of boats on wooden or steel cradles on shore. To the right of the main entranceway was a two-story office building with large windows overlooking the marina and the boatyard. A sign was affixed to the building above the main entrance. It read "Harbour House Marina Offices." Another sign hung over the exterior stairway to the second floor. It read "Mariggs Oceanography."

Across the drive was a large boat repair building fitted out with overhead cranes and covered with a shiny tin roof. Several other smaller metal buildings dotted the premises.

A tall, chain-link fence ran along the property's boundary line. Next to the open gate was a sign welcoming visitors to the Harbour House Marina. Two more signs hung below it. One warned that trespassing was not permitted. The other warned potential trespassers that guard dogs roamed the premises at night.

Through the open gate, Emerson drove his car and parked it in one of the available parking spaces. He had noticed that the *Southwind* was docked in the channel to his right as he pulled onto the property and decided to make it his first stop.

"Ahoy, anyone on board?" he shouted.

"Still looking for trouble?" a voice called from behind Emerson.

Emerson whirled around and saw the energetic Ratty approaching him. He was wiping his hands on a dirty towel.

"I found it."

"So, yous ignored my advice and have met Mr. Clarke."

"Actually, I was referring to you," Emerson teased the hardy Caymanian.

"I'd be the good kind of trouble to find. Like I told yous, Mr. Clarke is the bad kind of trouble."

"Ratty, I did meet your scary Mr. Clarke."

"Here, yous turn around for me." Not waiting for Emerson to move, Ratty began turning Emerson around, inspecting him from head to toe. He ran his hands up both of Emerson's arms. "Yous a miracle. I needs to start going to church, now," Ratty said as he stood back and looked at Emerson. He was now holding his pipe in his hand.

"A miracle?"

"Yes. Yous in one piece. I don't see nothing missing from yous!" He placed his pipe between his lips and inhaled.

"He wasn't such a bad guy after all," Emerson beamed.

"Yous count yous lucky stars that yous walked away all together. And yous don't go back to see him no more!"

"But, he was such a cordial host!" Emerson teased.

Shaking his head from side to side, Ratty cautioned, "Next time, maybe he not so cordial!"

"We will see. But, I do need your help."

"How's that?"

"Reid Dennis told me you had a boat."

"I do."

"I'd like to hire you to take me to a dive site off of Cobalt Coast Dive Resort."

"For a solo dive?"

"Yes."

"Haven't yous heard about the buddy system?"

Emerson had a guarded look on his face when he answered. "Yes, but I think I'm on to something. I'd like to do this dive quietly."

"Could be very quiet. Yous go down and no one comes up. Not a good idea. Yous take someone with yous and then I'll take yous."

"I'm not doing a technical dive. Just going down for a quick look see."

"What about yous friends at DiveTech? They have several dive boats."

"They follow the rules. They wouldn't let me do a solo dive." Emerson also didn't want anyone to witness this phase of his investigation.

The Caymanian looked skeptically at Emerson. "Yous really want to do this?"

"Yes. Here's my GPS reading." Emerson pulled out the folded paper from his shirt pocket and showed Ratty.

Ratty shook his head as he read the coordinates. "That's off the Wall. Yous have to dive with Trimix. And if yous are doing that deep of a dive, yous need to take someone with yous," he said firmly.

"Just take me and I'll do a shallow dive. If I need to go beyond that, I'll get one of my friends to go with me another day. And you can take me back there."

Ratty's eyes narrowed as he looked at Emerson. "Yous be taking a risk."

"I'll be careful," Emerson assured him.

"Okay, I'll take yous. When do yous want to go?" he asked the crazy American.

"As soon as possible."

Looking at his watch, the Caymanian said, "Be here at five o'clock and be sure to bring yous gear and tanks. I'll be over there on the *Sea Dog*." He pointed at a decrepit looking fishing boat.

Seeing the look on Emerson's face, he added, "Don't worry how she looks from here. She's meant to fool people. The engines, I assure yous, run like new." He grinned at Emerson, who seemed to relax at the comment.

"Good. I'll be back at five." Emerson looked at his watch as he walked toward the office building and saw that he had three hours before he had to return. He decided to climb the stairs to the second floor office of Mariggs Oceanography and see if Roger Rothman was in.

Mariggs Oceanography was headquartered on Grand Cayman and was widely known for its efforts to protect the underwater environment so that divers could enjoy it. They also were known for discovering shipwrecks around the world and bringing up treasure.

The door opened to reveal a large open office, which was filled with equipment, computers and stacks of reports. A door at the rear led to the executive director's office and next to it was a restroom. A fax could be heard printing on the fax machine. Standing next to it was Roger Rothman.

"Hello, Roger."

Rothman's smile flashed through his bearded face and his eyes sparkled behind his wire-rimmed glasses. "Hello stranger," he greeted Emerson. "What brings you to my neck of the woods?"

"I stopped by to see Ratty and thought I'd stop in and say hello."

"There's no one around here quite like Ratty. You heard the part about him not wearing..."

"Underwear," Emerson said as he finished the sentence for Rothman. "Yes, but I don't have any plans on confirming that piece of information. There is a limit to how far I go with my investigative work," Emerson kidded.

"He's a real trip to go diving with!"

"Oh?"

"Just rips off those trousers and straps on his gear.

"Am I to understand that he doesn't wear a suit?"

"Bare ass naked. He says it's the only way to dive!" Rothman chortled at the look on Emerson's face.

"Thanks for the warning. I'll make sure I don't go diving with him."

"Actually, I'm glad that you stopped by. Your timing is perfect," Rothman said with an air of mystery.

It wasn't lost on Emerson. "How so?" he asked with raised eyebrows.

"I was looking at the video from the *Murask*."

"The *Murask*?"

"Sorry. That was it's original name. I should say the *Reid Foster*."

"What about it?"

"I saw something in the background of one of the shots that I missed while filming."

"An eel?" Emerson guessed.

"No. Come over here and I'll show you."

They walked over to a worktable and took seats in front of a computer screen.

"Watch this." Referring to his notes, Rothman fast-forwarded to the portion of the video he wanted to show Emerson. It was the scene in the Captain's quarters. The film showed Emerson exploring the quarters while the light from Rothman's camera lit the room. At one point, he paused the video.

"I don't see anything," Emerson said as he studied the scene in front of him.

"To the right of you and on the wall." Rothman directed Emerson's attention to the wall, but he still didn't see anything unusual.

"What am I supposed to be looking for?" he asked, puzzled.

"I've spent a lot of time diving on the *Tibbetts*. It's the *Murask*'s sister ship and sunk offshore Cayman Brac."

"Yes?"

"It's the electrical breaker box on the wall."

"What's so unusual about that?"

"Here, let me load up some video I shot on the *Tibbetts*." It only took a moment for Rothman's fingers to fly across the keyboard and split the screen to display an interior shot of the Captain's quarters on the *Tibbetts*. "See the difference?"

"There's no electrical breaker box," Emerson said as he compared the two Captain's quarters.

"Strange, isn't it for two ships built off the same plans, that one has the box and the other doesn't?"

"Think there's something there?"

"Don't know, but I plan to check it out the next time I dive on it."

Emerson pushed his chair back from the computer screen and looked at Rothman. "If I dive on it before you, I'll let you know what I find."

"Take another look at the *Murask*," Rothman said as he zoomed in on the electrical box.

"What do you see?"

"It has two locks on it?"

"Yes. When was the last time you dove a shipwreck and saw a breaker box with a lock on it?"

"I haven't seen any."

"That's my point. Look at that lock. It's not the typical type of lock. There are two very serious, heavy duty locks on it."

Nodding his head, Emerson commented, "Must be something important there." He studied it for a moment. "I'd like to know what it is."

"Me, too."

"Maybe, we could dive it together?"

"Count me in. When?"

"Let's see what I have going on over the next two days and I'll call you."

"Just let me know when. Here's my number." Rothman held out a business card which had his office number as well as cell phone number.

They chatted a few more minutes and Emerson left to pick up his scuba gear and borrow a tank from DiveTech.

Later That Afternoon
Off Cobalt Coast Dive Resort

The low hum from the *Sea Dog*'s engines could be heard in the background as Ratty checked his GPS with the coordinates provided by Emerson. The sky was clear and the seas were calm. Both men were pleased that there seemed to be no adverse conditions to deal with in their respective responsibilities.

Emerson was on the stern and had already slid into his 3 mil wetsuit and booties. He called, "Hey, Ratty, are you ready to drop anchor now?"

From the pilothouse, Ratty answered, "Not here. We're over the North Wall. It's 6,000 feet deep here. And yous won't be going very far down in that gear. Yous need a submarine for that."

Emerson nodded in agreement, although he originally had considered doing a deeper dive on this trip. "I know. I just want to take a quick look-see around. If we have to come back another day, we can do that and I'll be better prepared for that – and I'll have Trimix."

"I tell yous now. If yous going to be diving Trimix, I'm not bringing yous back here unless yous have a dive buddy."

"I hear you loud and clear my friend." He would have to be content with the minimal depth that he could dive to on the air tank he had with him.

As Emerson lifted his BC and tank over his head and allowed his equipment to slide down over his back, he commented, "Good. I'm anxious to go down."

"Want to take this with yous?"

Emerson looked and saw Ratty holding a spear gun.

"Nope, although I'm supposed to be on a fishing trip, it's not that kind of fishing this time. I won't need it."

"Don't say I didn't offer," Ratty said. "Yous know, we're not too far from that Russian ship that sank, right?"

"The *Reid Foster*?"

"Yeah," he said as he pointed westerly. "She should be over there a few hundred yards."

Emerson spit into his mask to keep it from fogging up.

A few minutes later Ratty notified Emerson that they were finally on the proper GPS coordinates, so Emerson could throw out the weighted marker flag. The weight would sink, letting out a line that was tied to a dive flag that would float; marking the exact spot they would anchor. Ratty brought the boat around and dropped anchor near the flag. This area was where the reef should be below them and close to where the wall sloped down in gradual steps instead of a sheer vertical drop.

Making his way to the stern board, Emerson called back as he donned his fins and adjusted his mask, "See you soon." He did a perfect giant stride into the water, keeping his head above the surface. After turning toward Ratty and bumping his fist on the top of his head indicating he was okay, he descended into the warm, clear Caymanian water.

As he descended feet first, Emerson checked his compass to get his bearings and looked around to see if there was any marine life nearby. All he saw was a school of jacks seemingly frozen in the water column, facing into the current. When he looked down, he saw nothing but blue water and realized that Ratty had probably let out too much anchor line and the boat drifted out over blue water instead of remaining over the reef near the wall.

Emerson glanced at his depth gauge and saw that he was approaching the 130-foot level, which was deeper than what he'd wanted to be at this point in the dive since he was only diving on air and not Trimix. He knew that the shallower he stayed, the longer he could stay underwater and not suffer a case of the bends from absorbing too much nitrogen.

As he swam toward the steps of the North Wall, he ascended about 20 feet getting him to the 100-foot depth he'd planned for in his pre-dive plan. As he swam, his natural curiosity led him to examine the geologic formations and marine life on this section of the wall.

Once he got closer to the wall, he saw a number of small openings in the wall, which could lead to horizontal or vertical type caves. Most of these openings were somewhat camouflaged with beautiful stands of lacey black coral hanging from the tops of the openings and numerous whip corals reaching out into the blue. Emerson was pleased to see so much pristine black coral, reinforcing the notion that this area was not dived often.

The openings in the wall reminded Emerson of earlier underwater cave explorations he had made when he had completed his cave-dive training on Lake Erie and in Florida. As much as he wanted to enter any of these openings, he knew better. A simple solo dive in warm clear water would be fine for now, but no cave explorations without a buddy.

While doing his cave certifications, one memory stood out more than any other. Many of the caves had signs posted in front of them. Each one had a picture of the grim reaper and then words stating, "STOP. Prevent your death! Go no further! More than 300 people have died in Florida caves including open water scuba instructors. It can happen to you!"

This part of the North Wall seemed to be no different than other areas Emerson had dived. There were a number of lobsters poised in their nooks in the wall like sentries guarding their fortress. A green eel was tucked into a cranny with its mouth opening and closing continuously, showing its many razor-sharp teeth each time. Near the top of an upper ledge, a green sea turtle could be seen munching on a sponge.

After 45 minutes, Emerson glanced at his watch in frustration with the futility of this dive. He had found nothing to give him a clue as to why Clarke's men were diving it. He would need to begin his ascent and make his safety stops. During his ascent, he thought he heard the engines of an approaching boat, but they soon faded.

While he was hovering near the weighted dive flag line for his safety stop, he saw two divers break the surface. One spotted Emerson and motioned to the other. Then without warning, the first diver aimed his spear gun at Emerson.

Realizing that the divers' intentions were adversarial, Emerson quickly plunged downward. He was immediately followed by the two divers. Emerson zigzagged and returned to the Wall where he remembered the cave openings to be and looked over his shoulder at the approaching divers. The opening of the cave seemed quite ominous, but his options were limited at this point. His mind flooded with memories of his disastrous experience in the cave on Put-in-Bay as a teenager.

A spear ricocheted off the wall above his right shoulder, making the decision for Emerson much easier to make. Unclipping his flashlight from his BC, he plunged head first through the tunnel-like opening. Moving as quickly as he could, he reached the first turn in the narrow passageway.

As he made the turn, another spear harmlessly struck the tunnel wall from where he had just turned. After making the turn, he swam a short distance and found that the narrow tunnel opened into a wider chamber. He came up with an idea.

Emerson positioned himself above the opening to the chamber and waited for his attackers to swim through. He figured that he might have a chance to attack them from above when they began to enter the larger area. The only weapon he had was his dive knife, but it would have to do.

What seemed like hours was only seconds before he saw a light shine into the chamber from one of the diver's flashlights. The diver had made the turn and was approaching the opening. Emerson waited patiently as he held the knife, which he had withdrawn from the sheath on his leg.

When the first diver flew through the opening into the larger chamber, Emerson pounced. He dropped from above with his knife blade extended and sliced through the air hose of the diver's primary regulator, unleashing a stream of air bubbles. As the diver twisted to grab his auxiliary mouthpiece, Emerson tore the spear gun out of his grip and shoved the diver headfirst back into the narrow tunnel. Emerson wanted to block the second diver from coming at him and to also let the second diver see that the first diver was in distress and was no longer armed with his spear gun.

Emerson's plan worked. When the second diver saw the panic in the first diver and that his spear gun was missing, he immediately stopped in the tunnel without entering the chamber. As the first diver gained his secondary regulator, both divers used their underwater sign language and decided together to return to the cave's opening.

Meanwhile, Emerson waited in darkness at the tunnel's entrance to the chamber. He didn't dare turn on his flashlight to look at his gauges, but it didn't take long to realize that he was faced with a new danger. His last attempt to breathe from his tank was rewarded with nothing; no air. His tank had run dry.

Fortunately he had remembered to bring two small 13 cubic foot pony tanks as back ups. They were harnessed on either side of his main tank, each with their own separate regulator. He reached over his shoulder and turned the valve for the first auxiliary tank. He was thankful that his safe dive pre-plan included these supplemental tanks. Each tank might provide him with 5 minutes of air at this depth.

But time was running out and Emerson couldn't remain in the cave much longer. He hesitantly peered into the tunnel and thought about returning the way he came in. But he was unsure if the two divers might be waiting to ambush him as he emerged from the opening on the Wall. At that point, he heard a loud explosion and felt a great concussion in his chest.

There was no question now as to whether he could exit the way he came in. The opening had probably been blocked by the explosion. He would have to hope that this cave was like the ones he'd explored in Florida where many were interconnected. He only hoped that this connection would be near, and not miles away as some are in Florida.

Switching on his flashlight, Emerson began to explore the chamber walls as he moved vertically, searching for an escape route. Moving quickly, he flashed the light upwards on the wall. It didn't take but a few seconds before he encountered the cavern's ceiling. He swam all along the 10-foot high walls until he had returned to the tunnel opening.

Exasperated by his futile search to find another side tunnel, Emerson paused to illuminate and look at his dive watch. Time was running out for his air supply. His heart began to race as he realized the seriousness of his situation. Emerson remembered his initial dive certification training and talked himself out of any panic to calm his jittery nerves. He knew panic would cause him to use more air than he should and also cause him to lose concentration.

Realizing that there were no other tunnels around the perimeter of the chamber, he glanced upwards at the ceiling and decided to see if there were any possible exits that way. He began a methodical search of the ceiling. It wasn't long before he found a very small chute leading upwards, but it was too narrow for him to swim through. He flashed his light inside of it and saw that the chute continued upwards and did widen beyond the initial opening.

Knowing that this was his only option, he began to pull at the rocky coral around the opening to dislodge it and widen the opening. He was able to pull away some chunks of coral with his hands and when he ran into particularly hard pieces, he chipped away and pried at it with his knife blade. He was finally able to widen the hole enough that he'd be able to slip his body through it, but without wearing his gear.

He took his gear off and carefully pushed it through the opening, making sure to keep his teeth biting hard on the regulator to the pony tank so that he wouldn't lose his air source. He then squeezed his body through the opening and into the wider chute. There wasn't time to worry about putting his gear back on so he hugged it to his chest and thought about his swim upwards, hoping he would soon see real daylight instead of only the beam from his flashlight.

But then his first tank ran dry and he knew he didn't have much time. With only one pony tank left, he had to hope this tunnel would not turn into a dead end, literally. After 50 feet, the vertical chute angled 45 degrees away from vertical, but Emerson continued swimming. At least he had been ascending and getting shallower, which allowed his air supply to last longer.

Despite the warmth of the water, cold chills surged through Emerson's body. The close quarters were causing twinges of claustrophobia and again reminding him of his boyhood fear.

Finally, Emerson saw some daylight and the chute opened onto the reef, where he carefully emerged from its narrow confines. He quickly scanned the immediate area to see if his attackers were waiting for him. Seeing no one, he slipped his tank back on and began his ascent to the surface.

Once he got to 15 feet, he stopped and decided to breathe his last pony tank dry at that depth, and then make a safe out-of-air ascent to the surface. This would at least give him a partial safety stop. When his tank ran dry, he slowly and safely ascended to the surface.

Once on the surface, he kept a low profile and carefully looked around for any evidence of the attackers. He didn't see anything unusual, but was able to spot the *Sea Dog* so he began his surface swim toward it.

When he got within 30 yards of the boat he called out, "Ratty!" in hopes that a line would be thrown to him so that he could be dragged into the boat. He was tired from his near fatal dive. There was no reply from Ratty. All Emerson could see was the boat gently rocking in the waves.

When he got to the boat, Emerson warily swam around the stern to see if another boat might be on the other side of the *Sea Dog*, but fortunately none was there. He again shouted, "Ratty, are you there?" But there was still no answer.

Emerson swam to the swim platform at the stern and heaved his tank on board. Then, with a swift kick of his fins, he pushed himself onto the platform and carefully peered over the stern into the craft. What he saw made him chuckle for a moment, although it may have also been relief, having escaped from his own close call.

Squirming around on the deck and with hands and feet bound by duct tape was Ratty. Blood was smeared on the deck and dried on the side of his head. A piece of duct tape was stretched across his mouth. But the look in his eyes told the whole story. It was the look of a very angry, wild man.

Slowly, Emerson approached the squirming man. He was relieved that Ratty had not been harmed by their unexpected visitors, but he couldn't resist the temptation. With a grin on his face, he said, "Looks like you're all wrapped up!"

The comment was not well received. It was returned by a very hostile glare from Ratty's narrowed eyes. His legs kicked even stronger, accompanied by a very load moan.

Emerson deciphered the connotation of the moan. "You shouldn't swear like that, Ratty. Remember, I'm the one who can cut you free in a moment or allow you to writhe around on the deck like a fish out of water while I navigate us back to your dockage."

Ratty's eyes narrowed further and his head jerked violently up and down in anger. He moaned again, but this time there was a stronger tone to the moan. There was no mistaking this message.

Since Emerson needed Ratty's help, he decided that it wouldn't be in his best interests to continue to antagonize the cantankerous Caymanian. He reached down to the sheath, which was still strapped to his leg and withdrew his knife to cut the duct tape, which bound Ratty's hands and legs.

As Ratty reached to pull off the tape covering his mouth, Emerson commented, "Perhaps we should leave your mouth taped shut until you calm down a bit."

Ripping the tape from his mouth, Ratty seethed. "A little pepper burns hot!"

A perplexed look crossed Emerson's face. "I don't get it."

"Little things can be a big problem!" Ratty was furious. "Next time, it's not going to happen like this!"

"What did happen and who were those guys?"

"They were Jamaicans. They work for Pryce Clarke." Ratty had walked into the pilothouse where he opened a cabinet and produced a bottle of rum. "The only thing good about Jamaica is their rum." He twisted off the cap and took a swig from the half-empty bottle. Extending the bottle to Emerson, he asked, "Yous want a drink?"

Emerson thought to himself, I don't know where those lips have been, but what the hell. "Sure." He grabbed the bottle, tossed down a load and handed it back to Ratty. "So, what happened?"

"Their boat pulled up alongside mine. I was in the stern, looking into the water for yous. There were three of them. They started out friendly, but then they showed a hand gun and jumped aboard before I could run for my shotgun."

Emerson had noticed that a shotgun was lying on the deck.

"Yeah, that's my shotgun. They wanted to know what I was doing here and I told them it was none of their business. I told them to kiss off."

Emerson smiled as he pictured the tough seaman dealing with his boarders.

"They saw the diving gear and wanted to know who was diving below." It was Ratty's turn to smile, the first time since the tape had been removed. "I answered that it was Davy Jones. That's when one of them did this to me."

He turned his head so that Emerson could see the dried blood. "One of them hit me with the side of his pistol. I fell down and that's when they tied me up with that duct tape. Two of them went back to the boat and put on their diving gear and went over to look for yous. The third one found my shotgun near the bridge and held it on me."

As Ratty started the boat's engines, Emerson went to the bow to pull up the anchor line. Then they circled around to retrieve their weighted dive flag while Emerson relayed what had occurred underwater with his encounter and narrow escape.

Shaking his head, Ratty commented, "I told yous not to mess with this Pryce Clarke fellow. He breaks people's bones. They're never found again."

"Did the two divers say anything when they surfaced?"

"They thought yous was dead. They told the fellow on my boat that they had caved in the entrance to the cave so yous couldn't get out."

Realizing how fortunate he was to have found an alternate exit, Emerson took a deep breath. "I guess the diving gods were watching over me today."

"Yous need somebody watching over yous! Yous always get in trouble this way?" Ratty asked before taking another swig of the dark-colored rum.

Smiling, Emerson responded, "It just seems to follow me at times. But, I've always had someone up there, watching over me."

"And I had that other fellow watching over me. Before he left, he placed the shotgun barrel over my ear and told me that he should kill me, but he was going to let me live and that I should never tell anyone about what happened."

"I'd have thought they wouldn't have wanted any witnesses," Emerson mused.

"Not that easy. Tourist dying while scuba diving is explainable. Only an unfortunate accident. Killing Ratty is not so good for their business," he explained. "Too many people know me and would want to know what happened."

"So, I'm chopped liver?"

"Down here, yous are," Ratty grinned. "Yous nothing more than a tourist."

"Sometimes, that's not a bad idea."

"Yous right. And yous lucky."

"Why do you think they even came out here in the first place?"

"I think they wanted to run us off. Scare us away. There's something out here that they don't want anyone to see."

"And I'd like to find out what that is. It must be deeper because I didn't see anything at 60 feet," Emerson said as he turned and scanned the aqua blue water. "It must be pretty important."

"So yous want to come back here again and look for it?"

"Yes."

"Good. I'll bring yous, but next time we will be better prepared for them," the Caymanian said defiantly as he looked at his gauges to keep his boat on course for its journey back to its dockage.

Pryce Clarke's House
Morgan's Harbour

"He's dead?"

"Yeah. We sealed him in the cave," Slade beamed as he reported the results of their encounter.

"I don't want anyone to start an investigation," Clarke cautioned.

"They won't. We made it look like an accident. You know how the reports will go. Tourist diver goes solo diving and dies in cave mishap," Slade allowed an evil grin to cross his face. "It'll just trigger a bunch of stories on dive safety. Ratty will get caught up in it because he allowed the guy to do a solo dive."

"Speaking of Ratty, you did the right thing in not killing him," Clarke said as he looked across the harbour.

"Thought you'd be pleased with that. No need stirring up the police here with two deaths. They wouldn't buy any coincidence on that one."

"I agree. And he won't talk?"

"Not to the police. He might say something to his friends, but it won't amount to anything."

"Think he'll come over here?"

"No way, Boss. People don't want to mess with you. They know what happens."

"Good. We'll see what the news reports are tomorrow," Clarke smiled in anticipation of the headlines about Emerson's death. He reached for his tea and sipped slowly from the white porcelain cup with painted blue flowers as he gazed at the azure waters of the harbour.

The Next Day
On the Road to Ratty's House

As he drove from Cobalt Coast Dive Resort to Ratty's house, Emerson replayed the events from the previous evening. Arie had greeted him on his return with a phone message from Sam Duncan. The cryptic message had indicated that Sam was going to be unavailable for a few days and for Emerson to enjoy his diving adventures.

Relieved at having a communication from his adventuresome friend, Emerson had spent the evening at Cobalt Coast Dive Resort's Duppies Bar and Grill. He had linked into their wireless Internet and searched for additional information on Pryce Clarke.

As previously agreed with Ratty, he was now meeting Ratty at his house in West Bay. Emerson maneuvered the rental car down the narrow roads and onto Watercourse Road as he followed the hastily written directions from Ratty.

As he drove, he entered the small village known as Hell and pulled his vehicle into the post office where tourists typically mailed postcards, postmarked in Hell. He chuckled to himself as he walked past the scattered gift shops offering a wide variety of gifts from Hell and trekked the path to see how the area had secured its infamous name.

In front of him, he spotted the quarter acre of black and jagged ironshore, which jutted upwards like some of the ice formations he had seen that winter on Lake Erie. This area was devoid of life and reminded Emerson of Hawaii's black lava.

After returning to his car, he continued his drive to Northwest Point Road where he turned left and drove to Ratty's house. He followed a narrow lane for 100 yards until he spotted a faded pink, cement block house with white shutters. The front porch was in need of repair and a rusty anchor sat in the front yard. A rusting fence enclosed the yard.

Emerson elected to park alongside the road since the gate to the drive was shut. Parking the car, he walked up to the gate and pushed. It was unlocked and swung open easily on its well-oiled hinges. Emerson walked up to the house and knocked on the screened door. There was no response. He knocked again. When there was no response, he called, "Ratty, you home?"

There was still no answer.

Emerson placed his eyes to the screen and peered into the un-kempt house. It looked like it hadn't been cleaned in weeks, he thought to himself. He reached down and tested the doorknob. It was locked.

He then decided to walk around the house. As he walked into the backyard, a scene from the old TV show "Sanford and Son" greeted him. It looked like a junkyard! The yard was littered with engine, automobile, and boat parts. Under a low shed at the rear of the property, Emerson saw lumber stacked. It was par-tially covered by a torn, beige canvas tarp. A couple of old sail-boats and wrecked cars also dotted the backyard, which was filled with free-roaming chickens, pecking the ground for any food sources they could find. A grunt from behind one of the wrecked cars made Emerson walk over to investigate. There he spotted a rather large pig in a pigpen.

Another grunt behind him and near his left ear caused Emer-son to jump. Spinning around as he jumped, Emerson was greeted by laughter.

"Yous sure was surprised," Ratty guffawed. "Thought yous had a pig at yous back, didn't yous?"

"Not necessarily a pig, but something," Emerson retorted. "What in the world do you have here?"

"I call it the parts department. Yous need a part, I probably have it. If I don't have it, I can find it."

Emerson gazed around the cornucopia of junk on display and covered under tarps. "Quite a collection," he mused.

"A little bit of this and a little bit of that," grinned Ratty.

Looking at his wide array of "collectibles," Emerson asked, "What's the most unusual piece of junk that you have?"

Ratty looked at the mess in front of him and thought. "Well, there's one thing that my father found, it's probably the most unusual."

"What's that?"

"Here, yous follow me and I show yous," Ratty instructed. He turned and walked to the shed at the rear of the property. He motioned for Emerson to help him move a wooden boat, which lay up against some lumber, covered by a tarp. After moving the boat to the side, Ratty approached the tarp. "This is something that I don't show hardly nobody. But yous, I show because yous like this."

Grasping the tarp with both hands, he pulled it off. Emerson's eyes widened as he gazed on the remains of a plane. "What's this? A plane?"

"Yep. During World War II, my father was one of the Home Guards. They walked the North Shore and looked for German submarines. One day, he found pieces of this seaplane on the beach. It must have crashed nearby and broke up. Don't know where the engine is. It would have sunk."

Emerson ran his hands over the worn wings and pieces of fuselage. "It's German," he said as he saw the Swastika on the wing.

"Yeah, that's what he told me, too," the Caymanian said as he puffed on his pipe.

"What happened? Did they spot any more of the wreckage? Did they see a submarine or anything?" Questions spewed out of Emerson's mouth. He had recalled reading that in the later years of the war, some German submarines were capable of carrying small seaplanes.

"Nothing. The Home Guard went on full alert for two weeks, but nothing more came ashore." Ratty paused, then added, "One thing, though."

"What's that?"

"The guy who worked with my father found the tail fin and it still had its numbers on it."

"Really? I'd like to see that and try to trace the numbers."

"Can't talk to the guy."

"Why's that?'

"He's dead like my father," he replied stoically.

"Oh," Emerson said, disappointed.

"Yous could talk to his son, though," Ratty added.

Emerson perked up. "Well, let's do that."

"Got to find him. He's out in East End. Bad people out there. Run drugs with the Jamaicans."

"If you give me his name, I bet I can find him."

"How yous do that?"

"Don't worry, I'll find him," Emerson said mysteriously. "What's his name?"

"Percy Keenan."

"Can I use your phone?"

"Sure. Go in the back door. It's right inside."

Emerson started walking toward the house, scattering the chickens as he went. "If I can find him, will you drive me there?"

"If yous can find him, I'll do that."

Walking into the house, Emerson spotted the phone and walked over to it. He reached into his tropical shirt's pocket and pulled out the business card for Superintendent Fleming and was pleased when the receptionist immediately connected him.

"Fleming here."

"Superintendent, it's Emerson Moore. I met you in your office the other day and..."

Fleming interrupted him. "Yes, I remember, who you are. Still chasing the Clarke story? I've warned you to back off on that, remember?"

"Yes, I understand. But, I'm running down a lead on something else and wanted to see if you could help me."

"Perhaps. What is it?"

"I need to locate a guy named Percy Keenan. Lives out on the East End."

There was no reply.

"Are you still there?"

"Yes," Fleming answered warily.

"What is it? Is there something wrong?" Emerson quickly sensed that there was an issue.

"He's an associate of Pryce Clarke."

"Isn't everybody?" Emerson fumed quietly.

"You seem to be hitting on the right ones."

"Can you help me?"

"What do you want with him? More drug running questions?"

"No, this is different. It goes back to World War II." Emerson didn't want to give him the details.

"I guess there's no harm. Hold on a moment and I'll see what we have." Barely three minutes had elapsed before he returned to the phone. "I have his address." Fleming provided it and Emerson made note of it.

"Mr. Moore?"

"Yes?"

"When do you plan on visiting him?"

"This afternoon. Ratty's going to drive me over there."

"Do be careful," Fleming cautioned.

"I always am," Emerson responded. "Thank you for the information."

"I'm only giving you the address because you're a friend of Reid's. I must go now. I've got other calls to make."

"Thanks again. Good-bye." Emerson hung up as Fleming began dialing another number.

Proudly looking at the address in his hand, Emerson returned to the wreckage-strewn back yard.

"Got it!" he yelled to Ratty.

"Yous did? How did yous get it?"

"Investigative reporter secret," Emerson teased. He didn't want to alert Ratty that he knew Fleming.

"Well, it doesn't matter to me. I could have found him once we got to the East End. Some of the boys out there would have known where he was and told me," Ratty retorted.

"I will share one thing with you that I learned."

"What's that?" Ratty asked.

"Percy works for Pryce Clarke."

"I knew that. They are bad fellows over there in East End. That's where the drug boats come in."

"With all of this drug stuff Clarke's allegedly involved in, it's interesting that I really can't find negative stuff about him on the Internet."

"That's because no one would write anything and live long afterwards," Ratty offered.

Emerson nodded his head in agreement. "I bet. I found several items about his generosity on the island. He donates to this cause and that cause. But, I bet it's nothing more than a smoke screen."

Ratty had been watching one of his chickens scratching the ground. "See that chicken there?"

Emerson spotted the chicken whose feathers were covered in dirt and ruffled. It had seen much better days. "Yes."

"Even dirty chickens lay white eggs. Clarke puts on a good show here in the islands, but that's all it is. He's just as dirty as my chickens. One of these days, it'll catch up to him."

"I hope you're right." Emerson allowed his eyes to linger on the pieces of fuselage and wings from the German seaplane. "Shall we head for East End?"

"Sure." Closely followed by Emerson, Ratty walked to his faded blue Toyota pick up. "It won't take us too long. Yous go open the gate and close it after I drive through it."

Emerson did as he was instructed, walking to the end of the drive and unlatching the gate, then opening it as the truck drove through. Emerson noticed how the little engine seemed to hum - an indicator of Ratty's mechanical prowess.

They followed West Bay Road to the Harquall Bypass and onto Crewe Road, which connected them to South Sound Road.

Pointing to the right, Ratty mentioned, "There's good diving out there. Mostly from the dive boats. They've got places to take yous like Red Bay caves, Bullwinkle's Reef, Spotts Caves and Pedro Castle."

"Sounds like fun," Emerson commented with feigned interest. As much as he enjoyed diving here, he was focused on learning more about the German seaplane. His mind was racing with ideas as to how the seaplane may have ended up here.

They drove past Durty Reid's Bar and Grill in Red Bay and headed for Savannah.

"Oh, oh," Ratty said with concern as he looked into the rear view mirror. "He's coming up on us pretty fast," he said as his eyes moved from the mirror to the road in front of them, then back to the mirror. "We've got oncoming traffic, too."

His eyes widened as the speeding, dark green Toyota, carrying three male passengers, abruptly swung into the other lane. As they passed, two of the passengers glared at Ratty and Emerson.

"They looked real friendly. Must be part of the tourist welcoming committee," Emerson joked.

"Jamaicans," Ratty swore as he said it.

The passing car abruptly darted in front of their truck to avoid a head-on collision with approaching traffic. "Here in the Cayman Islands, we call that Jamaican Roulette."

Emerson nodded his head.

"Usually yous just see it at night after they've been drinking a while. Then they drive home, but not too good. They kill people and themselves all the time."

"They sure are in a hurry to get somewhere," Emerson observed.

As they drove through Savannah's round-a-bout, Ratty nodded to his left. "Yous know Steve Foster?"

"Yes."

"That's his new supermarket. It just opened."

"Nice," Emerson nodded as he recalled Foster from his visits to Durty Reid's. The tall, white-haired island entrepreneur and Emerson had hit it off from their first meeting.

They drove through Bodden Town, which fronted the azure waters on the island's south shore. It's solitary cannon pointed out to sea, guarding the original capital of the Cayman Islands from pirate attacks. It was here that the pirate caves were located and tourists searched for hidden treasure.

Through a beautiful sunny afternoon and bright blue skies, they drove past the Lighthouse Restaurant and the Blow Holes where water sprayed 15 feet into the air as the waves attacked the rocky coast.

"I can just imagine the pirates landing here and burying treasure," Emerson said aloud as he allowed his mind to wander. "I bet there are interesting stories about finding buried treasure."

"In the newspapers there are a few. But the more interesting ones are the ones that are not publicized."

"Oh?"

"That's right. Treasures are found all over the island, but not reported."

"Why? The government will confiscate it?"

"No, yous have to pay high taxes. That's why it goes unreported. It's whispered at bars at night."

"Really!"

"This Percy fellow. He was digging a foundation for an addition to his house and he found four skeletons chained together like a cross."

Emerson's eyes widened.

"Yeah, that's right. Percy goes to the foot of the cross and starts digging. He digs down three feet and hits something. So he works real careful like and he finds a small chest."

"What was in the chest?"

"I'm coming to that. He digs it up and it's got a few gold coins, several pieces of eight and a gold necklace."

"Interesting. What did he do with them? Sell them?"

"From what I heard at Durty Reid's place, he sold it a few pieces at a time when he visited Jamaica. That way no one was the wiser that he had come into some money. It paid for the addition to his house and then some."

"Have you found any buried treasure on the island?"

"No. I've looked for it, but I didn't find none. I'd rather find treasure from a shipwreck," he stated firmly. "I love being under the water and looking for stuff."

"Is that how you found that anchor?"

Ratty nodded his head as he passed a slow-moving vehicle on the narrow road. "I found it off the north shore. Winched it aboard and then brought it out to the house. Looks nice in my front yard," he grinned.

As they continued their drive, Ratty pointed to the water on their right. "Good diving out there, too. The dive boats can take you out to Ironshore Gardens, River of Sand, and Tunnels of Love. They got a nice site called the Grouper Grotto out there, too."

"Sounds intriguing."

"Out there is the most famous wreck in the islands."

"Ten Sails?" Emerson guessed.

"Yep. That's it, the Wreck of Ten Sails," Ratty affirmed.

"I've heard the name mentioned, but I haven't had a chance to research it. What happened?"

Adjusting his position behind the wheel, Ratty started his explanation. "It happened in February 1794. There were 58 ships in a convoy. They thought they had passed Grand Cayman, so they changed course northward. Well, they ran smack into that windward reef over there. There's a line of breakers here on the East End. Ten ships sailed straight into those breakers."

Emerson looked out to sea as they passed through Gun Bay. "How many were lost?"

"Funny thing about it. Only eight people. It was the worst shipping disaster in the Cayman Islands."

The truck slowed and turned into a narrow lane and began to drive up a rise. Suddenly, Ratty twisted the truck's wheel to the left as a car crested the hill in front of them and almost struck their vehicle as it passed. It was the same dark green Toyota, which had passed them earlier.

Ratty slammed on his brakes and brought his little truck to a halt just inches from a low wall, which framed a nearby yard. "I don't like this," Ratty said ominously.

"Neither do I," Emerson added as a knot began to develop in his stomach. He had a sinking feeling beginning to form in his mind.

"We're almost there," Ratty said as he backed the truck onto the road and changed gears to complete the short drive down the lane.

Using Emerson's directions, they parked in front of a small, single-story house. The house had been whitewashed and had a red tile roof with several of the tiles missing. A 3-foot high aqua concrete wall surrounded the house. The east side of the house appeared to be a relatively new addition to the main house.

"This would be Percy's house," Ratty offered.

"Let's see if he's home."

As the two men approached the house, they noticed the front door was ajar. "Looks like someone did a job on this door." Emerson was pointing at the door frame near the door latch. It had been splintered.

"Not good," Ratty worried. "Percy," he called through the door-way.

There was no response.

"We go in," he said as he entered the house's front room. "Not good," he repeated himself as he saw two overturned wooden chairs.

He and Emerson quickly searched the rest of the rooms, but found no one.

"Out back," Ratty suggested.

The two emerged from the back door and scanned the over-grown yard. Seeing nothing there, but a large, open-air shed where the bow of a boat on a trailer protruded, Emerson said, "Let's look there."

They walked over to the shed and past a collection of fishing nets and gear. Seeing two large 6-foot long aluminum tubs, filled with salt water, Emerson walked over to look inside.

"Yous be careful and don't reach in there."

"What's in there?"

"Jellyfish. So don't be sticking your hand in there."

"Jellyfish? What's he doing with jellyfish?"

"I heard he likes to keep them as pets. Crazy fellow. Why would yous want to fool around with them?"

"That's what I was just going to ask." Emerson peered carefully over the edge of the first elevated tub and saw several jellyfish floating in the water. "I never want to run into them."

"Yeah, they sting like hell," Ratty commented as he walked toward the stern of the fishing boat.

"Friend of mine was diving with me in Florida and she ran into one. She was in immense pain. Know how I relieved her pain?"

"Pissed on her!" Ratty said firmly.

"Exactly. She begged me to do it. And it worked. Got her to the hospital as quick as I could," Emerson said as he recalled the incident. "First time in my life I've done that to a woman."

"It's no big deal. They shit on us all the time," Ratty observed.

"Ratty, that's not nice," Emerson admonished. He was about to lecture Ratty about the virtues of women when he saw Ratty stop walking and stare at the floor. "Find something?"

Ratty looked from the floor to the aluminum tubs and back to the floor. "Funny. One of the jellyfish is here on the floor. I wonder how he got here."

As Emerson walked over, Ratty walked to the stern of the fishing boat. "Now, I know."

"What?"

"Come and see."

Emerson walked around the boat and stopped dead in his tracks. There before him and between the twin outboard motors was a man. His arms were outstretched and tied to the two outboards. On the concrete floor were two puddles of relatively fresh blood. The blood was still dripping from the slashes in his wrists.

"Looks like he died hard," Emerson reflected as Ratty stooped and looked up at the body's face. A gag had been stuffed in his mouth.

"That's Percy. It looks like someone tortured him first. They wanted to know something. Take a look at his face."

Emerson took three steps and stooped so he could look at Percy's face. Percy's lifeless eyes bulged out in horror. Red welts criss-crossed his face. "Jellyfish?"

"That's my guess," Ratty said as he looked around the work area.

"Looks like someone allowed those tentacles to spend some serious time on his face," Emerson said as he stood. "The toxins they release can cause paralysis, heart or kidney failure. They can do some serious damage to your nervous system, too."

"They probably used that pole to bring the jellyfish over here."

Emerson looked toward the pole at which Ratty was pointing. "Yeah, I bet they used that," he agreed. "Wonder what they were after."

"Like I told yous before. He's one of Pryce Clarke's fellows. Yous don't mess with these boys." Ratty looked around the covered area. "Who'd yous call to find out where Percy lived? This didn't happen a few days ago, yous know."

Not answering Ratty's question, Emerson guessed. "It was probably the boys in the dark green Toyota."

"Good guess." Ratty was smirking. "Now I know why yous such a good newspaper reporter. Yous put two and two together and get five," he said sarcastically.

"What's wrong, Ratty?"

"Yous getting people in trouble. Yous got me in trouble when I helped yous and now yous get this fellow killed."

"I didn't …," Emerson started, but Ratty interrupted.

"Who did yous call on the phone to find out where Percy lived?" Ratty demanded.

Emerson thought before answering. He did call Fleming for the address. Would Fleming be connected to Clarke? After all, Fleming had tried to discourage Emerson from doing a story on Clarke. Questions and suspicions raced through Emerson's mind. Emerson determined that he was not going to reveal the source of his contact to Ratty. "Just someone who shall remain anonymous," Emerson said.

"Well, yous tell yous Mr. Anonymous that me and my friends are interested in meeting him one night," Ratty was beginning to seethe with anger. He pulled back a number of boards when he spotted the tail fin of the German seaplane. "This is what yous came for!"

"Right," Emerson said as he walked over to the tail fin. From the side he was looking at, the number was faded. He turned it over, and was able to read the number off the other side. Pulling a small pad of paper from his shirt pocket, he wrote down the tail number.

"Now, yous got what yous came for. Let's go."

"But, what about Percy?" Emerson asked as they walked by the body hanging between the two outboards.

"We go now. I'll take care of it in a minute."

They walked around the front of the house and entered the truck. Ratty put the truck in gear and turned it around so that they could drive back to the main road. He navigated the truck down the main road to a small gas station and grocery store where he pulled in and shut off the engine. "Yous wait here," he said sternly to Emerson.

"Whatever," Emerson muttered quietly to himself.

Ratty disappeared into the store for a few minutes and then emerged. He looked down the highway in the direction from which they had just driven and was soon greeted by the sounds of sirens. Hearing the sirens, he walked over to the truck and entered it. He started the engine and put the truck in gear. "Now, the police will investigate what happened back there," he said smugly.

They rode in silence from East End and along the South Shore. The silence didn't last long.

As they passed through an intersection, a dark green Toyota pulled out and began to follow them at a discreet distance. As they approached a section of the road, which ran dangerously close to the edge of the cliff overlooking the sea, the Toyota sped up.

Glancing in his rear view mirror, Ratty commented, "Looks like we've got company."

Twisting around in the seat of the truck, Emerson looked behind them and saw the car. "What a surprise!" he said sardonically. "Think you can outrun them?"

"Not with this little four-banger," Ratty responded while accelerating the little truck.

The Toyota also accelerated. As it approached the truck, the driver targeted the truck's right rear corner and struck it hard as he drove by the truck on the right side.

"Hang on!" Ratty yelled as the force of the impact spun the truck. Ratty spun the wheel and applied pressure to the brakes as Emerson's eyes widened and he gripped the dashboard. It seemed that the truck was spinning in slow motion as it approached the edge of the cliff. Emerson's mind was racing about what to do when they went over the edge and hit the water.

They spun right up to the edge and the front wheel on Emerson's side hung in open space over the cliff's edge.

"I'd say it's time to bail," Emerson spoke quickly as he reached for the door handle.

"Not so fast. Here they come again," Ratty said as he saw the Toyota, which had turned around, racing toward them. "They're coming back to finish the job."

"We'd better get out of here!" Emerson stormed.

"Not quite yet," Ratty said as he feathered the engine. "I've got a little surprise in store for them," he grinned evilly.

Emerson swiveled around so that he could see the oncoming car. It had taken aim at the little truck and was bent on sending them over the cliff to the sea 100 feet below. Emerson could see the driver and the front passenger. They had sinister grins on their faces.

"Hold on!" Ratty yelled just before the Toyota struck the truck. He slammed the gas pedal to the floor and the truck shot backwards onto the road. The driver of the Toyota had counted on careening off the impact with the truck and back onto the highway. With nothing in front of them but open space, the Toyota shot out over the edge of the cliff. It began to turn in midair as it fell and crashed into a watery grave below, killing the three Jamaicans inside.

"Now, that's my version of Jamaican roulette," Ratty said, quite satisfied with himself as he shifted the truck's gears to first and eased up to the edge of the cliff. "Let's check it out," he said as he turned off the engine and opened his door.

Emerson exited the truck and joined Ratty at the precipice's edge. Below them, they saw rolling waves breaking on rocks.

They were in time to see the Toyota slide off the rocks on which it impacted and into the unforgiving sea.

"I sure would have liked to have had a chance to talk to those guys," Emerson said with an air of disappointment.

"The only conversations they'll be having is with the fishes and the bottom feeders. Even then, it'll be one-way conversation and they won't be doing the talking," Ratty snorted as he turned and walked back to the truck.

Emerson took a last look at the area where the car sank and made a mental note so that he could report it to the police. He joined Ratty for a very quiet ride to the marina.

Harbour House Marina
North Sound

"Think you can trace it?" Emerson asked Rothman. He and Ratty had stopped at the marina to talk with the scholarly Rothman. He needed Rothman's assistance in identifying the tail fin number.

"Maybe," he said as he stared at the number written on the paper in front of him. "You say it's from a World War II vintage German seaplane?"

"Right," Emerson responded eagerly. "With all of your contacts around the world, I thought that you might be able to track it down."

"Well, you've got one thing working in your favor," Rothman said as he peered at the number as if it were some key to unlocking a treasure chest. Little did he know what was in store for them.

"What's that?" Emerson asked.

"The Germans are very fastidious about their recordkeeping. Maybe we'll get lucky and the records on this weren't destroyed by any of the heavy Allied bombings toward the end of the war."

"Can you follow up on it?"

"Sure can. There's a guy I know in Munich, who may be able to connect with some other folks. Give me some time and we'll see what we can run down." Rothman turned to Ratty who had nearly knocked over a piece of equipment from one of the desks. "Careful there, Ratty."

Ratty responded with a sheepish grin. "Sorry, I was just looking at yous equipment."

"And where did your father find the plane?"

"The pieces were washed up on the north shore. He did take his boat out and try to find more of the plane, but it must have broke up outside of the wall. The engine probably sank in the deep. He never found anything else."

"How about the pilot's body?"

"I asked him about that, but it never turned up."

"What year was this that he found the pieces?"

Thinking for a moment as he recalled the date, Ratty answered, "Late 1944."

Emerson interrupted at this point. "What do you read into this?"

Sitting back in his chair, Rothman ran his right hand along his cheek. "It's either from a submarine or a German raider. During the war, German submarines patrolled the waters around here looking for Allied ships to sink. German raiders used to carry seaplanes as scout planes when they were trying to locate targets. It could have come from one of them."

Rothman ceased rubbing his cheek and looked directly at Emerson. "But, I don't understand why a raider or its seaplane would be this close to the Cayman Islands."

Royal Cayman Police Headquarters
George Town

"This is Denise, may I help you?"

"I hope so, Denise. It's Emerson. Emerson Moore calling."

The tone of her voice changed as she warmly purred, "Hello, Emerson. It's been a while since we talked."

"I know. That's part of the reason why I'm calling. Any chance that I could see you after work today?"

"Sure. Is everything okay?" she asked. She thought she read something in his voice.

"Sorry. I've just had a busy day." He brushed aside her question. "How about meeting me at JJ Breezes at 5:30?" It was the restaurant in downtown George Town where they had met during the start of Pirates' Week.

"I can do that. I'll see you at 5:30, then."

They hung up and Emerson thought about the day's events from the discovery of the seaplane remnants to the death of Percy to the near-death incident on the drive back to the discussion with Rothman. It had been quite a day. But most disconcerting for Emerson was a feeling that someone had tipped off Clarke's people that he was going to visit Percy. Emerson had a growing suspicion that Fleming tipped off Clarke. It wouldn't be the first time Emerson encountered police corruption.

And a number of other questions lingered in the back of his mind. Why was Percy killed? What did he know and who was concerned that Emerson would stumble across some information. Emerson hoped he would discover the answers.

After retrieving his car from Ratty's house, Emerson drove past Seven-Mile Beach on his way to George Town for his meeting with Denise. He'd have to be careful on how he posed his questions to her, he thought as he drove.

In a short while he found himself navigating the narrow back streets of George Town as he looked for a parking spot. He found one down a small lane and parked. Looking at his watch, he saw that he had time to kill and decided to tour the National Museum, which fronted the waterfront on Harbour Drive and was close to JJ Breezes.

As he approached the two-story museum, he eyed its white exterior and the wooden steps to the second floor. Years ago, the building had housed the courts on the second story. There were 12 steps leading to the second floor. The old Caymanian saying, "Walking the 12 steps," meant you were being taken to court.

Emerson entered the museum's first floor to the right of the stairs and was greeted by a cheery worker in the gift shop to whom he paid the modest admission fee. He had heard about a three-dimensional map, depicting the canyons, the wall and underwater mountains around the Cayman Islands. As he walked into the formal part of the museum, he spotted it right away. He stood in awe as he looked at the layout in front of him. The islands were the tops of mountains and the panorama showed the drop offs and sheerness of the wall.

Emerson walked through the museum, looking at the coral and limestone displays and history of rope making, turtling and shipbuilding. The Caymanians were sought after seaman by the shipping industry because of their reputation for outstanding seafaring skills.

As he turned toward the exit, Emerson glanced at his watch and realized that he had better hurry so that he wouldn't be late for his appointment. He bid the gracious gift shop employee good day and rushed down the street to the building that housed JJ Breezes. Taking the stairs two at a time, he rushed to the second floor restaurant and bar.

"May I help you, sir?" a young hostess asked as he walked into the lobby.

"I'm meeting someone. Mind if I take a look around?"

"No, go ahead."

As Emerson walked into the crowded restaurant, the six cruise ships in the harbor caught his attention. No wonder the street was so crowded, he thought to himself.

The sharp crack of a bullwhip next to his ear made Emerson jump to the side. Turning toward the direction from which the crack had originated, Emerson found himself staring into the bright blue eyes of a bandanna-wearing pirate, who loomed over him. His arms were massive and several of his teeth were missing.

"Got your attention there, didn't I, you scallywag?" the pirate boomed loudly as a motley crew of male and female pirates laughed from the bar where they were downing drinks.

Emerson relaxed as he then recognized the pirate from the pirate ship landing and the start of the parade a few days ago. He was one of the Seattle Seafair Pirates, a group of some 40 pirates, who promoted Seattle and served the community at a variety of events. One of the highlights of their year is the annual trek to participate in the Cayman Islands Pirates' Week.

The troupe members were attired in authentic pirate gear for the most part. Although some of the female pirates are dressed scantily in thigh high boots, short skirts and bosom baring tops like Bonnie, whom Emerson had met on board the ship he sailed on the first day of Pirates' Week.

"Yes, you did get my attention," Emerson grinned. "How's the week going?"

"Great, just great," the pirate replied as he began squinting. He moved his finger to his right eye as he adjusted the pale blue contact. "We've been all over the island for events."

Emerson recalled that each district sponsored daily pirate-themed events. "Where you off to tonight?"

"Bodden Town" he responded. "You want to join us for a little pillage?"

"I'd love to, but I've got plans for the evening." He saw Denise walk into the lobby. "In fact, my plans just arrived."

The pirate cast his eyes appreciatively in the direction Emerson was looking and commented, "Nice plans ! I hope ye and the wench enjoy the evening!" He turned to go back to his friends at the bar.

"I'm hoping to," Emerson grinned as he approached Denise. "Hi, Denise."

"I wasn't sure if I was going to have to come over there and free you from that nasty pirate," she teased as the two followed the hostess to a table on the balcony, overlooking the harbour.

"He'd probably want a hefty ransom to set me free," Emerson joked back.

"I'd pay your ransom any day," she replied as she looked directly into his eyes and smiled.

Staring directly into her eyes, Emerson responded, "I'd like that."

They placed their drink orders with the waitress, who had appeared.

"So, what's up? You didn't want to just meet and talk to me about pirates and ransom."

Get to the point, Emerson thought. He liked that in a woman. Especially in an attractive woman like Denise. "I wanted to ask you a few questions."

"Yes?" she asked as she sat straight up in her chair and leaned forward to Emerson, who was seated on the other side of the table.

"How long have you worked for Fleming?"

"Oh, I'd say about two years."

"Do you know where he lives?"

"Yes, over in Cayman Kai."

"Where's that?"

"Close to Rum Point. You've been there, haven't you?"

Emerson's mind wandered for a moment as he recalled Rum Point as one of the most beautiful places on this earth. "Yes, loved it." He went right back to Cayman Kai. "Is Cayman Kai an expensive area in which to have a home?"

"Very," she responded as the waitress placed their drink orders on the table and Denise reached for her glass to take a drink.

Emerson sipped his drink. How could a member of the police force afford a place there unless he was on the take, Emerson wondered to himself. "And from what you've observed, does he seem to be on the up and up?"

"Up and up?"

"Straight."

It was Denise's turn to react and she reacted in a negative manner. Shaking her head from side to side, she said, "I don't like you asking me all of these questions about my boss. Why are you doing this?"

"I'm suspicious."

"Suspicious of what?" she questioned with growing concern.

Emerson dropped the bombshell. "I think he might be working with Pryce Clarke."

Stunned and almost choking on her drink, Denise recovered. "And why do you think a good man like Superintendent Fleming would be working with Pryce Clarke?"

"A hunch." Emerson wasn't sure that he wanted to let her know yet about his suspicion that Fleming had tipped off Clarke about his visit to Percy, which in turn allowed Clarke to have Percy murdered.

"Personally, I think your hunch is wrong." She was miffed at the accusation. Denise reached for her drink and finished what remained. "And this is why you wanted to see me. Just to get information from me?" she stormed. "Is that all that I'm good for?"

Emerson was stunned by the reaction from the beautiful woman seated across from him. He realized that he had crossed her boundary. And she was right. The primary reason he wanted to see her was for information. "Let me explain," he started.

"I don't think I want to hear any of your explanations," she seethed as she pushed her chair back from the table and stood. Glaring at Emerson, she spoke with a harsh tone in her voice, "I've got to go. I've got things to do."

"But, Denise."

Denise turned and briskly walked away as Emerson watched her helplessly. Women! he thought to himself with exasperation. He seemed to be developing a knack for ruining budding relationships. He thought back to New Orleans and the Creole detective, Melaudra Drencheau. He had blown the start of a relationship with her, but he was thinking about making a return visit to New Orleans and looking her up.

Then, there was the elusive Martine, the attractive redhead he had met on Put-in-Bay. There had been a strong mutual attraction between the two, but it wasn't going anywhere since she was married. Since the death of his wife and 5-year-old son in a tragic auto accident in Washington, D.C., Emerson just couldn't get a relationship going. There had been plenty of women interested in him, but he was particular. At times, it seemed like too particular.

Emerson finished his drink and paid the bill. He turned his active mind away from Denise and thought about his next move with Pryce Clarke. Maybe it was time to pay another visit to Clarke.

Harbour Marina
That Night

"I tell yous, this is not a good thing to do!"

"Just this once. That's all I need your help for."

"Yeah, every time yous talk to me, yous say it's just one time," Ratty fumed as he took another tank from Emerson and placed it in the rack on board his boat.

"If you don't quit your complaining, you're going to get yourself so riled up that your blood pressure will soar and you'll have a heart attack!" Mad Dog called as he stepped aboard with the gear bags for Emerson and himself. "Why are you fretting so much?"

"I think he just likes to hear himself complain," Emerson observed.

The evening's plans had developed relatively quickly. When Emerson returned to his room at Cobalt Coast Dive Resort, he had called Mad Dog and learned that he had the night off. So, Emerson invited him to join him on his little evening sortie. Mad Dog was always up for an adventure at the drop of a hat.

Emerson then called Ratty, hoping that he could talk the Caymanian into providing his boat for this adventure. After much cajoling, he convinced Ratty to offer his services, but it was going to cost him more this time. Emerson had reluctantly agreed to pay the exorbitant fee. After all, if the story broke he would be able to clear the fee on his expense report.

With all the gear loaded on board, Emerson and Mad Dog cast off the lines and Ratty eased the craft from his dockage and headed slowly out of the harbor. As he navigated the craft, he looked overhead at the sky and cursed softly. A full moon would do little to conceal his boat on the evening's mission.

In the stern, Emerson and Mad Dog were talking quietly.

"You're not going to be able to get very close to this Clarke guy's estate, you know," Mad Dog said.

"I realize that."

"Here's what I'd suggest we do because you want to protect Ratty and his boat. Everyone knows his boat. And especially after Clarke's men boarded it previously."

Emerson listened.

"We'll go over the side a ways from the estate. Then, we'll have Ratty toss us a line to grab a hold of. As he gets near the estate, he can throttle back on the power as a signal to us and we'll let go of the line, submerge and swim in."

"I like it. Good idea, 'Dog'."

"Piece of cake," the burly, ex-navy SEAL grinned. "Done this kind of stuff before, you know?"

Emerson nodded as he began to pull on his gear. "What about pick up?"

Mad Dog thought for a moment and then responded. "How much time do you need there?"

"Depends. Depends on what we find and if anyone is around."

"Yeah, and if they find us first!" Mad Dog cautioned.

"Let's say an hour."

"Okay, then. I'd suggest we swim about half a mile south when we're done. With our backs to the estate, we can flash a light at Ratty as he approaches us. He can cut his engines and we'll climb aboard the dive platform."

"Sounds like a plan."

"Yeah, it does. I hope it works," Mad Dog said pensively.

"Let's tell Ratty."

The two walked toward Ratty at the wheel and updated him on their plans; then returned to the stern to finish pulling on their gear.

A short time later the two went over the side as Ratty idled the boat. In the water and with their masks hanging from around their necks, they looked up at Ratty, who now tossed a line to them.

As Ratty returned to the boat's controls, Emerson grinned at Mad Dog. "Let's rock and roll."

Mad Dog smiled back. He had his usual mischievous grin on his face as he gave Emerson a thumbs up and held tightly to the line as it began to pull taut from the boat's forward motion.

In seconds, the two were being pulled behind the boat and parallel to the shore. As they neared Clarke's estate, they felt the craft slow and relaxed their hold on the line, dropping into the water. The craft then picked up speed and moved farther out into the North Sound.

The two divers washed out their masks and slipped them onto their faces. They submerged and began swimming toward the estate. About 100 yards out, they surfaced briefly to get their bearings. That's when Emerson noticed the armed guard stationed at the end of the dock near the thatched tiki hut. The guard was periodically walking along the dock where one of Clarke's boats was tied.

The other boat, Emerson surmised, was off of Boatswain's Bay on its nightly nefarious business. At the end of the dock, Emerson spotted an inflatable with an outboard affixed to it. Pointing toward the dock, Emerson looked at Mad Dog who nodded his head, acknowledging that he understood the situation. Emerson motioned to submerge and the two slid quietly below the warm water.

Soon they reached the concrete wall, which fronted the main portion of Clarke's estate. Surfacing next to the wall, they listened before removing their mouthpieces and talking in hushed tones.

"There might be more guards," Emerson cautioned as he looked toward the beach. "And I don't think we want to go across that beach in this moonlight."

"That would not be a good thing," Mad Dog agreed. Spotting a ladder affixed to the concrete wall. Mad Dog added, "That might be a possibility, but we'd be as much in the open there as running across the beach."

Laughter from the tied boat caused them to swivel their heads in its direction. There they saw the guard laughing with one of the crew members aboard the craft.

"Let's see what we find at the end of this wall," Emerson said as he slid his mask in place and reinserted his mouthpiece. He submerged and began to follow the concrete wall with Mad Dog on his fins.

They had barely gone 20 feet when they encountered a 5-foot wide pipe with strong wire mesh guarding its entrance. The mesh was bowed outward to the North Sound. Excitedly, Emerson pointed at it and then tugged at it. The bracket at the top was loose and gave a bit.

The two divers surfaced and spitting out their mouthpieces talked quietly. "I think we can pull off the metal supports. Did you see how loose they were?"

"Yeah, as long as it doesn't take too long." Mad Dog was looking at his watch and calculating how much time they had until Ratty made his first pick up run for them.

"What do you think the pipe is for?"

"Tidal pool? I don't know. But when we go in, I'd suggest we don't use any lights. With my luck, I'd surface in the middle of a hot tub full of naked bodies," Mad Dog grinned.

They put their mouthpieces in place and dropped below the water's surface and began pulling at the top bracket, which secured the mesh. In minutes they were able to pull the bracket away and pull enough of the mesh aside that they could enter the pipe's opening.

Emerson entered the pipe first. As he swam into its dark and ominous opening, he felt a flashback. Despite the water's warmth, a chill ran through Emerson as he recalled his cave experience with his cousin as a 16-year-old in Put-in-Bay. It was something that would forever haunt him.

Trying to shake it off, he made his way down the pipe as he felt and used its rough concrete sides. He wouldn't allow his mind to worry him about what he could encounter as he made his way forward. Mad Dog followed closely behind him as they progressed 10, then 20 and 30 feet into the pipe. All of a sudden, Emerson's hands didn't feel the rough concrete pipe's walls. He was reaching into open water and, looking upward, could see lights, which he took as coming from Clarke's house. They were inside the estate, he smiled to himself.

Carefully, he turned to his left and felt for the wall. Rather than concrete, he felt a wall made out of rocks and it seemed to protrude into the tidal pool. Carefully, Emerson grasped the rocky wall and made his way upward.

He cautiously surfaced and began to scan his surroundings. On one side was the patio overlooking Morgan's Harbour and the concrete wall, which they had encountered. In front of him was the estate.

He looked to his side and saw that a wooden log obscured his view. He was about to climb out of the water and onto the log when Mad Dog surfaced next to him.

"What do we have going here?"

"All's quiet," Emerson said as he began to pull himself out of the water.

"Freeze," Mad Dog said as quietly as he could.

Emerson was able to stop his momentum and whipped his head around to look at Mad Dog. "What's wrong?" he hissed.

"Just do as I say and very slowly." Mad Dog was speaking in a very low, but firm tone. "Slowly ease yourself back into the water and don't make any sudden moves."

Emerson did as he was directed and slid back into the water.

"Now, carefully swim with me to the far side of this lagoon."

As Emerson swam, his eyes darted around the lagoon, trying to see what had alarmed Mad Dog. When they reached the other side, Mad Dog spoke first.

"I haven't seen one of those in a long time."

"One of what?"

"When you were about to climb out of the lagoon, did you notice anything that shouldn't be there?" Mad Dog was looking back in the direction from which they had swum.

"No, I couldn't see over the log."

"Exactly. Since when do logs have eyes?"

"You mean they had a spy camera embedded in the log?"

"Not exactly, my friend." Mad Dog let out a large sigh. "That was no log."

Emerson squinted his eyes as he looked back at the ledge and recalled how the Cayman Islands received their name. "Caiman?"

"Close. Would you believe salt water crocodile?"

Emerson gasped as he realized how close he had come to climbing onto that reptile. "But, there are no salt water crocodiles here."

"That's the point. I bet your buddy had it brought in as a pet." Pointing to the high fence surrounding the lagoon. "The fence caught my attention. Then I saw the croc. I could tell you all kinds of stories about salt-water crocs. Heard them during my SEAL days. You don't want to tangle with them."

A shudder ran through Emerson's body. "I seem to recall reading that they are territorial."

"Very!"

"Could I suggest to you that we find an exit from here?"

"My exact thoughts."

The two scanned the fence line and spotted a gate. Still wearing their gear, but carrying their fins, they crouched to maintain a low profile and walked to the gate. Finding it locked, Emerson pulled his knife from his leg scabbard and was able to jimmy it open. They stepped through and shut the gate behind them. They then slipped into the nearby shadows of the tropical landscaping.

"That was close."

"You have no idea how lucky you were," Mad Dog said. "That baby was about 12 feet long."

"So, you think Clarke had him shipped in?"

"Yeah. They usually live in the South Pacific or on the east coast of Africa. It's highly unlikely that one read the travel brochure for vacationing in the Cayman Islands and decided to swim over," Mad Dog joked as he took off his mask.

"Let's dump our gear here. We'll pick it up when we leave," Emerson suggested as he shrugged out of his BC and set the tanks on the ground.

They both scrambled out of their gear while keeping a watchful eye on the estate's grounds. They pushed their gear back further into the shadows and turned to plan their next move.

"So what exactly are you looking for?" Mad Dog asked as he scanned the rear of the house.

"Anything that implicates Clarke as a drug runner?"

"And you expect to walk in and find it on his desk?"

Emerson glared at Mad Dog. "Come on, Mike." He rarely called Mad Dog by his given name. "We'll have a look around and see what turns up."

"The things I allow you to get me into!" Mad Dog countered with mock indignation.

Keeping in the shadows and the landscaped vegetation, they moved along the wall to the house and its French doors. While Mad Dog watched the solitary guard on the dock, who had his back to the house, Emerson tried the door handle. He breathed a sigh of relief when the handle turned and the door opened quietly on well-oiled hinges. Emerson stepped in, quickly followed by Mad Dog.

They paused inside and quickly looked around the room. Spotting no one, Emerson led Mad Dog down the hallway and into the mahogany-lined study.

Closing the door, Emerson directed his friend. "Stay here and keep watch."

"Gotcha," Mad Dog said as he cracked the door and peered down the dark hallway.

Emerson pulled the drapes on the massive windows and walked over to Clarke's large mahogany desk. Producing a hooded flashlight from the utility belt around his waist, Emerson shone the light on the desktop and looked through the papers. Seeing nothing of interest he pulled the middle desk drawer. It didn't open. It was locked.

Retrieving his knife from his leg sheath, Emerson inserted the blade between the top of the drawer and wiggled it. When that failed to produce results. He leveraged the blade and was able to pop the lock. The drawer opened easily and Emerson carefully rummaged through the drawer futilely. He went through the remaining drawers quickly, not finding anything incriminating.

Turning away from the desk, he walked around the room, lifting the various photos on the walls to see if there was a wall safe hidden behind. Not that it would do him much good, as Emerson wasn't skilled at safecracking. His buddy, Sam Duncan, was an expert in that arena.

"Find anything?" Mad Dog called from his station at the door.

"Nothing that would help us," Emerson said exasperated.

"Time's running out," Mad Dog cautioned.

"Let's go upstairs and see what we can find."

"Okay dokey," Mad Dog responded as he cracked the door wider and peered out. "Coast is clear," he said as he opened the door and allowed Emerson to walk quietly by him.

The two approached the staircase to the second floor and took the stairs quietly. As they approached the entrance to Clarke's bedroom, they heard music playing and a woman moaning.

"Sounds like he's busy," Mad Dog grinned.

They heard the voices of two females and Mad Dog's grin broadened. "I'd say he's very busy."

The ringing of a cell phone froze Emerson and Mad Dog in their tracks.

The next voice they heard belonged to Clarke.

"What do you want? I'm tied up."

Emerson and Mad Dog moved closer to the closed bedroom door.

"Good. I'll be down to greet you. Good hunting!" Clarke hung up the phone. "If you ladies will excuse me, I've got a boat coming in and I need to greet it. I'll be right back."

Emerson and Mad Dog were halfway down the stairs when they saw that Clarke's second boat had returned. It had tied up at the dock and several men were carrying tubs as they were walked toward the house.

"Can't go out that way!" Emerson whispered as he heard the music from Clarke's bedroom grow louder, signifying that the bedroom door had opened.

"The front door," Mad Dog suggested as they whisked around the bottom of the staircase and charged to the front door. Without thinking, they opened the door and set off the security system.

"Oh shit!" Mad Dog lamented as they raced down the sidewalk and along the front of the building.

As they neared the garage, a voice called out, "Mr. Moore. Over here."

Emerson's head whirled around and he was staring into the barrel of a .38 held by Superintendent Fleming.

Before anyone could react, another voice called from the front of the house, "What's going on here, Fleming?"

Framed in the light of the doorway was Clarke. He was naked except for the bath towel around his waist. He was racking a shell in the shotgun, which he held in his hands.

Without waiting for a response, Mad Dog tossed two flash grenades, which he had been carrying in his utility belt. One toward Fleming and the other toward the house. "Cover your eyes," Mad Dog said quickly to Emerson as he jerked him off his feet and against the wall.

Two shots filled the air. One from Fleming's .38. The other from Clarke's shotgun. Neither found their marks.

When their eyesight was restored, Emerson and Mad Dog had disappeared. They had climbed over the wall and were running across the patio behind the house as the crew from the boat raced into the rear of the house to support Clarke. That is all, but one of the crew.

"Where do you think you two are going?" Slade asked as he spotted the two men in the tropical landscaping where they had raced to recover their gear, which was next to the fence surrounding the lagoon.

Emerson and Mad Dog looked up and into the barrel of a sawed off shotgun.

Mad Dog was the first to comment and he looked directly at Emerson. "Did you ever have one of those days when nothing seems to go right?"

Slade was motioning to Emerson and Mad Dog as he backed up. "Come on out onto the patio." He continued backing up, intently watching the two intruders in front of him.

"Lunch time," Emerson cracked at Slade.

Slade gave Emerson a puzzled look. Emerson nodded to Slade's left. Slade quickly threw a glance in that direction. He didn't realize that he had backed in front of the now open gate to the lagoon. At that moment a roar filled the air as the crocodile bellowed.

With his attention diverted, Emerson and Mad Dog rushed Slade. Mad Dog snatched the shotgun out of his hands as Emerson pushed Slade into the fenced compound and slammed the gate shut. It wasn't necessary as the croc quickly struck at its prey with its open jaws, trapping Slade between them with increasingly deadly pressure. The croc pulled the screaming Slade into the lagoon where it started its death roll.

"Hate to eat and run," Emerson called as he and Mad Dog raced to grab their gear and sprinted down the dock. They had virtually made it to the end of the dock when the French doors to the house burst open, discharging the crew and Clarke.

They ran to the lagoon where the croc was still rolling over with Slade still screaming each time he surfaced. Clarke shook his head. He unlocked the gate and entered the compound. As he did, he heard the Zodiac's engine spring to life at the end of the dock. Then they saw the inflatable racing away.

"Get them. I want them both now," Clarke ordered.

The crew ran down the dock and leapt aboard both of the vessels. They cast off their lines and pushed their throttles forward as they flew through the water to capture the two intruders.

In the meantime, Clarke walked over to the edge of the lagoon. When Slade's body came out of the water again and his eyes were wide in pain, Clarke casually pulled the trigger on the shotgun, putting Slade out of his misery. He then did something unexpected and on the spur of the moment. He took two steps into the water and, as the croc turned toward him, fired into its head.

"Sorry, my pet. But, I do need to be able to explain what happened here to the police."

When Clarke turned to walk back to the house, he saw the curtains to his bedroom pull shut. His two guests must have been watching. He called to his house servant. "Tell the girls that we're done for the night and have them taken home."

"Yes sir, Mr. Clarke." The house servant walked through the French doors to deliver his boss's instructions.

Clarke walked over to his patio and ripped off his towel. He felt like an animal in need and he would have his blood lust satisfied that night. He sat down in the chair with the shotgun and waited for his prey to be returned to him.

Beneath the dock, Emerson and Mad Dog had adjusted their masks and were preparing to insert their mouthpieces.

"I've got to hand it to you, Emerson. Starting that motor and locking it so that it'd go straight out in the Sound was a great idea."

"It seemed to work okay."

"Those guys took that bait and cleared out, didn't they?"

"I'll say," Emerson smiled. "Now, let's go meet Ratty."

They both placed their mouthpieces in their mouths and submerged for the uneventful swim to Ratty and return to the marina.

Cobalt Coast Dive Resort
The Next Morning

"You're kidding! How did you find all of that out?"

"This friend of mine has a friend in Berlin, who is a student of the Gestapo and their plans as the war began to fail. This is incredible news," Rothman said excitedly.

"I'll say." Emerson was stunned by his early morning phone call from Rothman. Rothman, in turn, had received an early morning phone call from his friend in Germany, which disclosed the good news. The tail number on the seaplane matched a seaplane assigned to a German Raider, the *Achilles*.

"What became of the raider?" Emerson continued with his questioning.

"It never surfaced again. Sorry, I couldn't resist." Rothman chuckled at his joke.

"No, seriously, was there any mention of what happened to the *Achilles* or what it was doing down here. It had to be down here if the plane was found here."

"No. I asked him the same questions. They couldn't find any documentation. It's like the raider just disappeared off the map."

"Think it might have been running stolen Nazi treasure to Argentina?" Emerson recalled that when the Germans realized that the tide was turning against them, they began to stash their stolen gold, jewels and paintings in South America, primarily in Argentina.

"Maybe. Who knows?"

"I'd sure like to know more. It'd be interesting to track it down."

"Then what are you going to do, search the entire ocean?" Rothman retorted as he tried to bring Emerson back to reality.

"No, no." Emerson thought for a moment. "I'm not jumping to conclusions, but it'd be interesting to know the seaplane's range. Then you could calculate an area from which it had flown." Emerson paused, then continued, "But, then again. You'd have to take in account the currents at the time and where the ship might have been headed. Did it sink or did the crew take off with the loot?"

"Or was the ship sunk by Allied warships?"

"True. I have a friend in Washington who could check a record of enemy sinkings in the Caribbean." Turning it over in his mind, Emerson concluded, "Let's forget it. It'd be like finding a needle in a haystack."

"Sure, I understand."

They chatted briefly and then hung up.

Emerson was leaving and in process of his shutting the hotel room door when the phone rang once again. He reentered his room and answered it.

"Hello."

"Mr. Moore?"

"Yes."

"I'm calling on behalf of Mr. Pryce Clarke."

Emerson's body tensed. "Yes?"

"Mr. Clarke has decided to honor your request to take you diving off of Boatswain's Bay."

Emerson thought before commenting. He was stunned to receive the phone call and suspicious. But throwing any serious concern aside, he responded, "I'd love to. When can we go?"

The next comment surprised Emerson. "Now. If you'll look out your window, you will see our inflatable awaiting you at Dive-Tech's dock."

Emerson looked out at the dock's end and saw the inflatable bobbing and waiting for him. One crew member was on board with a cell phone to his ear.

"I'll have to grab my gear."

"Mr. Clarke has gear for you to use. If you want to dive Boatswain's Bay with him to see this new wreck, you must come now. He's on board and waiting for you." The caller provided Emerson with a brief description of the wreck in order to entice him.

Looking farther out into the Bay, Emerson saw Clarke's boat at anchor. He couldn't tell if it was the *Turtle Dancer* or *Turtle Chaser*. It appeared to be in the same spot that the boat anchored each night. Emerson's intense curiosity took control and he hastily agreed. "I'll be right down."

Emerson left his room, locking it behind him, and raced down the stairs and past the pool toward the dock. As he walked by DiveTech's office, he saw Nancy Easterbrook and decided to let her know where he was going. He entered the office smiling. "Hi Nancy."

"Morning, Emerson. What's your big hurry today?"

"I'm going diving with Pryce Clarke. He said they found a new shipwreck around Boatswain's Bay on a ledge at 135 feet. He said the ledge is just above a beautiful stand of hanging coral on the wall. They're waiting for me at the end of the dock."

"Sure you want to do that?"

"Yes. Why?"

"You know his reputation?"

"Great guy!" Emerson teased.

"Dangerous guy is what the rumor mill will tell you, and anyway, I've not heard of any new wrecks in that area." She began to walk around the counter sliding her hand along the glass, and walked over to Emerson. "You give me a hug and I'll feel more comfortable about you diving with him."

Perplexed on how a hug would make any difference, Emerson complied with her request. As she hugged him, and without Emerson noticing what she was doing, she slipped a small object into the back pocket of his swim trunks.

Frowning, Nancy cautioned, "Be careful."

"I will," he said as he walked out of the office onto the dock and rapidly to the end.

"Mr. Moore?" the muscular, ebony-skinned crew member asked with a sinister tone.

"Yes."

"I'm Trinity. I'm the one who called you. Please come on board."

Emerson climbed down the ladder and settled aboard the craft whose engine was idling. Trinity cast off his line and pointed the inflatable in the direction of Clarke's boat. They raced through the oncoming waves to Clarke.

From DiveTech's office window, overlooking the Bay, Nancy watched the inflatable.

"Something wrong?" her husband, Jay, asked as he saw the look of concern on Nancy's face.

"Just a concern."

"How's that?"

"Emerson's diving with Pryce Clarke."

Jay grimaced. "Why would Emerson hang out with him?"

"I don't know and I don't like it." She continued to watch from the window as the inflatable pulled up to the stern. "We should probably keep an eye on them." She reached for her binoculars and focused on Clarke's boat.

"Woman's intuition?"

"You betcha!" she grinned at her good-looking husband before turning back to watch the boat.

As the inflatable bumped into the diving platform at the stern, Emerson began to pull himself onto the platform. Suddenly he screamed and jumped into the water as the salt water crocodile charged through the open stern passageway.

Laughter from those on board filled the air. Clarke was the first to speak as he stepped over the dead crocodile, which had been shoved through the opening at Emerson. Clarke extended a hand to Emerson. "No need to worry, man. This croc is dead."

Grasping the hand, Emerson allowed himself to be assisted onto the dive platform. Standing, he looked at the croc as Clarke spoke. "Unfortunately, someone left the gate open last night and I had to shoot my baby." Clarke was staring intently into Emerson's eyes, looking for a reaction. He didn't get one from the crafty reporter.

Instead, Emerson said, "I didn't think that there were crocodiles in the Cayman Islands."

"You are very correct!" Clarke said as he grinned and flashed his white teeth at Emerson. "This one was my pet. I've had it for several years."

"You said that you had to shoot it?" Emerson was grinning in-wardly.

"Yes. It ate something last night that it shouldn't have," Clarke replied stoically.

Emerson suppressed his grin.

"Last night was a rather difficult night at my place."

"Oh?"

"I actually had a break-in at my house last night."

"Really?"

"Two burglars."

"Did you catch them?"

"No, they got away. But they didn't get anything valuable."

"I'm sorry to hear that," Emerson commented.

Clarke's face flashed anger. "What do you mean?"

"I meant that it's too bad that you didn't catch them."

"They stole my inflatable," he continued as he pointed at the inflatable now tied at the stern. "But we were able to retrieve it. They left it running in the North Sound and apparently bailed out before we caught up to it."

Emerson again smiled inwardly at the false conclusion Clarke had drawn.

Changing the subject, Emerson said, "I appreciate you following up on my diving request from our first meeting."

"Mr. Moore, I do not forget. I have a memory like an elephant. Shall we get ready for our dive?"

"Sure." Emerson noticed the racks of tanks and expensive equipment on board. As he was directed to gear set aside for him, he noticed that only he and Clarke were preparing for the dive. "Are just the two of us diving?"

"Yes. I want to give you a dive experience that you will always remember. Wait until you set your eyes on this wreck."

A cold chill ran up Emerson's spine in reaction to the tone in Clarke's voice. Emerson realized that he would have to be careful. He was also concerned whether any of the others on board might suddenly appear underwater after they submerged.

"We'll be using Trimix so that we can do this deeper dive."

"Good. I'd like that." Emerson knew that there were a number of shipwrecks in the area and Trimix would allow a diver to go to a maximum of 260 feet.

Emerson slipped into a wetsuit and turned around as Trinity tested the tanks on the rack. He handed Emerson the Analox O2 E11 analyzer so he could test his own tank. The analyzer operated from an internal temperature compensated electro-chemical oxygen sensor.

Emerson tested his tank's gas levels and was satisfied that they were correct. Then he mounted a BC that Trinity was holding for him to the tank he'd just tested. He donned his gear, then turned his air on and looked at his gauges, only to find the tank was almost empty. "You need to be more careful here. This one is almost empty."

"Sorry. I will take care of it right away," Trinity said as he threw a conspiratorial glance at Clarke and grinned sinisterly as he pretended to test the second tank with the analyzer, while Clarke distracted Emerson by pointing to a dolphin swimming around the boat. "Here's a full one." He removed the first tank and affixed the second one filled with air instead of Trimix onto the back of Emerson's BC and stood back. "Try this one."

Emerson turned on his air supply, checked his gauges and said, "Much better."

"Yes, indeed. Much better," Trinity grinned at the crew members, who had observed how he had swapped the tanks.

Clarke walked over to Emerson and handed him a dive plan. "I had Trinity work this dive plan for us so that we are careful. Many accidents have happened to people, who do not pay attention on deep dives," he warned ominously.

One of Clarke's men chuckled and Clarke threw him a look that stopped the chuckle immediately.

With a growing uneasiness, Emerson scanned the crew members. He didn't like what he was seeing. His gut told him that he was in danger, but he put it aside. He was always up to a challenge and liked to tempt fate.

Picking up a spear gun, Clarke moved toward the dive platform. "Shall we?"

Emerson didn't like the fact that he was unarmed. Not only did he not have a spear gun, but also he didn't have a knife. He had always dived with a knife strapped to his leg.

"Coming?"

"Yes." He joined Clarke, who adjusted his facemask and jumped off the platform. Emerson quickly followed, knowing that he'd have to be very wary and alert.

Sinking along the face of the North Wall, they continued their descent. At the 60-foot level, Clarke pointed with his spear gun at an approaching Caribbean reef shark that checked out the two invaders to his world before swimming away.

A couple of large Caymanian lobsters on the wall cautiously watched the divers as they dropped past the 80-foot level.

Emerson saw that his depth gauge was reading 110 feet and saw that they were approaching what appeared to be a ledge and a small boat at about 135 feet. Clarke had paused and looked back to be sure that Emerson was following. He was grinning as he did.

Emerson was beginning to feel light headed as he swam ever deeper along the wall toward the boat. When a Green Eel swam close by, he pulled his mouthpiece out of his mouth and held it out for the eel to take a breath. The eel darted away and Emerson couldn't figure out why. Every animal needed to breathe.

Getting woozier, Emerson decided that he could swim like the eel by moving his body in an "s" motion and therefore didn't need his fins any longer so he proceeded to pull them off. He let them drop below and watched as they floated downward in front of him.

None of this was lost on the grinning Clarke. It was obvious that Emerson was oblivious to the fact that the deeper they went, nitrogen narcosis was setting in. He approached Emerson and motioned for Emerson to follow him closer to the boat. Then he wrote a message on his underwater pad and held it up for Emerson to read. It read, *Stay here.*

Emerson groggily nodded his head and found a rock outcrop to grasp onto near the bottom of the boat's hull and settled to wait for Clarke's next instruction. As he waited, he marveled at how beautifully the black corals below him waved in the current and decided to drop a little lower to check them out. He also began to notice how graceful all of the fish were as they swam about underwater.

Clarke began to ascend and occasionally checked below to make sure that Emerson was not following him. He swam around a corner of the wall, out of sight of Emerson, then made his planned decompression stops and surfaced near the stern of his boat.

"Everything go as planned?" Trinity called as Clarke swam over to the platform and hoisted himself out of the water.

"Exactly," he smiled. "If anyone finds him, they'll just consider it an accidental death. Another tourist making a diving mistake."

As he stepped aboard and the boat picked up speed, he continued, "Take her out a ways and we'll drop the croc overboard." The boat raced northeast to comply with his instructions.

Now 150 feet below the surface, Emerson decided to swim horizontally away from the outcropping. He was giggling to himself with the idea that he was going to play hide and seek with Clarke. He had swum out from the wall about 30 feet when he thought he saw something on another ledge below. No, I'm just imagining things, he chuckled.

As he hung in the water he continued to be amused by how confused Clarke would be when he returned and couldn't find Emerson. He decided to twirl around weightlessly and do some 360s while waiting for Clarke to return. As he began twirling, he felt something firmly grab both of his shoulders.

Smiling, he continued to twirl around some more to see what it was and came face to face with Nancy Easterbrook. She peered into his eyes and didn't like what she saw. He appeared to be disoriented and proceeded to pull his mouthpiece out of his mouth to offer her a breath of his air.

She quickly shoved his regulator back into his mouth and scribbled a note on her underwater writing slate while trying to keep Emerson's attention. The note read: *Are you okay?*

Squinting, Emerson read her note. He grinned and nodded. He then turned to point to the boat and the beautiful black coral he had been examining. When he did, Nancy's eyes widened when she realized that his fins were gone and Emerson didn't seem to care. She also noticed that the boat had no coral growth on it, meaning it had been put there recently.

Emerson had surely succumbed to nitrogen narcosis and obviously didn't realize it. Clarke must have somehow switched what should have been his Trimix tank for a plain air tank. As she forced Emerson to take her second Trimix regulator, she knew she would have to act fast as Emerson would have quite a bit of decompression time.

Earlier, Nancy had decided to follow her suspicion and had suited up for a deep dive at the end of her dock. Jay had helped carry her double 104 Trimix tanks with redundant regulators to the dock's end along with two extra deco tanks, one Nitrox and the other oxygen. She clipped the two extra tanks to her BC, then lowered the underwater sea scooter off the dock.

Nancy boarded the scooter and submerged. The powerful scooter propelled her forward as she began following the gauge in her hand, which guided her out to the Wall and directly to Emerson. The gauge would find the tracking device, which she had dropped in Emerson's back pocket in the office.

As Emerson breathed the Trimix Nancy had brought to him, he began to come back to his senses and realized what had been happening. He had definitely become narced and lost track of his own safety. The pair ascended to 100' and switched to the extra Nitrox tank as they approached their first deco stop according to Emerson's dive computer depths and times.

Their last deco stop would be on oxygen from the other tank Nancy brought. The use of oxygen would make this last stop much safer for both divers. Once they determined that their deco stops were sufficient in length, Nancy fired up her scooter and towed Emerson back to DiveTech.

When they surfaced near DiveTech's dock, Nancy saw that Jay was waiting anxiously at the dock's end.

"Is he okay?" Jay called.

"Now, he is," she responded as she guided the scooter against the dock. "You go first Emerson," she said as she pointed at the ladder leading upward and Emerson stepped out of his BC. "He may need some help," she cautioned Jay as he leaned over the dock and extended a hand to assist Emerson.

Shaking his head as he tried to clear the remaining cobwebs, Emerson had virtually returned to his normal conscious state. "I'm much better," he said as he grabbed the first rung on the ladder and missed the second. "Well, I guess that I'm not quite back yet," he grinned sheepishly.

Reaching again for the second rung, he connected and carefully continued up the ladder where Jay helped him through the final rungs and on to the dock. Emerson rolled over and laid there, resting.

Although he was filled with questions, Jay put them aside to finish the task of bringing the tanks, dive equipment and scooter onto the dock. In a matter of minutes the task was finished and they, with a recuperated Emerson, conveyed the equipment to DiveTech's office.

After setting down the equipment, Emerson plopped onto one of the nearby picnic benches. Nancy quickly joined him.

Turning to Emerson and Nancy, Jay asked, "How about a soft drink or ice cold water?"

"How about a good whiskey?" Emerson kidded. "No, I'll take water."

"Water for me," Nancy responded. She and Emerson waited quietly for Jay to return.

When he walked out with the cold beverage, he waited while the two took a drink. "Okay, you two, tell me what happened out there."

"Emerson, you go first. I want to know how you enjoyed your dive with Clarke," Nancy eyed Emerson carefully as she commented.

Emerson decided not to say anything about the crocodile, as it would lead to other questions, which he wasn't prepared to answer.

"When I had visited Clarke at his home a few days ago, I had casually mentioned that I wanted to go deep diving with him and he followed up with my request. That's how all of this started."

Nancy and Jay nodded their heads as they listened.

"You've heard the rumors about Clarke?" Nancy asked.

"Yes."

"And you still went diving with him?" Nancy asked incredulously.

"Yes. Sometimes you have to take a calculated risk," Emerson replied.

"Or a stupid risk!" she countered.

Emerson looked at his two friends and saw their concern for his personal safety in their faces. "I know. It's my curiosity and, sometimes, I like pushing the edge," he explained. He looked at them again, but could see that they weren't buying his explanation. He decided to continue.

"Clarke and I dove down to about 120 feet and, long story short, I began to feel woozy. I seem to recall doing some dumb things like trying to give a fish my mouthpiece, but some of my memory seems to have faded. I can only recall bits and pieces."

Nancy nodded as she spoke to her husband, "Nitrogen narcosis."

Jay asked as he turned his head back to Emerson, "But how could that have happened? You did check to make sure that you had a Trimix tank, didn't you?"

"Yes. It was on my BC. But when I tested it, it turned out to be empty. So one of Clarke's men replaced it for me."

"And you didn't check to make sure it was Trimix?" Nancy asked.

"No, I didn't even think about it."

"That was your problem from the start of this little adventure. You weren't thinking." Nancy interrupted. "You must always check your own gear before you dive. You've been taught that over and over!"

Emerson nodded his head. "I know. I made a mistake."

"Almost a deadly one," Jay interjected.

Emerson continued with his story. "I seem to remember that Clarke wrote a message and wanted me to stay there. I don't remember if he saw something or was going to spear something. I just don't recall clearly."

"Yeah, he wanted you to stay there so that you'd eventually be shark bait. I must have found you shortly after he left. I did hear a boat moving away while I was approaching you."

Emerson sat straight up on the picnic bench. "That's another thing. How in the world did you find me? That's a pretty big ocean."

"Stand up and turn around."

Emerson stood and felt her pat his butt. "Hey there, you're getting a little friendly aren't you?" He looked directly at her husband. "You've been here the whole time, I didn't say anything to provoke this type of reaction from your wife."

He and Nancy were grinning. Nancy plunged her hand into the back pocket of his swimming trunks and extracted a small device. She gave his butt one small pat and said, "Okay Sugar Butt, you can sit down."

With mock indignation, Emerson said as he sat, "I guess I shouldn't complain. Women just can't help but pat my butt."

After he said it, he groaned. He realized that it was something that his buddy, Sam Duncan, would say.

"If I were you, I wouldn't do any complaining, Sugar Butt. My wife saved your butt out there."

"Who's complaining?" Emerson said as he turned to face Nancy and saw her holding the small device. "What do you have there?"

"Your life saver!"

"Uh huh. What is it?"

"It's a tracking device. I dropped it in your pocket when you were leaving." When she saw the perplexed look on Emerson's face, she explained further. "I didn't have a good feeling about this."

Nodding his head, Emerson said, "I'm glad you did Nancy. Thank you."

"You better be glad. When I found you, you were just floating. Then, I saw you had an air tank rather than Trimix. I switched you over right away."

"Thanks."

"You know you're welcome. So, what was Clarke's plan? Just leave you there to die. And, why would he do that to you?"

"I'm not sure," Emerson replied to her. He still didn't want to let her know about his recent adventure at the Clarke estate.

"Well, this is pretty serious. We need to let Derek Fleming know about this." She reached for the nearby phone and Emerson stopped her.

"I'd prefer we don't."

"Why?" she asked with a look of surprise. "You've got his gear and me as a witness."

Emerson's mind was processing quickly. He didn't trust Fleming after bumping into him at Clarke's estate. "I'd rather handle it myself. Clarke could always say it was an accident as far as the tank switching went."

"And what about abandoning you below? How's he going to explain that?" Nancy pushed.

"I don't know. But, I'm sure that he'd come up with some excuse. It'd be his word against mine."

Both Nancy and Jay were shaking their heads.

Emerson stood. "I think I'll walk over to my room. I need to crash." Turning to Nancy, who was now standing, he hugged her. "Thank you both for your help today. The only reason I'm here is because you followed through."

"We're glad to help," Nancy responded as Emerson gave her husband a quick hug and started to walk to his room.

After watching him walk up the stairs and enter his room, Nancy's husband commented, "I don't like this one bit."

"Neither do I. I'm calling Derek." Nancy picked up the phone and punched in the number in George Town.

Two hours later, the phone rang in Emerson's room and woke him from his sleep.

"Hello?"

"Emerson?"

"Yes."

"It's Denise."

Emerson cleared the sleep from his mind as he sat up. "Hi Denise. What's going on?"

"I need to see you."

"That would be nice." Emerson then realized the serious tone in Denise's voice. "Is there something wrong?"

"Yes."

"What is it?"

"I can't tell you over the phone. I don't want Superintendent Fleming to hear."

Alarm bells began going off in Emerson's brain. "Is this about the diving incident with Clarke today?"

"Yes."

"Did someone call Fleming?"

There was a pause.

"Denise, are you there?"

"Hold on!" she hissed. "Yes sir. I'll get the file for you," she said to Fleming who had appeared next to her workstation.

"There's more to tell you. Do you know a Sam Duncan?"

Emerson tensed. "Yes. He's a friend of mine. I haven't seen him in a few days."

"I know why."

"Why?"

"Can't talk. Meet me at the Kaibo Yacht Club in two hours. I'm coming, Mr. Fleming," she responded as Emerson again heard Fleming's voice in the background.

"Is Sam okay?"

The only response Emerson received was the phone going dead on the other end.

Kaibo Yacht Club
Cayman Kai

The Kaibo Yacht Club was a 45-minute drive from George Town and located south of Rum Point on the north shore.

Beneath a thatched roof was the club's bar. The rustic bar was fronted with corrugated steel and the floor was done in a rough stone. The bar appeared to be built from pieces and parts washed ashore from area shipwrecks. Cargo nets and worn wood could be seen throughout the cozy and inviting bar.

It overlooked a pristine white sandy beach and the nearby docks where magnificent yachts were moored. Cayman Kai was an area where the very wealthy had palatial homes; many fronting on channels so their yachts could be tied conveniently to the house.

At the bar, Emerson glanced at his watch again. Scarcely had a minute elapsed since he last looked at it. Denise was now 16 minutes overdue and Emerson was worrying. Maybe she was caught in traffic. Nope, a highly unlikely scenario for the north shore.

What was keeping her he wondered as he took another drink of Seven and Seven. And what did she know about Sam's disappearance?

He looked at his watch another time, then looked toward the beach. That's when he heard the noise. It sounded like a small pop, but he knew better. Emerson stood from his barstool and raced out the entranceway. He charged around the bar to one of its parking lots and saw a body on the ground. Blood was flowing from a head wound.

There was a man kneeling next to her. He was holding a pistol in his hand. It was Derek Fleming. Seeing Emerson, Fleming stood to his feet. Emerson dove for cover when he saw Fleming stand.

"Mr. Moore, you don't need to hide from me," Fleming called as he began to walk to the spot where Emerson had stood.

Emerson didn't respond. Instead, he crawled through the lush underbrush toward Denise. He was counting on the parked cars and the late afternoon's deepening shadows to offer him protection from Fleming's eyes.

"Oh, come now Mr. Moore, you certainly don't think I did this do you?"

Emerson maintained his silence as he continued his forward progress.

"She's dead Moore. She took a bullet from a passing car. A kill and run job if I ever saw one."

Emerson still squirmed ahead slowly.

"She was coming here to see you. She wanted to come clean with you."

With people now coming into the parking lot, Emerson felt secure that with so many witnesses, Fleming wouldn't try anything. He stood up and saw that he had actually passed Fleming. "I'm here."

Fleming whirled in surprise with his pistol at waist level. It was pointed at Emerson.

"Going to pull the trigger, Superintendent?" Emerson tried to sound confident although he wasn't sure that he should trust Fleming. Fleming's next action provided relief to Emerson.

Holstering his pistol in his waist clip, Fleming said, "I'm sorry Emerson. She was going to tip you off."

With a look indicating his confusion, Emerson said, "How's that?"

Fleming put his arm on Emerson's shoulder. "Let's go inside for a drink and I'll let you know what has been happening."

"Mind if I take a look at her first?"

"It's not pretty."

"They never are, are they?" Emerson responded referring to head shots.

The two approached the body where one of the waiters was beginning to drape a white tablecloth to cover it. "Could you hold one second?" Fleming asked as he held up his finger to the waiter. The waiter nodded as Emerson knelt down to look at his dead friend. Still pretty in death, he thought to himself as he lamented her demise.

While Emerson was taking a last look at the woman, Fleming made a quick call on his cell phone to police headquarters and quickly explained what had transpired in the yacht club's parking lot.

"Let's go," Fleming said as he ended his call and Emerson approached him. Fleming also nodded to the waiter to cover the body as the two men walked away and into the yacht club bar.

Neither spoke except to place their drink orders. Once the waitress left their corner table, Emerson leaned forward and pushed hard at Fleming. "Okay, Superintendent, what gives? Are you working for Pryce Clarke or not?" Emerson wasn't sure that he was buying Fleming's story about a kill and run in the parking lot. He thought Fleming was the murderer.

"No, I'm not," Fleming replied as he looked directly into Emerson's eyes.

What Fleming said next caused Emerson to slump in his chair.

"She was!"

Emerson just stared straight ahead for a full minute before speaking. "How do I know that I can believe you?"

"You'll have to trust me. Didn't you see me holster my pistol in the parking lot?"

"Sure, in front of about 10 witnesses. Of course, you would. You're not stupid, Superintendent."

The waitress returned with their drinks and both men took a long drink. Fleming spoke next.

"I'm going to explain some things to you, but they are not for publication in your paper. Agreed?"

Emerson tilted his head and stared at Fleming for a moment before speaking. "Agreed."

"A few months ago, we noticed that Clarke was being tipped off about some of our investigations."

"And right away you suspected Denise?" Emerson said in stunned tone.

"No, we didn't actually. It wasn't until later. Then our surveillance team spotted her at Clarke's house on several occasions."

Interrupting, Emerson said, "Like my friend and I spotted you at the house the other night?"

"Surveillance."

"But you fired at us?"

"Not really. Your friend surprised me with the flash grenade. Not used to seeing those here. I accidentally pulled the trigger. It seemed like you also surprised Clarke."

"Yeah, he fired too. So where did you go?"

"In the rush and, if you remember, I was in the shadows. I just stepped back into the shadows and went to my car, which was parked nearby."

"I heard Clarke shout your name."

"Yes, it was unfortunate that he saw me. Now, he probably suspects we have him under surveillance."

Emerson wasn't sure that he was buying Flemings explanation. It sounded weak to him.

"And what were you and your friend doing at Clarke's house?"

"We had to check out something," Emerson responded.

"You knew that Denise was there, didn't you?" Fleming probed. Stunned, Emerson just stared at Fleming.

"By your reaction, I take it that you didn't know. She was probably upstairs."

A look of shock crossed Emerson's face as he recalled hearing the two women in Clarke's bedroom.

"Oh, don't be too surprised, Mr. Moore. There were things that Denise was pulled into despite her good character. In some ways, she had no choice."

"How's that?" Emerson asked with his forehead furrowed.

"She did a lot to protect her father and brother."

"Oh?"

"Her father was in prison in Jamaica. And her brother worked for Clarke there. When Clarke learned, in a conversation with her brother, that Denise was working for me, he arranged to meet her."

"And?" Emerson probed.

"He showed her a picture of her father in prison."

"So?"

"He was seated on a bench and surrounded by a group of tough prisoners. They were holding shivs and looking at her father."

"I get it. Clarke's men in prison. If she wanted her father to live, she needed to cooperate with Clarke."

"Precisely."

"So, how do you know all of this?"

"We had tapped her phone line at the station. That's how I knew that she was meeting you here today."

"But the stuff about her brother and father?"

"We interrogated her after her phone call with you today and she broke down. Once we told her all that we had on her, she agreed to cooperate with us."

"And you let her come out here to meet me?"

"Not exactly. She slipped out of the building before we knew it. I suspected that she was on her way here. So, I drove out. Looks like I got here a few minutes too late. Somebody tailed her."

"Yeah. A few minutes too late."

"She wanted to tell you about your friend, Sam Duncan."

Emerson stared directly at Fleming. "What do you know about Sam?"

"That's why we had to interrogate her. Sam was working with us on the Clarke case. He had been very effective in Jamaica running drug interdiction. He busted a big case over there that we suspect hurt Clarke big time."

Emerson thought back to the Jamaican hit men in Key West, whom Sam had mentioned.

"Where's Sam now?"

"He had disappeared and we were worried. Apparently, Denise picked up some information from her brother that Clarke's men had kidnapped a drug agent on Grand Cayman. He said that the guy, whose name was Sam Duncan, was the buddy of a reporter, who Clarke had killed."

"A reporter who Clarke thought he had killed. He didn't kill me although he tried," Emerson interjected.

"No, he didn't and I knew that thanks to a call I received."

"Nancy?"

"Can't say." Fleming said with a grin. "I will say that you're like a cat with nine lives."

Ignoring the comment, Emerson pushed. "Where's Sam?"

"Not exactly sure. All her brother told her was that he was close to Harbour Marina. We're running down buildings in that area. Then we'll make a raid once we have the appropriate paperwork from the court if we can get it."

"Yeah, and that'll take hours or days. Sam would probably be dead then," Emerson said angrily. "You need to move now!"

"Can't. These things take time."

"And it sounds like time is running out for my friend, Sam." Emerson stared at his drink glass as a plan formulated in his mind. He stood from the table. "Superintendent, I appreciate you telling me all of this, but I have to go."

Fleming also stood. "I understand."

"Do you? Do you really understand that my friend's life is in jeopardy?"

Fleming countered. "I do. My team is working on this as we speak."

Emerson threw some bills on the table. "That's to pay for the drinks. I've got to go."

Fleming looked from the bills strewn on the table to the rapidly departing Emerson. He smiled as he turned to walk away. His plan was working.

∽

Swerving through the gate, the rental car pulled to a stop near the main office building. Parking it, Emerson threw open the door and bounded from the car. He raced to the docks and breathed a sigh of relief when he saw that Ratty's *Sea Dog* was at its berth.

"Ratty," he shouted but with no response from the boat.

He called again. "Ratty." Again there was no response. Emerson was preparing to board when he was startled by a voice from behind him.

"Ratty sees yous coming and he went the other way. He says that yous is trouble for him."

Recognizing the voice, Emerson whirled around. "Ratty," he said when he saw his Caymanian friend approaching him. "I need your help."

Rolling his eyes, Ratty responded, "Every time I sees yous, yous are needing my help." He took his pipe out of his mouth and pointed the stem at Emerson. "Yous like this with all of yous friends?"

Grinning, Emerson replied, "No, not really. But seriously, I need your help."

"What is it this time?"

"I need to find a warehouse or building close to here that Clarke…"

Interrupting, Ratty firmly stated, "No more messing with Pryce Clarke. I shouldn't have helped yous last time. I'm just lucky that he hasn't figured out that it was me who helped yous last time."

"It's different this time. My friend was kidnapped and Clarke's men are going to kill him."

Puffing on his pipe, Ratty thought for a moment before replying. "Go ahead and tell me yous story. Maybe I help yous. Maybe I don't."

Quickly Emerson related what had happened to Sam in Key West with the two assassins and then moved to his almost tragic dive incident with Clarke. He wound up with what had transpired at Cayman Kai's Kaibo Yacht Club with the death of Denise and the conversation with Superintendent Fleming.

When he finished, Emerson allowed his eyes to follow Ratty's eyes, which were now gazing upon the *Sea Dog*. "That boat, she's my best friend. Anybody harm her and I'd cut off their balls."

Emerson didn't respond, he just waited.

Ratty squinted at Emerson and spoke, "Yous give me some time and I'll find out where yous friend is."

"We don't have much time," Emerson stated anxiously. "He could already be dead."

"Gimme a couple of hours."

"I'm not sure that we have that long," Emerson worried.

"Yous go upstairs and wait with yous friend, Roger."

"Okay," Emerson said as he turned and headed for the stairs to Rothman's second floor office. As he climbed the stairs, he saw

Ratty enter his truck, which had been parked nearby. The little truck backed out of his parking spot, and quickly exited the marina's driveway.

Rothman was studying an e-mail, which he had just printed, when the door burst open. Looking up, he saw Emerson standing in front of him.

"Perfect timing," he smiled.

"How's that?" Emerson asked.

"Just got another e-mail from my friend in Germany."

"Oh?"

"He found some old paperwork on that German raider. It showed that the ship was urgently ordered to return to port for a special mission. It showed that the ship returned to port, but that's when it gets strange."

"How's that?"

"There's no cargo manifest. The Germans were always so thorough about what they were carrying. In fact, there's a gap in the file until the next document. It read that the ship did not arrive at its destination and was presumed to be lost at sea."

"Interesting," Emerson observed, but then his mind turned to the crisis at hand. He quickly filled in Rothman as to what had transpired and Sam's dilemma.

"You're going to need help if you think you're going to go busting in there."

"Yeah, that's what I was thinking."

"What about your friends, Mad Dog and Durty Reid?"

"Good idea. I'll give them a call. Can I use your phone?"

"Sure," Rothman said as he pointed Emerson to a nearby chair.

Emerson didn't sit. He was too nervous. He quickly called Durty Reid's Bar and Grille.

Reid Dennis answered the phone. "You've got Durty Reid's."

"Reid?"

"You got me."

"It's Emerson."

"Hello stranger. I was just having a beer here with Mad Dog and telling him that we hadn't seen you in a while."

Emerson took Dennis through what had transpired and asked him for help in rescuing Sam.

"For crying out loud, I can get a few of the boys together to help you out," Reid advised after Emerson completed his story. "We'll be there as quickly as possible."

"Thanks, Reid," Emerson said as he hung up the phone and paced over to the window where he could survey the marina's grounds.

"Nervous, huh?" Rothman asked.

Emerson turned to face him. "Yeah, and frustrated. I'm kicking myself for not following up on Sam sooner."

"Quit being so hard on yourself."

Emerson was shaking his head as he thought about Denise's death and what may or may not have happened to Sam. He continued to pace as Rothman wisely maintained his silence.

Thirty minutes later, Emerson heard two vehicles pull into the parking lot. When he looked out the window, he saw Reid Dennis' thatched-roof Jeep followed by a Daihatsu van pull into the marina's parking lot. Emerson, closely followed by Rothman, ran down the stairs to greet the five arrivees.

"I brought some help," Reid said as he stepped out of the Jeep. Exiting the vehicles were Mad Dog, Steve Foster, Mark Rice, and a tall man. He had a graying mustache extending over the edges of his square jaw and a flattop haircut. He was carrying a long handled sledgehammer and had a sinister persona.

Foster introduced him. "Meet my friend, Big Foot."

Emerson looked down at the guy's feet and guessed he wore a size 15. No wonder they called him Big Foot, he thought to himself.

Foster continued. "No one wants to mess with Big Foot once he starts swinging that hammer."

"Yeah, I'm what you would call a home run hitter," Big Foot said stoically. "I never strike out."

A chill ran through Emerson's spine as he assessed the foreboding giant standing in front of him. Turning from Big Foot, Emerson worried, "We're going to need more than a hammer for this rescue."

Mad Dog had been watching Emerson. "I know what you're thinking. It's the Over the Hill Gang to the rescue."

Emerson was shaking his head. He didn't reply as he needed whatever help he could get.

Seeing his consternation, Mad Dog added, "Now, don't worry one second. We all did shots before coming over here – and they were spiked with extra doses of Geritol!" Mad Dog grinned as he spoke. "Reid, show him what you have there."

"Step over here," Dennis said as he walked to the Jeep's rear and lifted a tarp.

When Emerson peeked in the back of the Jeep, his eyes widened and a smile appeared on his face. "Where did you get those, Reid?" he asked as he surveyed the arsenal of weapons on display. There was a mixture of pistols, shotguns and extra rounds.

"I've got my ways," Dennis smirked all knowingly. "Brought these just in case we needed them."

"We can get more if you think we need them," Rice added.

"I would think this should get it done for us."

"And I came up with some more flash grenades," Mad Dog said as he produced them from a utility belt he was wearing around his taut waist.

"I meant to ask you where you came up with those," Emerson said as he remembered Mad Dog tossing them at Clarke's estate.

"It pays to have contacts." Mad Dog continued with a question. "How do you know we're not being set up? You comfortable with this Fleming guy?"

"I've been thinking about that myself. If he's in with Clarke, the two of them could be luring us into a trap."

"It seems strange to me that the police don't find out which warehouse he's in and bust in, all nice and legal."

"That's exactly what I was thinking Mad Dog. There's something amiss here. Why would he give me a tidbit of information and let me run with it?"

It was Dennis' turn to speak up. "I think you guys are on the wrong track. I've known Fleming for the last couple of years. He's as straight as they come."

Emerson looked at the scruffy bar owner. "I hear you, but money can do funny things to people. If he's on the take and we're getting too close to his money source, I'd think he'd want to have us taken out of the picture."

It was Foster's turn to speak. "My brother, it wouldn't be us. It would be you he'd eliminate."

"He's right," Rothman added. "He wouldn't know that you got us together to help you."

Nodding his head in agreement, Emerson concurred. "I guess that's true. I think all that he'd suspect is that I might go to Ratty."

"Exactly," Mad Dog agreed. "They set you up and take you out. It's all over with, nice and neat!"

"Or, does Fleming want it all for himself?" Rothman asked.

"What do you mean?" Emerson answered with a question.

"Maybe, Fleming wants you to do his dirty work for him, taking out Clarke so he can run Clarke's drug business," Rothman ventured.

"Roger has a point, there," Mad Dog agreed.

"I don't know. I still think you guys are barking up the wrong tree," Dennis suggested.

Their conversation was interrupted by an approaching pick up. It was Ratty, returning to report his findings.

Stopping his truck next to the group, Ratty exited and reported. "I think I've found yous friend. They've got somebody hanging from an overhead chain. His arms are tied and above his head. They've got a couple of chainsaws on the floor near him. Looks like they're waiting for someone before they start to cut him."

"Sorry Ratty. I wasn't thinking," Emerson said as he pulled out his Blackberry and scrolled to the picture icon. He selected a picture, enlarged it and showed it to Ratty. "Did he look like this guy?"

"From what I could tell, yes."

"How many people did you see?"

"There were six inside and a guard outside. He had a shotgun. I sneaked around some boats in cradles and was able to get by him and look in the window."

"Could you draw the layout of the building and grounds?" Mad Dog had picked up a stick and handed it to Ratty.

Taking the stick as the group crowded around him, Ratty drew a rough outline in the sand. "Here's how it's set up." He continued sketching. "They'd get real suspicious if they see a bunch of trucks pull up in front."

"You did," Mad Dog pointed out.

"No, I parked over here by another warehouse and sneaked through here." He pointed to his circuitous route.

"What's over here, Ratty?" Emerson asked.

"That's the canal from the North Sound."

"That's our way in," Emerson pronounced.

"Huh?"

"Yeah, Everyone knows you, Ratty. We'll come in from the water. The noise from your boat will help distract their attention on the canal side of the building." Emerson quickly outlined his plan.

"That just might work," Mad Dog said as the others nodded their heads.

"It better work," Emerson said with an air of determination. "Let's load up."

The men picked up the small arsenal of weapons and marched to Ratty's nearby boat as the sky began to darken. A storm was brewing in more ways than one.

Clarke's Warehouse
One Hour Later

"Just be ready for me when we get there," Clarke's voice ordered through the radio. He had just boarded his boat to make the trip from Morgan's Harbour across the North Sound to the warehouse. "You have the tools?"

Simpson, the Jamaican in charge of Clarke's men at the warehouse, allowed a thin smile to cross his mouth as he glanced back at the two chainsaws below the dangling Duncan. "Yes, boss," he replied as it thundered outside and lightning flashed. "We're ready for you."

"I'll be there shortly," Clarke said before signing off the radio and peering through the tropical downpour, which had just started. The brunt of the storm was passing over Morgan's Harbour and veering to the northeast.

Simpson walked out of the small office and to the work area where his victim was hanging. He picked up the electric cattle prod, which they had been using off and on over the last 24 hours as they tortured Duncan. Simpson walked over to Duncan and jabbed the prod at the base of Duncan's neck. "Still with us?"

Duncan opened his eyes and glared at Simpson. His body was weak from the physical abuse he had endured, but his inner spirit remained strong. "I'll still be with us for a lot longer than you ever will, chump!" He virtually spit out the last word.

"Still got some fight in you?" Simpson asked as he ran the end of the cattle prod across Duncan's bare chest and stopped over his heart. "I could turn up the power and touch you right here," he said perversely. "Just think what the effect would be on your heart!"

He trailed the edge of the prod down to the waist of Duncan's slacks. "Take these off him." He ordered one of the men who had been watching Simpson.

The man moved quickly and began to undo Duncan's belt. When he did, Duncan quickly brought his knee up and connected with the man's groin, causing the man to fall to the floor in pain.

Just as quickly, Simpson switched on the cattle prod and applied it to Duncan's knee before Duncan could react. Duncan yelled and twitched violently from the pain.

"The three of you, take his pants off," Simpson ordered two nearby men and the one who had recovered from the groin kick. Duncan fought them as well as he could, but he was no match for the three Jamaicans.

"His shorts, too," Simpson said as he anticipated using the prod on Duncan's privates.

As the men prepared to tousle with Duncan again, the outside guard stepped in the doorway from the light rain and shouted, "We've got company. Boat coming down the canal."

Simpson looked at his watch. It was too soon for Clarke's arrival. "It's not Clarke. Do you know who it is?" he asked as he dropped the cattle prod on the floor and pulled out a .45 from his belt. "Let him go," he said to his men as he began walking toward the door.

"Looks like Ratty's boat," the outside guard responded.

"What in the hell is he doing over here?"

All of his men grabbed their weapons and began following Simpson to the door. As the one Jamaican walked by the dangling Duncan, he suddenly jabbed his rifle butt into Duncan's exposed kidney. "Payback," the Jamaican sniggered quietly as a loud moan escaped Duncan's lips.

"What's going on back there?" Simpson asked as he looked over his shoulder.

"Nothing. He's just a wimp," the Jamaican said as he caught up to Simpson.

"Everybody stay here. Go see what he wants and send him away," Simpson directed the outside guard.

The guard walked through the gentle rain and approached the slowing boat. As he walked, he leveled his shotgun toward the boat's stern.

Minutes before and using the rain to obscure visibility, Emerson, Mad Dog, Foster, Rothman, and Rice armed with shotguns along with Big Foot and his sledge hammer slipped aboard a moored boat when Ratty slowed the *Sea Dog* and brought it abeam of the other craft.

Once his passengers had disembarked, Ratty and Reid Dennis continued down the canal toward the warehouse.

Meanwhile, Emerson and his team of rescuers ran furtively from the moored boat to the rear of an empty building, which was next to Clarke's warehouse. They slowly edged their way along the rear wall to the edge of the building where Emerson stopped them.

"Guys," he cautioned as he looked at his wet team, "we have to do this as quietly as possible. We don't need anyone turning around and firing a bullet into Sam."

The team murmured their understanding.

"If you see someone point a weapon in Sam's direction. Take him out without hesitation."

"Got it," Mad Dog said, speaking for the entire group.

"Okay, let's get over to the building." Emerson turned and began to head to Clarke's warehouse when he stopped and pushed the group back. "Wait!"

"What's wrong?" Rice asked.

"There's another guard. He's patrolling the backside of the building."

Mad Dog peered around Emerson and saw the guard. He was walking with his head down in the rain. In his hand, he was carrying an AK-47. Mad Dog pulled back and looked at the group. "I want that 47!"

"Then, go get it!" Emerson responded to his ex-SEAL friend.

A smile crossed Mad Dog's face as he turned and waited for the guard to turn and walk in the other direction. When the guard turned, Mad Dog dashed after him. As he ran, he counted on the rain to mask the noise of his approach. It almost worked.

He was within 10 feet of the guard when the guard stopped abruptly. He thought he had heard a noise. He turned and seeing something out of the corner of his eye, began to raise his AK-47. When he faced Mad Dog, he saw a wild-eyed man with a fierce grin on his face, barreling down on him. Before he could react, Mad Dog tackled him and he dropped the AK-47 in the mud.

The two rolled in the mud as they fought. The guard was able to roll free of Mad Dog and began to reach for his weapon. Mad Dog, who had bounded to his feet, stepped up and gave him a sidekick in the ribs, splintering two ribs. When the guard groaned and rose to his knees, Mad Dog charged in again with a kick to the man's crotch, which sent his privates up to his lungs. As the man doubled over, Mad Dog completed his mission with a knee to the man's face. The man crumpled unconscious to the muddy ground.

Bending over to pick up the AK-47, Mad Dog quipped, "Every day above the ground is a good day!"

He turned and saw that the rest of the team had crossed the open space while he was subduing the guard. He saw Emerson was fidgeting with the locked door to the warehouse. Thinking quickly, Mad Dog bent over the guard and searched his pockets. He found a set of keys, which he carried over to Emerson.

"These might help," he snickered.

Taking the keys and inserting them one at a time until he heard a click, Emerson said, "Enjoy your brouhaha?"

"Oh yes. Reminded me of the time a jealous husband came up on the Round House stage and I had to kick his..."

"Later." Emerson cut him off as he slowly opened the door. He looked inside and saw stacks of boxed goods, some nearly reaching the ceiling.

"Let's go in quietly and take them out quietly," he reminded the team. "We've got to protect Sam. If everything goes right with Ratty, we should have this over shortly."

On the canal, everything was going according to plan. When the guard approached the slowing boat, he yelled, "This is private property. You need to move out of here."

"I can't. This lady's husband is sick. Yous need to help her," Ratty called from the helm as he nudged the *Sea Dog* against the dock.

The guard's attention was drawn to the tall, beautiful Caymanian woman, who was emerging from below deck.

"Can you help me?" Keisha purred as she looked at the guard with her big brown eyes.

The guard caught his breath as he saw the woman. He glanced back at the building and signaled that he was going on board, and not waiting for a response, he followed the woman below.

"He's in there," she said as she pointed to the bow cabin and stepped aside. She allowed her body to brush against the wet guard's body as he moved into the cabin. She knew how to disarm men.

The guard saw someone on the berth and approached him. As he got close, the figure on the bed moaned and rolled over. The guard suddenly found himself staring into the twin barrels of a sawed-off shotgun held by Reid Dennis.

"I wouldn't think about doing anything sudden-like. I have a very itchy finger on the trigger," Dennis said as Keisha took the guard's weapon from his hands.

"Nice job, Keisha," Dennis said as he smiled to himself at his idea of having her join them on their rescue attempt. She was great eye candy and no man could resist her.

"Any time, Mr. Reid. Any time." She flashed her winning smile at him as she pushed the guard to a sitting position on the deck.

From the warehouse doorway, Simpson fumed as his outside guard disappeared below deck without waiting for approval. He was watching Ratty, who did his best to stay within Simpson's sight. He didn't want them to get nervous and charge the boat. He glanced around to make sure that his shotgun was in easy reach.

As he watched the outside guard descend below deck, Simpson swore and said to his men, who were gathered nearby, "I don't like this." He turned to the Jamaican who was kicked by Duncan. "I want you to go inside and be ready to kill Duncan when I tell you to."

The Jamaican grinned as he willingly accepted his assignment. "My pleasure." He began to walk toward Duncan.

"Not a scratch on him unto I tell you to. Is that clear?" Simpson asked.

"Yes. Not until you tell me too," the Jamaican replied.

"You two, go find places to hide in here in case there's trouble. The rest of you stay with me," Simpson said as he turned his attention back to the *Sea Dog*.

From their hiding places, Emerson and his team watched the two guards find hiding places. The first guard walked near Emerson, who stepped out from behind a stack of boxes and knocked the guard unconscious with his shotgun butt.

Across the building, the other guard met the same fate when Big Foot's sledgehammer connected with the guard's temple, killing him instantly. The noise from the rain falling on the roof aided in masking any sounds caused by the actions on the two guards.

Emerson moved closer to Mad Dog. "That one by Sam is going to be difficult."

"I'll say." Mad Dog's eye swept from Duncan to his guard to the three men at the door, looking at the *Sea Dog*.

"We need a break," Emerson said.

They got it.

From the doorway, Simpson called in to the guard next to Duncan. "Watch him! We're going to see what's going on."

"This one isn't going anywhere," the guard called as he glared at Duncan.

"We'll be right back." Simpson and the other two, with their weapons leveled, exited the building and approached the *Sea Dog*.

"Got to move fast," Mad Dog said as he handed his AK-47 to Emerson. "Be careful. The safety is off," he grinned as he began to approach Duncan's guard from the rear. Emerson quickly followed him.

From where he dangled, Duncan saw Mad Dog and Emerson surreptitiously making their way toward the guard. When the guard began to turn around, Duncan diverted his attention back to him as he yelled at him, "Next time you get close to me, I'm going to slit your throat and watch your blood pump out of you."

His plan worked. It worked a little too well as the Jamaican struck a glancing blow at Duncan's head with his shotgun butt. "I should off you right now. I'll just tell Simpson that you tried to escape. Besides, I owe you."

Duncan shook his head to recover from the blow. His plan was working. The Jamaican's attention was entirely focused on Duncan and Duncan could see his two friends moving in. "What do you mean you owe me?"

"One of the men you killed at your trailer in Key West was my brother." He raised the gun butt in preparation of striking Duncan again. The shotgun was ripped out of his hands from behind by Mad Dog and passed to Emerson.

Mad Dog reached down and grabbed the top of the man's head with one hand, placing his other forearm under the man's neck and tilting the head backwards so he could look into the man's eyes.

"You shouldn't have hit him like that."

The man's eyes bulged in fear as Mad Dog rotated his forearm upward from the elbow, levering the man's jaw while keeping a tight grip on the top of the man's head. In a moment a resounding crack was heard from the man's neck. His bulging eyes receded and went blank. As his bowels released, the air was filled with a repugnant odor.

"You stink," Mad Dog observed as he let the lifeless body drop.

The rest of the team appeared and assisted in releasing Duncan from the chains.

"You okay?" Emerson asked his friend as Foster and Rice supported Duncan. The blood surged through him as he tried to stand.

"Oh, man. I hurt so bad that my shadow hurts," Duncan said as he took a few wobbly steps.

"Thanks, guys." Duncan said as he flexed his stretched arms. He looked toward the spot where Emerson had been standing and saw that he was gone. "Hey, where's Emerson?"

Emerson had run to the doorway and saw the men approaching the *Sea Dog*. He saw one of the guards begin to board the *Sea Dog* and saw Ratty tuck and roll as he grabbed his shotgun. Ratty fired at the boarder, killing him.

Before Simpson and the remaining guard could fire, Emerson yelled, "Drop your weapons!"

When the two turned and pointed their weapons at Emerson, Emerson pulled the trigger on the AK-47, sending a spray of bullets at the two. They both dropped to the ground as the bullets penetrated their bodies.

"Hey, what's the racket out here?" Mad Dog asked as the rest of the group with Duncan in tow emerged from the warehouse.

The firing of the AK-47 carried down the canal to Clarke's boat, which was now reversing its engines and backing out of the canal. Clarke was on the radio, but no one was responding from the warehouse. Clarke feared the worst and ordered the craft back to his estate. His mind began working overtime as to the consequences, which he might face.

"They wouldn't listen," Emerson said. "Nice weapon you've got there," he said to Mad Dog as he handed the AK-47 back to him.

"You did that? I'm impressed," Duncan said as he surveyed the two bodies. Rice and Foster were helping him walk.

"Now what?" Mad Dog asked.

"I'd suggest that we get out of here before the police come," Emerson said.

"Or Clarke," Duncan added "He was on his way over here. I heard him on the radio. Probably to kill me."

Emerson turned to Duncan. "You've got some explaining to do, my friend."

"Glad to. Once we're on board."

Suddenly Mad Dog shouted, "Down Emerson!"

Big Foot saw it too and jumped behind Emerson. The bullet struck him in the back of the head as he fell. Mad Dog opened fire with the AK-47 and killed Simpson, who wasn't quite dead. He had got off one shot at Emerson.

"My mistake," Mad Dog lamented. "I should have made sure that he was dead."

The rest of them were gathered around Big Foot, but there was nothing they could do. He was dead.

"Big Foot was my friend," Foster said he as he stood over him. "We grew up together here," he added.

"Good man," Rice concurred.

"I'm sorry. I should have checked myself," Emerson was mad at himself.

"It was his time," Foster said stoically as he led the men in transporting Big Foot on board. "We'll take him home."

"That's not good," Dennis' voice came from the cockpit where he stood with his captive and Keisha.

"The plan worked pretty well," Emerson said.

"Yeah, especially with my idea to bring Keisha along. Nice work, girl!" Dennis grinned as the beautiful barmaid smiled back at her boss. When Reid had called her at the bar, she had driven quickly to the marina to join them on their rescue mission.

Ratty interrupted, "If yous don't mind, we better be getting out of here."

"Sounds good to me," Emerson agreed as Ratty turned the craft around in the canal and pointed it toward the North Sound.

They were barely 100 yards down the canal when a figure stepped from a car. He walked through the dwindling rain to the bodies on the dock. After seeing the bodies, he entered the warehouse and looked at the bodies strewn inside. Messy, he thought to himself.

As he passed the small office, he heard a voice on the radio. It was trying to contact Simpson.

"Simpson, are you there?"

Getting no answer, the voice repeated itself. "Simpson, are you there?"

Smiling, the man recognized Clarke's voice. He walked to the radio and pressed the mic key. "It's over." He replaced the mic and turned off the radio. Chuckling to himself as he imagined the consternation on Clarke's face. He pulled a handkerchief from his pocket and wiped off his fingerprints from the mic and the on/off knob.

Seeing a phone on a nearby desk, he walked over to it and picked it up. He dialed police headquarters and reported gunshots at the warehouse. Quickly he wiped off his fingerprints on the phone's handset and placed the handset in the cradle. He walked out of the warehouse and back to his vehicle.

Getting into his vehicle, he drove off. He didn't want to be discovered on the premises when the police arrived. Or it could raise questions that he didn't want to answer.

Superintendent Fleming turned right after exiting and drove toward George Town. He felt like the puzzle master. He'd only give out the pieces when he thought it'd be necessary. No one would see the entire puzzle assembled, but himself. At least for now. He drove on with a growing smile on his face.

The Sea Dog
North Sound

Only a few minutes had elapsed since the *Sea Dog* had left the rescue scene and entered the North Sound. The rain had ceased and the sun was setting in the western skies.

Emerson was the first to turn to Duncan, looking for answers. "Okay Sam, you owe us an explanation. How did you end up in that warehouse and what were you doing with Clarke?"

"It's a long story, but I'll try to give you the *Reader's Digest* version," Duncan responded as he took the shot of whiskey from Keisha and downed it. "Thanks, Keisha. I'd like another," he smiled.

Keisha refilled his shot glass and handed it back to him. Duncan threw it down quickly as the others waited for his story.

"It started about a year ago. I had an assignment to help bust a drug ring in Jamaica. It was run by Pryce Clarke from what I could tell, but I couldn't tie him directly to it. He was smart. Ran his transactions through several intermediaries and hid his involvement. And when you arrested his men, they wouldn't talk."

"Arrested? You were arresting people?" Mad Dog interrupted.

"No, not really. It was a joint law enforcement effort. I was just there as an advisor."

Mad Dog nodded his head.

"We seemed to be making headway with our investigation. We had several witnesses to help our case, but then that all changed. They all died suddenly. Then, our liaison with the Jamaican police department died."

"Somebody took them out?" Emerson asked.

"Exactly." Duncan held his shot glass up for a refill and Keisha obliged. Before continuing, Duncan threw it down. Smacking his lips, he said, "That hit the spot!"

Reid Dennis called out, "Geez Keisha, that's enough of that free stuff. Start charging him."

The group tittered at the crusty bar owner's comment.

"We suspected Clarke, but again couldn't prove it. The probe was put on hold and I returned to Key West. Emerson knows this next part, but I'll update the rest of you. I had two Jamaican assassins break into my home. I got them before they could get me. Then my good friend here," he looked at Emerson, "invited me to join him in the Cayman Islands. It was an opportunity for me to be near the lion's den."

"So that's why you were disappearing so much? You were checking out Clarke?" Emerson asked.

"Yes, to an extent. It was on my little side trip to Jamaica that things went wrong."

"Oh?"

"I went over there unofficially, so to speak, to see what I could piece together quietly without anyone knowing what I was up to. I was watching them load one of those Jamaican canoes when I was surprised by two of his men. It was as if they were waiting for me to appear."

When Duncan saw Emerson nodding his head as if he knew something, Duncan asked, "Okay, what gives. What do you know?"

"You said you went over there unofficially?"

"Right."

"But didn't you meet with Superintendent Fleming here?"

Duncan paused before speaking. "Yes. How did you know that?"

"He told me."

Everyone's attention shifted to Emerson.

"That was confidential," Duncan responded with consternation.

"He shouldn't have told me then, right?" Emerson didn't wait for Duncan's response. "Ever think he might have told other people?"

"What are you getting at?"

"I think he's dirty. I think he's either working for Clarke or trying to take over Clarke's business."

Duncan was quiet. He was thinking about Emerson's supposition.

"How well do you know him?" Emerson probed.

"I barely know the man."

"All I know is that Clarke seems to be getting tipped off and I believe it's Fleming doing the tipping. He tried to tell me it was his secretary, but I'm not sure that I'm buying into that story." Emerson then related the incidents with Percy's death, the failed attempt on Ratty and himself before talking about the death of Denise at Cayman Kai.

"I tell you that you're wrong," Dennis spoke up. "I've known the man for the last two years and he's straight. You're wrong on this one, Emerson."

"Time will tell, Reid."

"You ought to question the guard we locked up below." Dennis was still fuming. "He might give you some information."

"I'll get him," Foster volunteered as he stood and descended below deck.

"And I'll help him talk," Ratty said as he throttled back on the engines and allowed them to idle as the boat bobbed gently in the sound.

Foster returned, pushing the guard in front of him. The guard was still wet from the rain and tripped as he walked onto the deck. He went sprawling and slid into the middle of the group. Ratty appeared magically at his side and bent over the guard. His knife was in his hand. Foster and Rice quickly pinned the guard so that he couldn't squirm away.

Ratty looked up at Emerson and said, "Yous asks him the questions. I'll make sure he answers." Having said that, Ratty pricked the guard's face with the tip of the knife's blade. A small trickle of blood appeared and made its way down the nervous guard's face.

"E, I'd like to ask the questions if you don't mind. This one is the one who captured me in Jamaica. He brought me back here," Duncan said as he edged closer to the guard.

"Sure, go ahead," Emerson urged.

Turning to the guard, Duncan posed his first question. "We know Clarke is behind all of the drug running here. Where does he stash the drugs?"

The guard said nothing.

"I'm going to ask you one more time, where does Clarke stash the drugs?"

The guard didn't respond.

But after a moment, Ratty responded. "I think maybe he is deaf. I fix that." He grabbed the guard's hair and pulled his head to the side, exposing the guard's right ear. "Hmmm, just as I thought. Yous ear looks blocked. I'll just stick my knife in here and sees if I can make it better for yous."

The guard began to twist and jerk, but Foster and Rice restrained him in their viselike grips. Ratty began to insert the sharp tip of his knife in the guard's ear, pricking it as it slid in. It didn't have to go in far before the guard began to scream.

"Stop! Stop! I'll tell you what you want to know!"

Ratty withdrew the blade and sat back. He had a grin on his face as he turned to face Duncan. "They always talk for me!"

Duncan smiled back and turned to the guard. "Answer my question."

The guard's words rushed out like a torrent. "There are two safe houses. One is in the East End. The other in West Bay."

"I want the addresses."

"Keisha, give us a hand here," Dennis said to his barmaid. "Write this down for us, okay sweetie?"

Keisha answered by grabbing a nearby notebook and pen. She was ready to write.

"Tell her," Duncan said sternly.

The guard provided the addresses to Keisha.

Duncan continued. "Now, where does Clarke keep the cash?"

The guard shook his head from side to side.

"Having a reoccurrence of that hearing loss?" Duncan asked as he glanced at Ratty and nodded his head. Ratty approached the guard. His knife was pointed toward the guard's ear.

"No, I don't know."

Emerson interrupted. "Sam, if he's on the ground in Jamaica, he might not spend time here. He wouldn't know."

"Is that true?" Duncan asked.

"He's right," the cowering guard responded. "I help make the deliveries here and oversee some of the crop growing in Jamaica."

Ratty pointed his knife at his ear again.

The guard screamed. "That's the truth. I can't change that!"

Ratty sat back. "What he says is true. I can tell this."

"You're not going to get much from him," Emerson said. "But I have a question for him."

"Go ahead, E," Duncan urged.

Turning to the guard, Emerson asked, "What's going on in Boatswain's Bay?"

Clarke's Estate
Morgan's Harbour

Seething with anger since hearing the gunfire and getting the cryptic radio message, Clarke had been turning the evening's events over in his mind. All he could piece together was that something of catastrophic proportions had occurred. And whatever it was, it did not bode well for him. It was time for him to take evasive action and lie low. He'd make one more trip to Boatswain's Bay and then head to a safe house he owned in Jamaica and ride out the storm.

His wrath had exploded after the radio message, sending his three crew members scurrying for cover. Clarke's temper had a tendency to translate into physical harm to those in his immediate vicinity. His bloodlust was well known.

"Ten minutes, I want both boats ready to go with fresh tanks," he yelled as he bounded off the boat when it bumped against the estate's pier. As his men rushed to complete their tasks, he walked rapidly toward the house, barking orders as he went. He needed to retrieve his computer's hard drive and the papers he had hidden in a wall safe behind the mahogany paneling in his study.

Clarke burst through the French doors and strode down the hallway to the study. As he walked, he hit speed dial on his cell phone. The phone on the other end rang six times, before it was answered.

"Yes?" a voice answered unhurriedly.

"I need to lease a large boat to transport some of my merchandise."

The voice on the other end perked up at the opportunity to make a handsome profit for what sounded like an emergency lease from Clarke. It wasn't the first time that the two had brokered deals.

"Of course, Pryce. I would be more than happy to accommodate you."

Clarke didn't like what he was sensing. It sounded like this time he would have to pay an exorbitant fee. His sense would soon prove accurate.

"Where are you going?" the voice asked in order to determine the size of vessel which would be necessary.

"I'm running a large load to Kingston. I'll need something over 50 feet and I'll need it for a few days."

"I think I have just what you want. Where should I deliver it."

"To my pier at the house. I need it now!" he demanded.

Seeing further opportunity to take advantage of Clarke, the voice said, "There's an extra charge for rush service."

Clarke unleashed a series of expletives in response. He was in no mood to play negotiating games.

"Temper. Temper. Talking to me like that might cause a delay as I try to find someone to deliver it to you."

Realizing that he wasn't in the driver's seat on this transaction, Clarke chilled. "Okay. Let's just get this done and now. What's the damage?"

The voice on the other end responded, doubling what he was originally going to charge. "$50,000."

"$50,000! You're out of your freaking mind! I'm not paying $50,000."

"Good-bye."

The phone clicked on the other end.

Entering his study, Clarke found it difficult to contain his rage. He picked up a small statue on his desk and threw it through the front window, shattering glass onto the ground outside. He stormed to the wall and opened the secret panel. He spun the dial on the wall safe and quickly opened it. Inside were the papers he needed as well as stacks of bills. He picked up his cell phone and redialed.

The phone on the other end was answered on the first ring. The voice asked, "Change your mind?"

"I'll pay your frigging $50,000."

"Oh, I am sorry. There's been a slight price increase."

Clarke bit his tongue. He was ready to lash out again, but realized that it would be futile. "How much?"

"It's the law of supply and demand. It's $100,000 now," the voice said calmly.

"All right. Bill me!" Clarke fumed.

"No, cash in advance."

"How?"

"Have one of your men deliver the cash to my office. I'll send the vessel to your place, but will have them stand off until I receive and count the money. Then, the vessel is yours. Deal?"

"Deal!" Clarke continued to storm inside.

"I'll be waiting."

Before Clarke could respond, the phone line went dead. Clarke started to slam his cell phone against the wall, but realized he might need it before the night was over. He reached into the safe and pulled out $100,000 in bundled bills. He placed the money in a briefcase and locked it. Then, he had one of his trusted men join him in his office.

He handed the briefcase and key to the man and gave him detailed instructions on making the delivery immediately. The man acknowledged Clarke's instructions and left to fulfill them.

Island Boat Leasing
The North Sound

What Clarke didn't know was that the man from whom he had just leased the boat was now placing his own call. He saw an opportunity to make more money on the transaction.

"Fleming here," the phone answered.

The voice on the other end spoke. "I have a piece of information which you might be interested in."

"Oh?" Fleming responded as he recognized the voice.

"I trust that it's worth something to you."

"Depends."

"It's about Pryce Clarke," the voice teased.

"I'm interested."

"I thought you would be." The voice paused to build up Fleming's anticipation. "It'll cost you $25,000 and one stipulation."

"What's the stipulation?"

"You can't take any action until I meet with one of Clarke's messengers. He has something for me."

"Playing both sides again?" Fleming asked.

The voice wouldn't answer. The only response Fleming received was a chuckle.

"I thought so," Fleming said. "You let me know when you meet with the messenger and I'll honor your stipulation."

"And the $25,000?"

"That too. I'll get it to you."

"Deal?"

"Deal. Now, what's the information?"

"It appears that Mr. Pryce Clarke is under duress. He is highly stressed and must leave the Cayman Islands."

Fleming was listening closely as his eye narrowed. His plan was indeed working and much better that he could have ever hoped. Clarke was feeling the pressure.

"Where's he going?"

"Kingston. Or that's at least where he told me he wants to take the boat he just leased from me."

"What's the cargo?"

"He didn't say."

"Wouldn't be drugs. He wouldn't take the time. They're replaceable," Fleming wondered.

"My exact thoughts. But it must be something that you'd be interested in under the circumstances."

"Definitely. Thank you."

"I'll be waiting for my payment."

"I'll make sure it gets to you. Call me when I can make my move." Fleming hung up and began to plan his next steps.

The caller sat back in his chair and smiled to himself. It had been a very profitable day.

The Sea Dog
The North Sound

"I don't know," the guard responded to Emerson.

"He's on to something. Why would Clarke or his men spend so much time out there?" Duncan asked.

"I don't know," the guard repeated.

"Yous want me to see if I can make him talk the truth?" Ratty asked.

"He's telling the truth, E," Duncan interjected. "Remember he works in Jamaica and runs the drugs here. He doesn't spend time here, isn't that correct?" Duncan was staring directly at the guard.

Ratty approached him with his drawn knife. The guard, seeing it, responded quickly, "That's correct. I don't know what he's doing there!"

Emerson shook his head. "There's something going on there. I just know it."

"What do yous want us to do with this guy?" Ratty asked.

"Feed him to the sharks," Mad Dog suggested with an evil sneer on his face.

Glancing at his watch, Rice added, "Yeah, I'd say it's about feeding time."

"I don't know, he looks like he'd be tough meat," Rothman chimed in.

The guard's head was swiveling quickly around the group as the suggestions flowed. His anxiety level was rising rapidly.

"We'll take him with us," Emerson decided.

"Take him with us where?" Mad Dog asked.

"To Clarke's place, right, E?" Duncan asked.

"You got it." Turning to Ratty, he asked, "Okay with you?"

"Tonight, I do what yous want." Ratty went back to the helm and thrust the throttle forward. They were on their way to Clarke's estate.

Clarke was standing outside of his crocodile's lagoon, giving instructions to four armed men. "I want it all carried to the boat I just leased and stored aboard. Radio me when you're ready to leave and I'll give you rendezvous instructions."

Pointing to one of the men, he said, "Logan, you're in charge."

A short Jamaican with a broad chest nodded. "Okay, Mr. Clarke."

"Anything goes wrong, I'll kill you."

A shudder ran through Logan. He knew that Clarke meant business. He had seen him do it to others, who had failed in completing his orders.

Clarke left the men at their posts and strode to his waiting boats. In a few minutes, both boats were headed through the North Sound and bound for Boatswain's Bay.

Scarcely had 15 minutes elapsed when the *Sea Dog* began approaching the pier at Clarke's Estate. The pier was lit by one solitary light at its end, in contrast with the grounds of the estate, which were bathed in light.

Ratty was at the helm and Clarke's guard was on the bow. Next to the guard and with her left arm around him was Keisha. Her right hand was raised as she waved at the four men near the lagoon. In her left hand, she held a small revolver whose barrel she had firmly pressed against the guard's lower back. "Wave to them," she directed her captive. In response, he anxiously raised his left arm and waved.

Crouched in the cockpit and out of sight were the remainder of the rescuers. They were all armed and ready to overpower the four guards. The *Sea Dog* slowed as it neared the pier and the guard in charge, Logan, began to walk down the pier. Since Clarke had not told him what boat to expect, he mistakenly assumed that this was the boat they were to load.

"What are you doing on board?" Logan asked as he approached.

"Tell him something!" Keisha hissed quietly.

"I caught a ride on it," he offered weakly as Logan walked along the craft. He was keeping a watchful eye on Ratty at the helm.

Ratty smiled and waved. "Come aboard. I have a surprise for yous."

Logan brought his shotgun to bear on Ratty.

"No need for that," Ratty said as he idled the boat's engine. "Let me tie her up," he said as he jumped onto the pier next to Logan and secured the stern line to the pier.

From the bow, Keisha called to Logan, "It's a beautiful night for a swim."

Her plan to distract him worked. As Logan swung his head to look at her, Ratty moved behind him and place the tip of his knife against the base of Logan's skull as he grabbed Logan's belt at the base of his back.

"Live or die. The choice is yous."

Thinking for one brief nanosecond as the knife's blade pricked him, Logan wisely answered, "Live. What do you want me to do?"

"Call yous friends over here. Tell them yous needs help," Ratty instructed.

Nodding his head slowly in acknowledgement, Logan called out to the three men at the lagoon. "Come here. I need your help."

"Now, yous come with me and we go on board," Ratty said as he prodded him forward with his knife blade. Giving no resistance, Logan stepped aboard and over the bodies of the men lying on the deck with their weapons slightly raised and pointed toward the pier.

Ratty and Logan moved to the opposite side of the *Sea Dog* and stood waiting.

Mad Dog spoke as he saw Logan drop the barrel of his shotgun so that it was pointing straight down. Straight down at Mad Dog's head. "I'll just relieve you of that weapon if you don't mind. Just don't like something like that aiming at what little brains I've got left." Mad Dog took the shotgun from Logan, who relaxed his grip.

"Feel better?" asked Duncan, who was on the deck next to Mad Dog.

"Much."

The three guards walked along the pier, ogling Keisha as they walked by. She returned their looks with a flirtatious smile and a wink from her large brown eyes. The guards drew abreast of the boat and saw Logan standing without his shotgun. Before they could react and bring their weapons to bear, the men laying on the deck sat up with their weapons pointed at the three.

"Drop your weapons," Duncan ordered as the guards, with surprised looks on their faces, gazed into an arsenal of gun barrels leveled at them.

One of the guards decided to play beat the odds. It was a mistake. A fatal mistake. He fired, missing Duncan by inches. In return, the men of the *Sea Dog* retaliated with a broadside, knocking the three backwards and off the pier into the warm water.

"I guess we don't have to worry about them anymore," Duncan said as he sprang to his feet and looked toward the house to see if there were any other guards coming.

As the others stood, Emerson asked the guard, "Is there anyone else here?"

The guard didn't answer until he felt the prick of Ratty's knife. Then, he answered quickly, "No one else. They all left."

At that moment, Keisha appeared with her captive. "I'll let you guys have this one back," she said as Rice took their prisoner.

"Nice going, Keisha," Dennis said appreciatively as the others echoed his comments.

Keisha smiled demurely in return. "Thanks Reid," she commented to her boss.

"So where did everybody go?" Emerson asked Logan.

"They left." When Ratty pricked his skin with the knife blade, he decided to provide a fuller answer. "They went to Boatswain's Bay."

"And what's so special about Boatswain's Bay?'

"I don't know."

Ratty pricked him a little deeper.

"I said I don't know and I don't. They go there at night and come back in the morning. I don't know because we all have to go to the front of the house when they return. We aren't allowed to see what's going on."

"You don't go out diving with them?"

"I don't dive."

Emerson turned to Duncan. "What do you think?"

"It could be a number of things." Duncan turned to Logan. "Guys talk. Certainly the guys from the dives talk to you, don't they?"

"Not here. Mr. Clarke would cut their tongues out. He's done it before."

"You notice anything kind of funny when we came in?" Duncan asked Emerson.

"What do you mean?"

"Notice where all the guards were?"

"Up by the croc's lair?"

"Yeah. With no one around the estate, if that's true." Duncan threw a glance at Logan who nodded his head that it was true, "Then, why do they have armed guards by the crocodile enclosure?"

"Good question." Emerson looked at Logan. "Can you answer that?"

Rather than answer the question posed to him, Logan caught everyone off guard and twisted away from Ratty, who had relaxed his grip on him. He stepped up on the gunwale and dove toward the water to escape from his captives.

Before his body sliced into the water, a shotgun blast caught him in midair, driving his body sideways and changing a well-executed dive into a loud splash as it hit the water.

"I guess his gun was loaded after all," Mad Dog said as he held Logan's smoking shotgun.

"I guess that will make it a little more difficult, " Emerson said as he turned from looking at the spot where the body had sunk and began to step on the pier. "Let's go see for ourselves."

Everyone followed Emerson to the croc's enclosure.

Ratty shouted as they walked. "This Jamaican here doesn't know anything. I'm positive he'd have told me if he did." He was guarding the guard, whom they had captured at the ware-house.

"Thanks, Ratty," Emerson called as he approached the enclosure. "Looks like somebody was going to be carting something somewhere," he observed as he saw four hand trucks near the enclosure's entrance.

"Let's have a look-see," Emerson said as he opened the gate and flicked on a light switch, which turned on floodlights aimed into the enclosure. Emerson walked in, followed by Duncan, Mad Dog, and Rothman.

"Keep your eyes open in case that dead croc has a brother," Mad Dog warned as they walked through the area. They searched the lush tropical foliage without finding any hidden areas or compartments.

In a corner was a 4-foot high shelter. It was about 30 feet long and covered with corrugated steel. It had a steel-barred door, which could be raised or lowered. The door was in the raised position. The four men stared at the shelter.

"What do you think? Something in there?"

"Like the croc's brother?" Mad Dog asked again.

"What better place than there to cache valuables!" Emerson suggested.

"Well, E, let's find out then," Duncan said as he walked over to it and carefully peered inside. He was ready to jump back if a pair of croc jaws came snapping at him, but nothing happened. He dropped to his knees and looked in more closely. "I don't see anything? Anybody got a flashlight?"

"There's one in Ratty's boat. I'll get it," Foster volunteered and returned to the *Sea Dog*.

"I'll just go on in," Emerson said as he laid his shotgun against the shelter and got down on his hands and knees.

"Whoa one second," Duncan said.

"What?"

"You better take this." Duncan handed Emerson a .45 automatic.

Taking it, Emerson grinned, "Thanks." He began to crawl into the shelter as Duncan, Rothman and Mad Dog took positions near the shelter's entrance.

After a few seconds, Emerson yelled from within the shelter. "Hey, you guys can relax. There's nothing in here but bones and crocodile dung. And I've got it all over my hands and knees," he said as he crawled out of the shelter. "Let me wash this off." With that, he dove into the lagoon and began scrubbing the dung off his hands and knees.

When he surfaced, Mad Dog cautioned him one more time, "You just better be sure that that croc didn't have a brother!"

He no sooner said it that Emerson's body gave a jerk, Emerson screamed and he disappeared from the surface.

"Emerson!" Mad Dog yelled as he brought his weapon to bear on the spot where Emerson had been pulled under.

Duncan had waded into the water and was shouting, "E! E!" as he scanned the lagoon for Emerson.

Just then Emerson's body shot from the bottom of the lagoon and out of the water. When he dropped back into the water, Emerson was laughing, "Had you, didn't I?"

Mad Dog racked his shotgun. "I have half a mind to take you out for worrying us like that."

"You're right on one part of that!" Emerson chuckled.

"What do you mean?" Mad Dog growled.

"You have half a mind!" Emerson chortled before he dove again. He stayed under longer this time and when he resurfaced, his countenance had changed. He was very serious. "Hey guys. Come into the water with me. I think I just spotted something interesting."

"What? Is this a joke?" Mad Dog asked as he placed his shotgun on the ground.

"Nope. Not this time." Emerson took a deep breath and submerged. He was closely followed by Duncan, Mad Dog and Rothman.

When they found him, he was at the deepest part of the lagoon. There stacked on top of each other were roughly 200 hundred aluminum containers. Emerson pointed at one and the four of them grasped the four handles. They swam to the surface and dragged it to the beach.

"Must be something pretty valuable to go to all this work to safeguard it." Emerson said as he caught his breath.

"E, what do you mean, all this work?" Duncan asked.

"There's a drain at the bottom of this lagoon. I bet we can find a pump which drains the water out so that you can retrieve whatever you hide at the bottom."

"What about water flowing in through the pipe we swam through to get into the lagoon a few nights ago? If you try to pump this out, the water from the harbor will replace it," Mad Dog observed.

"I didn't say anything to you when we swam in that night, but I noticed a steel door on this side of the pipe. I bet they just close that door when they need to pump out the lagoon. And I'd bet that they'd lock the croc in that shelter behind that barred door." The pieces were coming together in Emerson's mind.

"Let's see what's inside." Mad Dog was anxious.

"Here's the flashlight," Foster said as he returned from the *Sea Dog*.

"Don't need it now," Emerson said as he tried to open the container, which was locked. "I need a hammer and chisel."

"Got the hammer," Foster said as he walked into the enclosure. He was carrying Big Foot's sledgehammer. "Thought I'd bring it up here just in case anyone might need it," he smiled as he handed the hammer to Emerson.

"Let me try first," Duncan said as he produced a pocketknife.

"Where did you come up with that?" Emerson asked.

"Found it on the *Sea Dog*. I just borrowed it for a bit."

Duncan went to work on the lock with the knife blade. Watching Duncan work the lock reminded Emerson of the time a few years ago when Duncan and he had broken into the Stone Lab on Gibraltar Island and Duncan had picked a lock and cracked the safe. He smiled as he watched his friend at work.

"Got it!" Duncan exclaimed as the lock turned. He opened the container and inside were gold bars.

"Whoa! Where do you think these came from?" Duncan said as he gazed upon the bars.

Emerson guessed, "I'll bet that Clarke has stumbled on a virtual gold mine. Must be a shipwreck. And judging by the quality of the container, it didn't happen that long ago."

The others crowded in to take a peek.

"And what a great place to secure this. The bottom of a lagoon guarded by a croc! No one is going to venture in there to look!" Emerson said in awe.

"What's next, gang?" Mad Dog asked.

"I'd still like to see what Clarke is up to. Why don't the four of us head over to DiveTech and borrow some equipment, then swim out and investigate?"

"Sounds good to me," Duncan agreed as Rothman and Mad Dog nodded their heads.

"Ratty, why don't you and the others stand guard here the rest of the night and we can figure out what we need to do with this gold in the morning?"

"Okay."

"Reid, put that bar back," Emerson said as Dennis extracted one of the bars from the container.

"I just wanted a souvenir," he whined as he teased Emerson and replaced the bar in the container.

"Planning on an addition for your bar?"

"It'd help," the mischievous bar-owner said with a twinkle in his eye.

"We'll need a vehicle," Rothman said.

"Follow me." Emerson responded as he headed toward the garage. "I remember seeing a couple of vehicles in the garage when I was here the first time. He led the three to the garage's back door and tried the door handle. It was unlocked. He opened the door and turned on the light switch.

"There's our wheels," Emerson said nonchalantly.

As the rest of the group walked into the garage, they marveled at the vehicle in front of them. It was Clarke's silver Bentley. From the day he bought it, Clarke had babied the car, keeping it spotless and well waxed.

"Let's go cruising," Duncan said as he walked to the car, opened the door and sat in the left front seat. The others piled into the back as Emerson commented, "I need to make a call."

He walked over to the wall phone and called DiveTech, waking Nancy and Jay. He explained that he needed to borrow equipment right away and that he'd tell them more when he got there. They agreed to help him and said they'd have everything ready for him when he arrived.

Emerson replaced the receiver on the wall and walked to the car. Sitting behind the steering wheel, he saw that the keys were in the car.

"It's an adjustment driving on the other side of the road, isn't it?" Duncan said as he watched Emerson quickly scanning the instrument panel and locating switches. He found the headlight switch and turned them on.

"Always," he said as he started the luxurious car and listened to it purr. He then began looking for the garage door opener. Duncan helped.

When they couldn't spot it, Duncan volunteered, "I'll get out and open it."

"Hang on one second," Emerson said. "I have a better idea. Hang on!" He shifted the car into drive and slammed his foot on the accelerator.

A second later, the tranquil evening was interrupted as Clarke's pampered Bentley crashed through the garage door, sending debris flying through the air and causing numerous scratches and dents to the vehicle's pristine exterior.

As the car hurled forward, its jovial occupants were screaming wildly.

From the back seat Rothman yelled, "Way to go, Emerson!" and Mad Dog added, "It's about time you loosened up a bit, Emerson!"

Duncan, who had braced his arms against the dashboard, relaxed them and commented with a smug look, "That's my boy, E! That had to feel good for you!"

From the back, Mad Dog interjected, "Was it as good for you as it was for me?"

Duncan howled and Rothman chuckled as Emerson grinned, "All I can say is that the accelerator stuck!"

The Bentley turned right at the next intersection as it went quickly to DiveTech. Because of their turn, the Bentley's occupants just missed seeing three black cars driving at a high rate of speed toward Clarke's estate. The cars' passengers were wearing black garb and heavily armed.

DiveTech
Off Boatswain's Bay

The damaged Bentley pulled to a stop in front of the Cobalt Coast Dive Resort and discharged its occupants.

Looking at the vehicle as he stepped out, Duncan quipped, "Ought to put a sign in the window. 'For sale. Special scratch and dent price'." He chuckled at his feeble joke when he noticed that the other three weren't laughing. "Gee, doesn't anyone have a sense of humor?"

"Not tonight, my friend," Emerson replied as the three men raced through the hotel lobby and past the swimming pool. As they approached the DiveTech office, Emerson pointed offshore. "There they are!"

His three companions cast glances seaward and saw two fishing boats at anchor.

"They're in for a surprise tonight," Duncan smiled.

"Hi, Nancy," Emerson called as they neared the office. They could see that Nancy and Jay had been busy. Tanks filled with Trimix and underwater gear had been assembled for their use.

"You two have been busy! " Emerson observed. "How you two did this on short notice is beyond me!"

"It's just because we like you," Nancy teased.

"Four underwater scooters are already at the end of the dock," Jay offered.

"Thanks guys," Emerson said as he and the three others began stripping to their shorts and pulling on gear.

"It's Clarke, isn't it?" Nancy asked pensively.

Emerson looked directly into her eyes. He couldn't mislead her. "Yes, I think we're on to something big."

"Need help?" she asked eagerly. "You did last time."

"And I thanked you for it."

"You better not, Nancy," Duncan interrupted. "We need you as part of the rescue team if this falls apart on us."

Nancy's brow furrowed. "I don't think I like where this is heading."

Emerson caught her attention. "If it makes you feel better, why don't you give me your homing device and I'll slip it in my pocket."

"That would be better," she smiled weakly. She still wasn't at all happy how this was going down. She walked into the office and reappeared momentarily with the homing device. "Here you go, Emerson." She handed the device to Emerson.

"Thanks, Nancy," Emerson said as he turned to his suited teammates. "Let's roll."

Carrying their fins, the four began to walk to the end of the pier and to their waiting scooters as Nancy and Jay leaned against the office wall and watched.

About 20 minutes had elapsed since Emerson and his three diving friends had departed the estate. Dennis was getting antsy, just standing next to the container of gold. He decided to take a look at the two pools by the patio. He laid down his shotgun and took a stroll.

"That looks interesting," Dennis said as he wandered over to Clarke's built in aquarium with its artificial reef. Foster, Rice and Keisha had walked over with him, leaving Ratty with their prisoner. "Look at that sea life."

"Yes, look at it!" an approaching voice called.

The four of them looked toward its source and saw Fleming walking toward them. Behind him were 12 tough-looking men, dressed in black and holding semi-automatic weapons. The weapons were pointed at the four.

"Ratty, drop your weapon," Fleming ordered. "We wouldn't want any accidents to happen now would we?"

Ratty quickly took in the odds and the potential risk to his four friends. He dropped his weapon.

"That's the way. And what do we have over here?" Fleming asked as he spied the open container. He briskly walked to the container, kicking Ratty's weapon away as he walked by. Stopping at the container and seeing the gold bars, Fleming murmured, "This is better than I expected."

"Derek, what's the meaning of all this? I thought we were friends," Dennis began to fume.

Abruptly, Fleming spun around to face Dennis. He reached into his pocket as he did.

Approaching Clarke's Boats
Boatswain's Bay

The hum of the generators on Clarke's boats sounded almost deafening and it was hard to tell underwater just how close they were to the boats. Seeing Emerson stop his scooter, the others stopped theirs and then joined Emerson at the surface to survey how close they were to Clarke's boats. They could see a crew at work with the winches and apparently loading one boat, which was sitting much lower in the water than the other.

"We'll have to be careful now. Remember, no lights," Emerson cautioned the others before sinking below the surface to continue his journey. The others followed.

As they neared Clarke's boats, they saw the glow of work lights deep below. Emerson decided to investigate and began his descent, followed by the others. Their descent took them to 140 feet and Emerson paused as he saw where Clarke and his crew were working.

In front of him and on a ledge was a sunken shipwreck; much different than the little boat Clarke had taken him to in his attempt to stage Emerson's "accidental" death.

Seeing a smoke stack and steel superstructure, Emerson gauged the age of the ship to be somewhere in the mid 1900s. He guessed she was a freighter and about 500 feet in length. Through the light he saw several pieces of armament. Then, Emerson saw something below her waterline, which raised his curiosity to a higher level.

As he looked over the deck, he saw that Clarke's divers were focused on their work. The ship's cargo covers were opened and Clarke and his team were swarming over it like an army of ants. They were transporting containers from the cargo hold to the deck where they deposited them in waiting cargo nets. The nets were then being winched to Clarke's boat by the surface crew. They certainly were not expecting visitors to their dive site, especially at this time of night.

Watching them load the containers, Emerson wondered if the containers held gold since they appeared similar to the ones at the crocodile's lagoon. Turning, Emerson motioned to Rothman to join him and signaled Mad Dog and Duncan to remain where they were. He had them hold their two scooters so they could approach this wreck in a quieter fashion.

Carefully, Emerson and Rothman dropped down and then swam toward the ship's bow. As they approached it, Emerson's eyes widened. There in front of him were two torpedo tubes. When he took these in consideration along with the deck armament, it appeared to Emerson that this was a World War II German surface raider.

Excitedly, he turned to Rothman, who had already drawn the same conclusion and was nodding his head. This was probably the mother ship for the wrecked Henkel seaplane. They would learn later that is was the *Achilles*.

What Emerson didn't know was that Clarke had been mining this underwater treasure vault for the last several weeks. The load this night was the last of it.

Emerson and Rothman returned to Duncan and Mad Dog. With his back to the sunken raider, Emerson wrote a message on his dive slate for Duncan and Mad Dog. He flashed a small underwater penlight on it so that they could read it. It read: *Sunken German Raider. Stealing treasure.*

Duncan and Mad Dog nodded their heads in understanding.

Wiping the underwater slate clean, Emerson wrote another message and showed them. It read: *Go to surface. Commandeer their boats.*

In the faint light, Emerson saw smiles break out on the faces of Duncan and Mad Dog. It was action time! They nodded their heads as Emerson wrote one more message. It read: *Lure two divers to surface.*

They both gave an okay sign as Emerson wrote one final message. *Good luck!*

They acknowledged it with a smile and nods, and handed the extra scooters back to Emerson and Rothman. But before the pair ascended, Rothman got their attention and pointed to the Forespar WL-1 floating strobe water light and reel hanging from his BC. Duncan and Mad Dog nodded their heads to show that they understood that Rothman would deploy it, if necessary, to mark their position.

Mad Dog and Duncan commenced their ascent as Emerson and Rothman turned around to watch the activity below as they waited for their plan to take shape.

Since Mad Dog and Duncan had not been down at the 130-foot depth for an extended period of time, they would only need a 3-minute safety stop at 15 feet. Once that was completed, Duncan and Mad Dog surfaced near the bobbing vessels. They pulled their masks down to their necks to get a clearer look at the two boats.

"How many are there?" Mad Dog asked.

"Two from what I can see," Duncan answered. "And they're just on the one boat. It doesn't look like they're loading anything on the other."

"Too bad."

"Too bad?"

"Yeah, I wish they had about six more aboard."

"Six more? Why?"

"Then, they might have a chance against us," Mad Dog quipped. "This is going to be a walk in the park."

He watched as the whirring noise from the winch floated across the water toward them and a dripping wet cargo net filled with containers was raised from the sea and swung onto the boat's deck. Working in low light, the two men on the boat, quickly emptied the net and dropped it over the side where it was lowered back to the group waiting below.

"Let's drop our gear on the swim deck." Duncan was pointing at the unmanned boat.

"Right."

The two swam toward its stern. When they reached it, they shucked their gear and placed it on the swim platform, then tied their scooters to the stern ladder. Putting a finger to his lips, Duncan said, "Watch the other boat and crew. I'll check out this one."

Mad Dog nodded his head in understanding as Duncan pulled his body onto the swim platform. He rolled over and moved to a crouch so that he could peer into the craft. Seeing no one, he stepped onto its deck and furtively padded into the pilothouse. It was empty.

He glanced over to the other boat to make sure that they were focused on their work and saw the men talking quietly as they waited for the signal to raise the net with another load of the booty.

Carefully, Duncan descended below deck and found the cabin unoccupied. He returned to the main deck and reentered the pilothouse where he grabbed a fire extinguisher. Carrying it as he walked in a crouch, he returned to the swim platform and eased himself into the water.

"No one on board?" Mad Dog asked.

"Nada," Duncan responded.

"What are you planning to do with that?" Mad Dog asked as he eyed the red colored extinguisher.

"Got an idea." He quickly outlined his plan to Mad Dog. After Mad Dog made a couple of suggestions, they put their plan into action.

A few minutes had elapsed before the two men aboard received the signal to raise the next load. One man walked to the winch's controls and shifted the lever, causing the winch to begin raising the loaded net. Its engine whirred as its load made its way to the surface. The winch operator stood next to the winch while the other man stood at the gunwale, so that he could pull the loaded net from above the water to over the deck where it could be emptied.

From the stern of the boat, Duncan and Mad Dog waited patiently for the net to approach the surface. When they saw it nearing the surface, Duncan quickly swam down toward it and situated himself on top of the net. As the net broke the water's surface, Duncan saw the look of surprise on the face of Clarke's henchman. Duncan was holding the fire extinguisher. Its nozzle was aimed toward the man's face.

As the man reached for his shotgun, Duncan pulled the trigger on the fire extinguisher, shooting a stream of foam into his target's eyes and over his body. Meanwhile the winch operator began to level a hastily grabbed weapon at Duncan. It was the wrong move.

The distraction that Duncan had created by his surprise appearance, had allowed Mad Dog to board the *Turtle Dancer* without being noticed. He pulled his dive knife from his leg sheath, and then had quietly slipped behind the winch operator. Before the winch operator could fire his weapon, Mad Dog spun him around. The man's eyes widened in fear as he stared into Mad Dog's wild eyes and saw the dagger.

"Naughty, naughty," Mad Dog said as he shoved the knife blade up through the winch operator's jaw and into his brain. His body twitched violently for a few seconds and then was still. Before allowing the body to drop to the deck, Mad Dog pulled his bloody knife out and wiped it on the operator's shirt.

"Drop!" Duncan yelled.

Faster than he had moved in his life, Mad Dog hit the deck. A shotgun blast from the other man went wide as he staggered and fell over the gunwale, plunging into the water. A knife was buried to the hilt in his back.

From the deck floor, Mad Dog had seen the knife protruding as the man fell overboard. "Nice throw!" he observed as he stood to his feet.

Duncan jumped from his precarious position on top of the swinging net onto the deck. "You got to do what you got to do," he grinned.

Duncan noticed a tug on the net's guide line, which ran to the shipwreck's deck below. "Our friends below are getting anxious."

"I imagine it won't be long before someone comes up to inspect."

"For Emerson's sake, let's hope it's two someones," Duncan said as he looked around the craft.

"I'll cover your back," Mad Dog said as he picked up the fallen shotgun and took a position in the darkness of the pilothouse.

Duncan peered overboard and saw the floating body of the man he had killed. A plan formed quickly in his mind and he eased himself into the water. Swimming to the body, he pulled out his knife and peered down into the water below.

Soon he was able to see a diver approaching and knew he would only have one more safety stop before surfacing. Emerson would be disappointed, though. Only one diver was surfacing. As the diver hung at 15 feet, Duncan mimicked the dead man floating next to him, breathing from under his armpit while keeping an eye on the diver.

When the diver's head broke the water's surface he tilted his mask and looked at the boat, then at the two bodies floating in the water. He recognized the one body as his crewmate, but he didn't recognize the other body. He threw a quick glance at the boat again and then turned his attention to the other floater.

He approached the body and began to turn it over to see who it was. As the body turned, its right arm came out of the water. In its hand was a knife. In one swift continuous motion, the knife plunged into the diver's exposed neck.

During the last second, the diver had tried to push himself away from the now life-filled death machine in front of him, but he didn't have enough time as the cold steel of Duncan's knife sliced through the carotid artery.

Feeling the body go lifeless, Duncan released it and turned toward the boat.

"Where's diver number two?" Mad Dog shouted as he peered into the watery graveyard.

"Only one came up," Duncan said as he swam to the swim platform. "Too much blood in the water. It's time I get out of here." He pulled himself on board. "Why don't you stand guard? I'm going to check these two boats out and see what we really have here."

"Gotcha!" Mad Dog replied.

Meanwhile, Emerson and Rothman had been waiting patiently underwater as they watched the activity on the shipwreck. They noticed that the divers seemed to have become agitated that the net had not been returned to them in the same timely fashion for another load. That's when one diver began to surface.

This disappointed the pair. Rothman looked at Emerson, held up two fingers, and then bent one back down indicating that only one diver had surfaced. Then he shrugged like, *What's next?*

Emerson put his two forefingers together, then separated them meaning that they would have to divide and conquer. Rothman understood and gave an OK sign back to Emerson.

Rothman thought a moment and then looked at his GPS. He realized that they weren't too far from the sunken Russian frigate *Reid Foster.* He looked at Emerson then pointed toward the *Reid Foster* and made a vertical circle with his finger to remind Emerson about the circular structure that's mounted on the bow of the *Reid Foster.*

Emerson got the idea and motioned with his hands that they lure the remaining divers to the Russian frigate. This would also get them away from the lighted shipwreck.

On the German ship, Clarke was beginning to fume at the delay in raising the last containers of gold. There were only two more loads to get topside. He continually looked upward, hoping to see the cargo net descending. The longer he waited, the more a dire concern grew in his gut.

Suddenly, he noticed two divers approaching them on underwater scooters. He shook his head, as he couldn't let them see the shipwreck and tell others. When his two men looked at him, he drew his hand across his throat as if he was slitting it. Then, he pointed at the approaching divers.

Clarke's two men nodded their heads to show their understanding. The three of them boarded their underwater scooters, which had been secured to the deck of the shipwreck, and headed toward Emerson and Rothman. Their larger and more powerful scooters were equipped with underwater floodlights, which they switched on to be able to catch up to the two intruders. They also had two spear guns affixed to each scooter.

Seeing that their ploy had worked, Emerson and Rothman turned and headed toward the sunken Russian frigate, with Rothman in the lead.

It wasn't long before Emerson realized that the water around them was becoming very illuminated. He turned and found himself staring into the bright floodlights of the pursuing scooters, and they were getting closer.

Rothman had also turned and noticed, but felt secure as a large shape was quickly looming out of the dark water. It was the *Reid Foster*.

Seconds later, Emerson was startled when he heard and saw a spear whoosh by his scooter on the left side. He again peered over his shoulder and saw that the three scooters were gaining more ground on Rothman and him. But, Rothman and Emerson were passing over the circular structure on the bow that Rothman had alluded to earlier.

The pair soared across the rest of the bow, over the double-barreled fore cannons, and headed up toward the wheelhouse. Rothman pointed his scooter toward the bridge and drove it through one of the glassless windows where he parked it. As

Emerson followed him, the sharp point of a fired spear struck the metal mullion to his right.

Emerson parked his scooter and followed Rothman down the passageway at the rear of the wheelhouse. They spotted a set of stairs and descended them. At the base of the stairs, they went in different directions. Emerson headed toward the Captain's cabin. Rothman swam through an open doorway, which led back to the ship's foredeck where he tethered his floating strobe light to the port side handrail and released the strobe to float to the surface.

On the surface, Mad Dog kept his eyes sharply peeled for any danger from below. When the flashing strobe emerged, Mad Dog saw it floating and remembered that Emerson and Rothman would use it to mark their position if it changed.

"Sam, we'd better move these boats!" Mad Dog called as Duncan completed his exploration and subsequent task.

"What do you mean?"

"Look out there!"

Duncan looked in the direction in which Mad Dog was pointing. "Looks like they moved! I wonder why."

"Think we should go back down?"

Duncan thought for a moment and then answered. "No, not yet. Let's give them a while. But, we better move these boats over there."

They released the lines, which had kept the boats together, and weighed anchor. Then they started the engines and moved both boats slowly to the point where the strobe was floating. Shutting down the engines, they retied the lines and lowered the anchors.

Meanwhile, the underwater pursuers had entered the bridge area and dismounted their scooters. Each carrying a spear gun, they split up. Clarke swam down one passageway while the other two divers swam down the other, and then down a set of stairs. At the base of the stairs, the two split with one swimming out onto the foredeck.

As he began searching the foredeck, he heard metal striking metal. He cocked his head toward the sound and heard it again. It was coming from the forward gun turret. With his spear gun held out in front of him and his finger on the trigger, he decided to investigate the source of the noise. He carefully approached the forward gun turret.

Upon reaching it, he paused. He didn't hear anything, but he was sure that he had found one of the intruders. With his left hand, he reached down and grabbed his flashlight. Switching it on, he began to open the door of the turret.

As soon as he opened the door, he sensed movement to his left and quickly pointed both the flashlight and spear gun in that direction, but immediately the glass in his mask shattered.

The Great Barracuda was very territorial and did not take kindly to surprises by invaders. It struck quickly and with such force that its strike broke the mask's glass and the infuriated barracuda clamped its jaws on the nose and eyes of the intruding diver.

Frantically the diver dropped his flashlight and spear gun and grabbed at the barracuda's body as it viciously sliced through cartilage of the diver's nose. The diver's fright and panic carried him out of the turret and onto the deck. His regulator dropped from his mouth and he slumped in a heap as he drowned.

From behind the turret, Rothman emerged. He replaced his knife, which he had been using to tap against the turret's wall, in its sheath and retrieved the diver's spear gun and flashlight.

He looked about and, now armed, reentered the passageway in search of Emerson and the other two divers.

In the Captain's cabin, Emerson saw the breaker box on the wall. It had two massive locks, which were rusting. He remembered talking with Rothman about investigating what was locked in the breaker box. He reached over to one of the locks and examined it. He just might have a chance at opening it.

He swam out to the passageway and looked in both directions. He didn't see anyone coming, so he backed into the cabin and slowly shut the door. He returned to the breaker box and withdrew his knife from its sheath. Inserting it in the first lock, he began to turn and twist it. He was surprised when the lock gave way and opened. That's one, he thought to himself as he attacked the second lock in the same manner.

But the second lock wasn't as accommodating. After a few futile moments, the work of the salty seawater in corroding the lock's inner mechanism and the intrusive force of Emerson's knife blade combined to pop the lock open.

Emerson smiled as he removed both locks and opened the breaker box. There he found a small metal container. It was about 4 inches long and 1 inch wide. There were two words written on it in Cyrillic. Emerson glanced at it and then very carefully slipped the container in his BC pocket.

Suddenly, he heard a noise and spun around as the cabin door swung open. It was the other diver shining a bright UK Light Cannon nightlight directly into his eyes. And he was holding a spear gun, which was quickly rising, toward Emerson's chest.

Emerson dodged sideways while scanning the captain's cabin, but there seemed to be nowhere to hide or escape from this certain spear attack. Emerson immediately decided to go on the offensive and charge the armed diver. It was his only choice.

He quickly braced his feet against a wall and launched his attack before the diver could react. Curiously, before Emerson reached the other diver, his spear gun dropped and his body shuddered and awkwardly leaned to the left of the doorway. As it moved, Emerson saw a spear protruding from the diver's side, just under his BC.

Emerson swam over and looked in the direction from which the spear appeared to originate. There, he saw Rothman. Rothman was reloading his captured spear gun. Emerson nodded his appreciation and looked back at the other diver, who had escaped down the passageway and onto the deck. The injured diver inflated his BC to begin his ascent to the surface.

Meanwhile, Emerson picked up the fallen spear gun and joined Rothman. He held up three fingers, and then folded two over, leaving one finger to indicate that they only had one more to go. The two armed divers, who had been the prey, were now the hunters. In searching for their prey, they swam through a number of passageways without finding anyone.

A minute or two later, Mad Dog and Duncan saw a body rocketing out of the water, then splashing back to the surface. Mad Dog jockeyed the boat around so that Duncan could use a nearby grappling pole to drag in the floating body. Blood was streaming from the diver's mask and mouth and a spear was still sticking through his side.

On his way up, the diver had blacked out. Since his BC was still inflated, his ascent rate kept increasing exponentially as the volume of air in his BC also increased. This was due to the lower ambient water pressure at the shallower depths. His lungs had burst for the same reason and the pair on the boat figured the diver probably suffered an air embolism as well.

Below water, Emerson and Rothman were on the verge of a deadly encounter with the third diver. As they swam back to the bridge, Rothman suddenly jerked and grabbed at his calf. A spear had penetrated his calf and its sharp end was protruding from the other side.

Emerson looked around Rothman and saw the diver reloading his spear gun. The other diver glanced at Emerson.

Emerson could see a smile form on the diver's face as Clarke recognized Emerson. Knowing that it was Emerson he was targeting and would be killing, brought a strong sense of satisfaction to Clarke.

Turning back to Rothman, Emerson motioned to him to ascend. Rothman reluctantly agreed, dropped his spear gun at Emerson's feet and swam out of the wheelhouse to begin his ascent.

Then, Emerson quickly aimed his spear gun at Clarke and fired. When he missed, he dropped his spear gun and grabbed Rothman's loaded spear gun. But when he looked back up he saw that Clarke had disappeared.

Emerson looked above him to make sure that Clarke was not pursuing Rothman and was satisfied that he wasn't. Emerson then began to swim down into a nearby passageway. He held his spear gun in front of him, ready to fire.

Minutes later, Emerson rounded a corner and a spear fired by Clarke narrowly missed him. Reacting rather than thinking, Emerson fired back in the direction from which Clarke had fired, but the spear sped off over the railing into dark water. When he went to reload, he realized that Rothman's spear gun did not have any more spears. Lucky for him, neither did Clarke's.

Emerson drew his knife from its sheath and slowly swam down the passageway where Clarke had last been seen. It was then that he heard the sound of a slamming hatch. Emerson approached the closed hatch and carefully opened it. He wasn't sure whether Clarke would be waiting for him or not.

He peered around and saw nothing. But when he looked up, he noticed movement above him. It was Clarke quickly swimming toward the surface. He decided to follow him slowly at a safe distance. Clarke leveled off at 15 feet for his safety stop and looked around in hopes that Emerson had missed his escape. He didn't see Emerson anywhere and slyly hoped that the pesky reporter was still searching the *Reid Foster.* Little did he know that Emerson was biding his time doing a much slower ascent with plenty of air left for his own safety stop that he'd make after Clarke finished his and surfaced.

Both Clarke and Emerson took abbreviated safety stops. Clarke was the first to reach the surface. Clarke smiled when he saw the two boats had been moved and that it appeared that all the divers were tending to Rothman on the *Turtle Dancer*. It appeared that the *Turtle Chaser* was unoccupied. Clarke also noticed that someone had been careless in securing the two boats together as the *Turtle Chaser* had drifted 20 feet away from the *Turtle Dancer*. He began to swim to the boat's swim platform.

When he reached the platform, he quickly pulled off his gear. Not wanting to make any unnecessary noise, he left the gear in the water and dragged himself onto the swim platform. Keeping a low profile, he slowly made his way to the pilothouse.

From below, Emerson angled his ascent and emerged from the water near the stern of Clarke's boat. He had seen Clarke discard his equipment and he had followed suit. He knew that he'd have to settle up with the folks at DiveTech, but he couldn't lose any time. He reached the edge of the swim platform and rolled onto it just as the boat's engines sprang to life with a loud roar. He hung on as the boat accelerated through the water.

The *Turtle Dancer*'s occupants turned in surprise when they heard the other boat engine come alive.

In the early twilight, they saw Clarke at the helm. His face was turned to them and a victorious smile filled it. He turned back to focus on his escape and realized that the *Turtle Dancer* wouldn't be able to catch him since it was laden with the gold.

Looking at the escaping boat, Duncan moaned.

"What's wrong?" Mad Dog asked.

"Look there. On the swim platform. Isn't that Emerson?"

Mad Dog and Rothman, who was now standing, looked.

"Damn! It's Emerson," Mad Dog grimaced.

Duncan raced to the cockpit and started the *Turtle Dancer*'s engines. He shoved the throttle forward and the boat leapt out of the water in pursuit of Clarke and Emerson.

As the *Turtle Chaser* planed, Emerson was able to make his way from the swim platform to the boat's deck. He began to rush at Clarke, but before he reached him, Clarke must have sensed him and he spun around.

The two men grappled to the deck as the boat charged through the water. Each man pummeled the other's body and made several connections to the head as they fought. Rolling away from Emerson's grasp, Clarke reached for a flare gun.

Seeing that there was no way he could close the distance between them before Clarke would have time to fire it at Emerson, Emerson raced to the side of the moving boat and dove overboard.

Irritated, Clarke threw the flare gun on to the boat's deck and turned his attention back to the helm. It was then, that he realized he had a way to kill not only Emerson, but also the other three divers. He looked over his shoulder as he slowed his craft and pointed to Emerson, who had now surfaced.

"He's overboard!" Rothman yelled from the pursuing craft.

"Yeah, I see it," Duncan responded as he began to slow the boat to rescue Emerson. He eased the boat up to where Emerson waited, bobbing in the clear blue sea. He cut the engines as Emerson swam to the stern where Mad Dog waited to assist him aboard.

"You wimp. You let him throw you overboard, didn't you?" Mad Dog teased.

Emerson just smiled as he was helped to his feet. He felt exhausted.

"Yeah, the Good Samaritan in front of us pointed at you in the water to be sure that we picked you up," Duncan said uneasily.

"I wonder what he's up to," Emerson said as he looked toward Clarke.

"Now, what's he doing?" Rothman called.

The other three turned their attention to see that Clarke had stopped his engines and was standing in the stern. "I'm not done with you bastards, yet! Think you can screw with me and get away with it? No one does!"

In his hand he had been holding a small device. He smiled as he depressed the button. When nothing happened, he depressed it several times. His anger surged at the perceived failure of the remote detonator.

"Maybe this one works!" Duncan yelled to Clarke. Duncan had a huge smile on his face as he held a second remote detonator in his hand.

"What's this about?" Emerson asked, puzzled.

"Working with drug interdiction like I have, I've seen dealers use two boats. The first boat has the drugs, but unknown to its crew, it also has explosives hidden aboard. That way the drug boat is exploded if the drug deal goes sour."

"It's a nasty business," Emerson said, shaking his head from side to side.

"The guys in the second boat, the chase boat, will also explode the first boat if it's stopped by the Coast Guard."

"So, the guys in the chase boat are clean because they don't have any drugs on board," Emerson reasoned as he watched Clarke who was staring at them with his face full of hatred.

"Exactly."

"So, I guess we have explosives on board our boat and Clarke is on the chase boat!"

"You're partially right and he is on the *Turtle Chaser*. How ironic!"

"How am I partially right?" Emerson asked.

Grinning conspiratorially, Duncan responded, "While we were waiting for you to complete your underwater adventure, I checked out both boats. When I found the detonator on Clarke's boat, I realized it was the chase boat. So, I returned to this boat and found the explosives."

"You bet we found them. We put them on Clarke's boat!" Mad Dog chimed in with a hearty snicker. "He has no idea what he is sitting on!"

"Here, you take this." Duncan handed a remote detonator to Emerson.

"Where did you come up with this?"

"There were two on board Clarke's boat. I deactivated the other one to be safe." Duncan looked toward Clarke who was staring at them from the stern of his boat. "And Clarke thinks he's right all the time. This time the Pryce isn't right. Go ahead, Emerson. Do it!"

Examining the detonator, Emerson looked up at Duncan and then toward Clarke. He thought for a moment about the carnage for which Clarke was responsible and made a decision. "This is for Denise Roberts," he said as he pointed the remote toward Clarke's boat and depressed the button.

The signal was instantly transmitted to the explosives in the bow of Clarke's craft. The craft burst into fiery pieces, which were scattered in a radius of 100 feet. The early morning sky was illuminated by the brilliant explosion.

"Well, I guess that takes care of that," a satisfied Emerson said as he threw the detonator into the sea.

"Yeah, Clarke was just like Rudolph the red-nosed reindeer."

The other three just stared at Mad Dog.

"He just went down in history!" Mad Dog chuckled at his joke.

"Or up!" Duncan said as he started the boat's engine and headed the boat toward DiveTech's dock.

Emerson joined Rothman near the stern. "How are you doing?" he asked as he looked at the leg.

"Good. Your ex-SEAL buddies had some training in field dressing. They found a first aid kit and field dressed the wound. I can have someone run me into town and take a look at it. Probably should get it sterilized since Mad Dog touched me. You don't know what kind of bacteria that boy might be carrying," Rothman teased.

Emerson chuckled and then edged closer to Rothman. "Remember that day in your office when you showed me the photo of the breaker box on the *Reid Foster*?"

"Yes. What about it?"

"While I was in the captain's cabin, I broke into it."

"But it had two locks on it!"

"Guess I was lucky. When I opened the box, I found a sealed tube. It was about four inches long and an inch wide."

"Did you open it?"

"No, I didn't have time and I wasn't sure that I wanted to open it."

"Why?" Rothman asked.

"There was a warning written in Cyrillic."

"You read Cyrillic?" Rothman asked, astonished.

"Just a bit. I learned a few key words when I was covering the Serbian-Croatian conflict in Yugoslavia years ago."

"I didn't know you were there."

"I was, but that's a story for another day." Emerson paused and then continued. "It read Danger. Poisonous. It also had the universal skull and crossbones."

Rothman sat up. "Let me see it."

"I don't have it any longer. When I was fighting with Clarke, I slipped it in the back pocket of his swimming trunks. If it was dangerous, I surely didn't need it. I shouldn't have brought it to the surface anyhow."

"That's an interesting story, Emerson. While doing maritime research, I found several references to the Cuban Missile Crisis and what the Soviets were willing to do."

"Oh?"

"Yes. It was rumored that they would go as far as releasing bacteria such as bubonic plague in the United States. Some say Miami was a primary target. So was Washington, D.C."

"How would they deliver the virus?"

"Couriers from Havana. The stuff was so infectious; they were worried about sending someone with it from Moscow. It had been rumored that several secured vials had been hidden on Soviet naval vessels. That might be one of them. We would have had the proof that they had really done that."

Frustrated with himself, Emerson moaned, "And I gave away the evidence."

"Under the circumstances, I wouldn't be moaning about it. You wouldn't want to take a chance of unleashing it here in the Cayman Islands, or for that matter, anywhere else. You're fortunate that you didn't open it and expose yourself."

Before Emerson could comment, Duncan called to him.

"Need a little help here," Duncan yelled as he pointed to the stern line. Emerson saw that they were nearing DiveTech's pier and that Mad Dog was on the bow with the bowline, ready to secure it to the pier.

As the craft nudged the pier, Emerson and Mad Dog secured the lines while Duncan shut off the craft's engines and assisted Rothman onto the pier. The four men walked down the pier toward DiveTech's office.

As they neared the office, Nancy emerged. "You better join me in Duppies. You'll understand when we get there."

The group walked to the nearby restaurant. As they rounded the corner, they came to an abrupt stop. Leaning against the bar was Derek Fleming. Seated at the bar were Jay Easterbrook, Reid Dennis, Mark Rice, Ratty and Steve Foster. They all look tired. It had been a long night. Behind the bar, Cobalt Coast Dive Resort's owner, Arie Barendrecht, was serving drinks to everyone.

"What can I get you boys?" Arie asked as Rothman eased the pain in his leg by sitting on a nearby bar stool.

The new arrivals placed orders as they eyed Fleming.

"I guess I have some explaining to do," Fleming said in response to the looks he was receiving.

"That's an understatement if I ever heard one," Emerson said as he glared at Fleming.

"What I've been telling you has been the truth. Denise Roberts was not who you thought she was. She was feeding information to Clarke."

"Then why did she want to meet me at the Kaibo Kai Yacht Club?" Emerson asked.

"We were tapping her phone line. She found out about the capture of your friend, Duncan here, and wanted to tip you. I think that Clarke was getting suspicious of her, because he knew I was conducting an investigation on him. He wasn't sure if she had turned on him and he's not someone who likes to worry about being betrayed. I believe that he had her taken out at the yacht club. The timing may have just been coincidental."

"What about you? What were you doing at Clarke's house the night we busted in?" Mad Dog growled.

"Coincidence. I was checking on my team. They were concealed on a stakeout."

"But, you sure didn't do a good job of concealing yourself!" Mad Dog churned.

"It was unfortunate that Clarke saw me. He knew then that we were closing in on him if we had him under surveillance."

"Then, why did you fire at us?" Emerson probed.

"It was accidental. When I saw two men run out of the house. I withdrew my hand gun. Your flash grenade caught me by surprise and I accidentally discharged it."

"As did Clarke!" Mad Dog added.

"Yes, he did. I melted back into the shadows and retrieved my team. We figured Clarke would be conducting a search of the area, so we packed up our surveillance team and left."

"All this to build your case? Why didn't you move sooner? Couldn't you work with a judge here and expedite your records search?"

A smile crossed Fleming's face. He glanced at his watch. "Pryce Clarke has been a very slippery criminal to nail. Every time we have tried to make a case on him, he's either been tipped off or we couldn't get a court order to move forward. I can tell you now, that my men are arriving at the homes of two of our judges. They are being arrested for conspiring with Clarke and taking bribes from him in exchange for tipping him and blocking our efforts. There were things that I couldn't do, but you did them for me. I was always in the shadows watching your movements."

"You used us!" Emerson stated with irritation.

"It was a bit cheeky of me, wasn't it?" Fleming said as he looked from the restaurant toward the sea and then scanned the people gathered at Duppies. "You did things for me that I couldn't do. And I thank you. I thank all of you," Fleming said sincerely.

"I guess you know about the gold in the lagoon since Reid, Mark and Steve are here?"

"Yes. My men are recovering it as we speak."

Pointing to the boat at the end of the pier, Emerson said, "There's more on board and down below waiting to be brought up from a sunken German raider."

"I'm sure that I can engage the services of Nancy and her team at DiveTech to assist in bringing up the remaining gold," Fleming said as he looked at Nancy, who nodded her head affirmatively.

"Ratty, it looks like we found the source of your crashed seaplane. It came from that raider."

"Good. I always wondered where it came from. Thank yous," Ratty replied as he puffed on his pipe.

Emerson took a sip from his drink as he looked around the restaurant filled with his friends. Then he gazed out on Boatswain's Bay and thought about the events over the last few days. He began to outline, in his mind, a story to e-mail in to his editor.

The Turtle Chaser's Debris
Boatswain's Bay

Earlier, as Duncan had headed the *Turtle Dancer* toward DiveTech's pier, a severely burned arm emerged from the water amid the fiery debris from Clarke's boat, the *Turtle Chaser*. It was followed by the head and shoulders of Pryce Clarke, who was gasping for breath.

All of his facial hair had been burned during the explosion. His leg was broken and dangled as blood from a severed leg artery pumped into the water. Clarke spotted an inflatable raft floating nearby and feebly swam the three strokes toward it. He clawed at the rope pull, which would inflate it. After several attempts, he was able to pull it and initiate the rafts inflation.

Realizing that his strength was being sapped and that he needed access to the raft's first aid kit, he slowly hoisted his body onto the inflating raft. Looking around, he couldn't find the first aid kit, but he did feel something in the pocket of his swim trunks. In pain, he rolled to one side and, using his good arm, he reached into the pocket and withdrew the cylindrical object. It was about 4 inches long and 1 inch wide.

He turned it over as he tried to recall how it ended up in his pocket. Clarke couldn't figure it out. He also tried to read it, but it was futile, as he didn't understand the strange markings.

He decided to twist it open and see what it contained. Grunting in pain, he twisted. It didn't budge. He tried several more times, finally opening it, and releasing the bacteria from the black plague. Clarke held it to his nose and sniffed, unknowingly inhaling the bacteria. Angry at it being nothing of value, he threw it overboard where it began to sink to the bottom of the Caymanian Trench.

Clarke didn't realize what he had done, but it wasn't going to matter. His attention was distracted as he realized that the raft was sinking. It had been damaged during the explosion. As the raft sunk, his bloody leg found itself awash in the bay.

The blood in the water attracted several nearby sharks, who began to circle the sinking raft. It was not going to be a happy ending for Pryce Clarke as the raft sunk underneath him, dumping him in the water, and the sharks moved in on their prey.

The Presidential Protection Unit
U.S. Secret Service
Washington, D.C.
Several Months Later

"Looks like we'll be heading to the islands," the agent said as he finished his phone conversation and turned to his partner.

"Caribbean?"

"Nope. Lake Erie Islands."

The other agent paused for a moment as he thought. "Something to do with that bio-terrorism problem on the Great Lakes?"

"They didn't say, but that would be my guess. Something or some body is killing the fish. The President is having a conference on one of the islands with Canada's Prime Minister." He checked his computer's e-mail, but didn't see the message he was expecting. "The Chief of Staff is having someone e-mail information to us shortly."

"When's the meeting scheduled?"

"Just before the national convention in Cleveland."

Coming Summer 2009

The Next *Emerson Moore* Adventure

Tan Lines